Claire's career as an author began in earnest at the end of the Second World War, during which she served in Fighter Command in the Filter Rooms on secret duties. Encouraged by her mother, the bestselling author Denise Robins, she began writing light romantic novels under her maiden name, Patricia Robins. However, in 1970 she started writing her magnificent family sagas and thrillers under the name Claire Lorrimer. She is currently at work on her eighty-first book. Claire lives in Kent.

Find out more about Claire: www.clairelorrimer.co.uk

Twitter: @ClaireLorrimer

Also by Claire Lorrimer and available from Hodder

YOU NEVER KNOW

An autobiography

CLAIRE LORRIMER

HODDER

First published in Great Britain in 2006
by Pen Press Publishers Ltd

This paperback edition published in 2016
by Hodder & Stoughton
An Hachette UK company

1

A CIP catalogue record for this title is
available from the British Library

Paperback ISBN 978 1 473 63398 8
eBook ISBN 978 1 444 75275 5

Typeset by Palimpsest Book Production Ltd, Falkirk, Stirlingshire
Printed and bound in Great Britain by Clays Ltd, St Ives plc

Hodder & Stoughton policy is to use papers that are
natural, renewable and recyclable products and made from wood
grown in sustainable forests. The logging and manufacturing
processes are expected to conform to the environmental
regulations of the country of origin.

Hodder & Stoughton Ltd
Carmelite House
50 Victoria Embankment
London
EC4Y 0DZ

www.hodder.co.uk

For my much loved children, grandchildren, my sister, Mel and all the friends who have brought so much happiness to my life.

INTRODUCTION

As children we all wonder what the future will be like. Will I be a train driver, a vet, a nurse? Will I marry a fair or dark man? How many children will I have? The future of course is unknown. Often there are choices to be made – this job, that career, this vote, that holiday destination? Some people find it hard to make these leaps into the unknown but I was born impulsive and have nearly always known what I wanted. Looking back, I see I made some wrong choices but I'll never know what life would have been like had a different choice been made, any more than any of us know what awaits us just round the corner. Two paths through the wood. Is one full of danger and only the other safe? We can never know. There is an inevitable lottery to life, but it is that which lifts it from the mundane to the exciting. If you can truly believe you have chosen the right path, then like me, you can look forward with enthusiasm to tomorrow.

Claire Lorrimer
Edenbridge, 2006

CONTENTS

CHAPTER ONE

It was a cold February day when the nanny wheeled her small charge along the Brighton promenade. The little girl's mother was pregnant with her third child and for once would be resting on her bed rather than sitting up at her desk typing one of her romantic novels.

The wind was fresh but despite the cold, the nurse stopped to listen to the bearded man standing on a box surrounded by a crowd of angry men. The orator was in full voice as he urged his audience to take note of the fact that they were being exploited by their government; that he – and he alone – was not a slave.

'Raise your hands if there is one among you poor down-trodden workers who can call himself free?' he shouted.

There was a murmur of agreement amongst the men whose mood was becoming dangerous. Suddenly a small voice piped up:

'I'm free!'

I had just had my third birthday and was proud of my advanced age.

The mood of the men changed instantly and laughter now rippled through the crowd as my nanny turned the pram round and hurried me home.

Obviously I don't remember the incident but it was recalled in the family whenever the word 'free' came up in conversation.

On August 12th of that year, 1924, my younger sister, Anne, was born, my parents' third child and – to my mother's everlasting distress – the baby was yet another girl. Her first born, Eve, although not the son she had wanted, was nevertheless a remarkably pretty baby, blue eyed, golden haired, like a little doll. I, on the other hand, was not only the second girl but was scarlet faced, bald and heavy enough to have caused my poor mother considerable discomfort when she brought me into the world on 1st February, her birthday, too. By the time Anne came along, my mother vowed to give up her hopes for a boy and devote herself to her career.

At that time, only six years after the end of the First World War, the country was in a severe economic depression. There were over six million unemployed and my father, a corn broker on the Baltic Exchange, was as a consequence far from well off whereas my mother's (Denise Robins) love stories were in great demand by D.C. Thompson of Dundee's popular weekly magazines. A very deaf registrar had put my father's occupation on my birth certificate as that of a pawnbroker – a subject of mirth in later years in the family – but which might have been far more economically beneficial in 1924 than his employment as a corn broker.

Although my father was far from happy about it, it was obvious that my mother's financial contributions were much needed. As her literary career developed, she began writing novels and our family was soon able to move from the tiny flat in Adelaide Crescent in Hove to a small county cottage in Haywards Heath from whence my father commuted each day on the steam train to London.

At the time of Anne's birth my parents' wartime marriage, which had begun so romantically, was already proving less than idyllic. My mother, a young, very pretty VAD (women's Voluntary Aid Detachment) had nursed my father who was convalescing following a severe leg wound. Fair haired, blue eyed, handsome and extremely courageous, he epitomised the romantic hero of her dreams. He was, however, not only very young and inexperienced but shy, reserved, in many respects inarticulate and although he loved her devotedly until the day he died, he could not offer her the somewhat unrealistic demonstrative adoration she craved and brought to life in the fictitious heroes of her novels.

In those early years, she was still loving towards him and one of the nicest of her gestures, which I learned about many years later, was in the Depression when they were so hard up, my father was obliged to pawn his treasured pair of Purdey guns in order to pay the bills. Receiving a handsome cheque for one of her magazine serials, she went secretly to the pawnshop and redeemed them for him as an unexpected birthday present.

Eve, not quite two years older than me, was a shy, rather timid child who, when she could not be close to the mother she adored, tended to look to me for assurance as, right or wrong, I was never in doubt as to what I wanted to do. She was a remarkably pretty child. Having been a pretty baby she was now a lovely little girl, essentially very feminine and even then as a presage of things to come, attracting admiring glances from the opposite sex. My mother loved to dress us in pretty clothes, nearly all of which enhanced Eve's charm whilst emphasizing my short sturdy frame and tomboyish demeanour. Shopping with our mother for new clothes was always a nightmare for me, knowing that whilst Eve would look lovely in her dresses I would look untidy and plain. Had I but been born two generations later, I would have been in seventh heaven in a pair of torn-at-the-knee jeans!

By the time we moved to Haywards Heath, we had a governess to look after us as my mother was busy most of the day in the special hut she'd had built in the garden to use as her study. Her first novel, *Sealed Lips*, was published by Mills and Boon, to be followed shortly after by *The Marriage Bond*, *The Inevitable End*, and others, all of which were hugely popular. Towards the end of her long, successful career, she told me that Charles Boon had fallen in love with her – not surprising as she was a very beautiful young woman with perfect bone structure, expressive green eyes and chestnut brown hair. She was quite often likened to the film actress Marlene Dietrich. Too strictly brought up by her Catholic convent to contemplate an affair with the publisher, they did enjoy a flirtation and it was really he who started her meteoric rise to fame.

She was rapidly becoming a household name. In 1927, the actor, composer and playwright Ivor Novello welcomed her suggestion that she should turn his latest successful play, *The Triumph of a Rat*, into a novel. This was published in 1927 and Ivor wrote to congratulate her and thanked her for writing it.

By then I was six years old. Having had a lonely and unhappy early childhood, our mother had found security and happiness as well as receiving an excellent education from the convent in Norwood where she was a boarder. Thinking that Eve and I would be equally happy in a similar environment, she dispatched us to a nearby convent run by a closed order of nuns. Even the reception room where parents handed over their offspring was partitioned off with a grill through which the nun would communicate; and parcels were placed in a revolving cupboard so that she would not have to touch the hand of a male parent.

My memories of the year I spent there remain very acute. There was a large bathroom in which several baths stood in line. We were each given a voluminous rubber cape beneath which we undressed and, still wearing it, climbed into the bath where our ablutions were supervised by a nun. I don't recall how we managed to dry ourselves under the sodden cape which, wet, cold and clammy, clung to our bodies.

I had a vivid imagination and a tendency to take everything I was told very literally. The story of the crucifixion and the mental picture of the horrifying walk Jesus took with the crown of thorns round his head and the heavy cross on his shoulders, kept me awake at night. It worried me to death that I could not go to confession as the Catholic girls did every Friday and have my ever-growing mountain of sins forgiven me. Even more worrying was the story I was told of babies who, because they died unbaptised, could never go to Heaven. A kindly nun consoled me with the news that if I repeated the names of Jesus, Mary and Joseph, a baby would be able to leave Limbo and go to Heaven. From then on (until I suppose I forgot) I spent every spare minute muttering a shortened version of the heavenly names – i.e. Jes-May-Jo, comforting myself with the mental image of little round, pink babies floating skywards into the arms of the Virgin Mary whose pretty statues placed all over the convent, compensated slightly for the body of Jesus dripping blood that also dominated the convent rooms, school rooms and corridors.

I do not recall anyone being unkind. We slept in dormitories with each bed partitioned off from the next; presumably yet again to keep us from seeing each other's bodies. I never questioned the oddity of this, nor why my parents should have been asked to remove me (for polluting the minds of the Catholic children) when I was caught doing the dance of Hiawatha with only a towel round my waist and my six-year-old chest exposed to my giggling audience. Eve told me that her friend Angela had been expelled when she was in the sanatorium with chicken pox and was caught trying to see in the mirror the spots on her bottom. I was, however, reprieved and was determined to be less sinful in the future.

I don't recall being particularly unhappy at the convent although I was often afraid. However, one bitter memory returns even these long years after, of a beautiful doll, which was to be given to the girl who best remembered the lengthy catechism we had just been taught. Having a good memory, I answered most questions right. However, the doll was not to be mine because, so I was told, it was intended for a Catholic not a Protestant child.

I did think it very unfair (and still do!) but I did not mind all that much as I wasn't into dolls – I preferred stuffed animals and my teddy bear.

Eve, unlike me, was hardworking, obedient and although homesick, had settled down philosophically to boarding school life. When we went home for the holidays, she preferred my mother's company to mine and as Anne was still too young to be a playmate, I wished fervently for a brother. Meanwhile, my cousin, Buzz, a year old than me, was a substitute. When he visited us, I followed him round like a puppy. I envied him the fact that he wore shorts, not tiresome skirts and dresses which I always seemed to get torn or dirty; and most of all I envied him the snake belt which kept his shorts up! To possess either, I realised, one had to be a boy, *not* a girl.

The possibility of this radical sex change was presented to me during my second term at the convent. With sufficient faith, anything could be achieved, a kindly nun told me. Did I truly believe in God the Father, God the Son and God the Holy Ghost? I wasn't too keen on the Holy Ghost and secretly hoped never to meet him. However, I did believe in his existence as well as that of God the Father and Son and now in my prayers, begged all three to change me as soon as possible into a boy.

Having no brothers, I was unaware of the difference between males and females but as I woke each morning without short hair, or shorts and a snake belt on my bedside chair instead of my uniform dress, I realised that no miracle had occurred in the night. In due course, I reported this tragedy to my sympathetic nun.

'God must have other plans for you, child!' she said.

Naturally I wanted to know what plans she thought God had in mind.

'He may wish you to become a nurse,' she volunteered. 'Or a missionary, or . . .' she added with inspiration, '. . . he may wish you to become a nun like me.'

'But how will I know whether he does or doesn't?' I persisted.

'You will hear His voice calling you to take Holy Orders,' she replied.

This struck me instantly as being a very desirable occupation. The nuns could order any of us to do whatever they wanted and we had to obey. If I was a nun . . .

I decided to waste no time in trying to achieve my objective, I must now listen at all times whenever possible in case I missed The Call. In class I sat as near to a window as I could so I could hear God's voice, which, I reckoned, would be pretty faint anyway coming all the way down from Heaven. I stopped talking to people except when I was obliged to speak in lessons; I stopped people talking to me. The only person who benefited from this was my sister Eve, who was fed up being pestered by me with questions.

I was still listening intently when we went home for the holidays. I opened the windows in any room I was in so I could better hear The Call. It was a very short time before my father, a staunch Protestant, asked if his middle daughter was heading for the lunatic asylum, which happened to be a mile or so down the road. This brought about a speedy end to Eve's and my life at the convent and we were sent instead as day girls to the P.N.E.U. (Parents National Education Union) school in Burgess Hill. Here my desire to be included in the hockey team supplanted any idea I might have had to be a nun, although I did still crave a snake belt. (The memory of this featured in one of the short stories in *Variations*, a book I had published in 1988, and which is still being read in the libraries today).

During the year Eve and I were at the convent, life in the outside world moved on. In 1927, a thousand people a week died in a 'flu epidemic. Poverty was rife as a consequence of the General Strike the preceding year. Women were now permitted to vote at the age of twenty-one instead of thirty and 1928 saw the introduction of one pound and ten shilling paper notes – not that Eve or I were aware of such things. We were very vaguely aware of the Wall Street Crash in 1929 and of the two million unemployed only because at Christmas we were asked to select a number of our toys to go to the children of these poor people. I am ashamed to say I bitterly resented being made to part with my favourite teddy bear – a particularly large one – demanding an explanation as to why I was not old enough to stay up as late as Eve but too old to keep the toy I wanted. 'It's not fair!' was a frequent cry in my childhood.

My mother was now writing her fourteenth book and was beginning to know a number of people important in the literary world. At the age of thirty-two she was a remarkably pretty woman whose frustrated ambition to become an actress now assisted her publishers' wish to give maximum publicity to her books. She was in demand by magazines for stories by newspapers for articles; and for personal appearances at fêtes, luncheons and charity events. She acquired a flat in London in Whitehall Court where she could socialise without having to commute to our country house. My father who was still suffering the effects of the serious leg wound he had incurred at Gueudecourt near the Somme in the war, preferred a quiet life, gardening, shooting and training his gun dogs, to my mother's social whirl. He was a very reserved man who got on better with his dogs than with people.

Being something of a tomboy, I think I was in some ways compensation for the son he never had. It was I, not either of my sisters, who creosoted the garden shed with him;

shinned up the apple tree; hammered in nails, or sawed wood. Doubtless he was also trying in his quiet way to make up for the fact that Eve was unquestionably my mother's favourite. The preference was understandable because not only was Eve very pretty, she was always happy to fall in with my mother's wishes whatever they might be. Moreover, Eve never argued.

My relationship with my mother was extremely difficult. She was given to fantasising and, indeed, her novels were pure escapism, so my constant questioning was obviously an irritant. 'But yesterday you said we could stay up for supper with you and Daddy!' 'But you said you'd take us to the seaside tomorrow!' And so on. I had a prodigious memory for conversations and although I knew arguments would always end in my being sent to my room and having to apologise, I would only apologise for upsetting my mother, not for the point I had been trying to make. 'It's not fair!' was much in evidence.

Despite my jealousy of Eve's relationship with my mother, I did not in any way blame my sister. She was invariably patient with me and often succumbed to my pleas to go out and build a house or play games despite having no wish to do so! My younger sister, Anne, now became my constant companion. Three years younger than myself, she was a pale, skinny little girl, blonde, blue eyed like Eve and pretty, but was even less in favour with our mother than was I! Not only had she been the third disappointing girl but she was a natural mimic and had many of my father's mannerisms. I often felt that she was being reproached or punished unjustifiably and in my haste to defend her, would bring my mother's disapproval once more upon myself. I spent many a long hour confined to my bedroom for not minding my own business!

My determination to see Fair Play at all costs meant quite high costs for me but nevertheless did earn me my little sister's adoration. At the age of five, she was old enough to comply with my eight-year-old plans for our mutual amusement. We both loved animals and spent time with our pets. When we were required to stay indoors to be introduced to a visitor – this meant sitting quietly on the sofa and speaking only when spoken to – I would make up stories about a tiny family who lived behind the cushion – (pre-empting *The Borrowers*?) using a squeaky voice to pretend they were real. The fact that she believed in these little people unreservedly, added to my own enjoyment. Neither of us was much interested in my mother's erudite friends.

One most frequent visitor was the playwright Roland Pertwee, who my parents had met five years earlier when we lived in Hove. He wrote a play using much of the plot of my mother's novel *Heat Wave* which had run in the West End with excellent reviews. My mother adored him but he was not in the least interested in us children or we in him! Nevertheless we liked his two sons, Michael (later to become a playwright himself) and Jon, who became an actor, best remembered as one of the Dr. Who's and Worzel Gummidge.

Jon, as much the black sheep of his family as I was of mine, was given to showing off and once, trying to be clever, pushed me off a punt in the boathouse intending to perform a daring rescue by pulling me out of the water and saving me from drowning. As I fell between two boats which closed together after I had fallen in, I nearly did drown. However, I bore him no grudge as I felt sorry for him. He so desperately wanted to be noticed, but his father, Roland, had no intention of moving from centre stage, so like me, Jon was always in trouble. We also liked Coby, Roland's stepson who was as quiet as Jon was vociferous, a studious, gentle, smiling little boy who ultimately became a professor of Tropical Medicine in Edinburgh.

Herbert Marshall, Edna Best, Ronnie Shiner, Val Geilgud, George Sanders, Jack Hobbs the cricketer, Jack Strachey (who wrote 'These Foolish Things' and always played and sang the song on my mother's Blüthner piano when he visited) were all famous in those days and among the weekend visitors to the house my parents had bought by the lake at Slaugham, in Sussex. At one end of the long drawing room, Roland and my mother put on many amateur dramatic shows in which we children had little interest. Their fame meant nothing to us but the fact that they were 'important' visitors meant a tiresome change into pretty dresses, clean socks, clean fingernails, best behaviour and an hour or so of boredom whilst they talked about themselves.

I have to admit that I did welcome Jack Strachey's visits. He had a lovely singing voice and I decided it would be nice to marry him when I grew up so he could play the piano and sing to me every day. However, being aware one could not have two husbands, let alone three, Jack came third in line, my cousin Buzz being second and the man who came to service or repair our gramophone-cum-wireless set coming first. He had a test record of 'I want to be Happy' and deeply in love with him as I was, I could listen to it with him however many times he had to play it before the gramophone worked to his satisfaction. I think that record drove my mother mad!

I think my father must have been as bored as we children were during these weekend parties, although he was always an excellent host. He owned his own shoot beneath the South Downs which he enjoyed and shared with his friends.

We now had a new governess, a young girl called Joan Ashworth who remained with us until after the start of Second World War. I think it would be true to say she was more of a mother to Anne, who adored her. I liked her as she was sympathetic when I was in one of my tearful bouts following yet another violent blow up with my mother. Retrospectively, I have realised several things. First, that parents in those days did not psychoanalyse their children as they do today! Children were well behaved or naughty and I came into the latter category, not so much to gain my mother's attention but because all too often I had one of my 'Good Ideas' which invariably ended in trouble for me.

An example of a perfectly well-intended idea which went wrong was as follows: It happened one day when Joan had taken Eve to the dentist in Brighton and my parents were out as well, that Anne and I were left to our own devices, with only the servants to supervise us. So Anne and I had the run of the house since those who were not on duty were in the kitchen. We had recently been given a toy telephone that worked off a 6-volt torch battery. Having set this up in the nursery and with each of us standing in adjoining rooms, it quickly became apparent that we could hear each other just as easily without the telephone receivers. What we needed, I said, was more electricity so that we could be in rooms much further apart: but how to get more electricity? I had a good idea. We had a generator (mains supply was not yet available locally) which for some obscure reason I knew provided 220 volts. All we had to do to get about forty times more volume, I told my sister, was pull the wires out of the 6-volt torch battery and stick them in the wall socket.

Anne wasn't keen on the idea, sensing trouble, but I chose not to heed her warning. Bang! The lights went out, the room filled with acrid, evil-smelling smoke, there were shouts from the kitchen where the cook and parlourmaid had been enjoying a quiet cup of tea and I was in Trouble, with a capital T – even more so when my parents returned and subsequently received a hefty bill for major repairs to the generator.

Another such good idea involved a catapulted flight. One of the big beech trees in the nearby spinney had long branches sweeping down to the ground. It was a good tree to climb but once climbed, it lost its allure. Studying it on one occasion, I realised that if I grasped the pliable end of a branch, held on to it as I climbed part way up the tree, the branch doubled backwards would be under great tension. If I then jumped off the tree, the branch would swing upwards and outwards and my weight would bring it and me safely down to earth. I jumped and it did – but not safely. I was catapulted skywards so violently I lost my hold on the branch and fell heavily to the ground. I came to with metal clamps in my head behind my ear and a severe telling off for leading not only myself but also my sisters into such danger.

I think it was about then that my mother decided it would be better if my 'good ideas' were used as story plots rather than as games for my sisters and me to enjoy. She gave me an old portable typewriter and suggested that I might follow her example and become an author. Realising this would raise me in her estimation as well as being something Eve could not do, as she wasn't given to 'good ideas', I immediately set to work.

I think that was probably the start of my writing career.

CHAPTER TWO

Furnace Pond Cottage, our home in Sussex, was a lovely old house, which had originally been three Tudor cottages on to which my mother built another wing. It overlooked the lake known as Furnace Pond. It had six bedrooms, a nursery, a dining room, a study, a large drawing room, a big kitchen and a maid's room, a swimming pool (unheated), a grass tennis court and a large garden. Taking care of all this was the cook, a housemaid, a lady's maid cum parlourmaid, my father's valet, my mother's secretary, our governess and a full-time gardener. Although we enjoyed these facilities, the house was fairly isolated. The nearest public transport, a bus service to Haywards Heath, was two miles away.

Lacking any local friend to play with, my favourite occupation was to go to the house of the friend I had made at the convent – a little girl my age called Margaret Pepler. The youngest of six children, she lived in a big, rambling house on Ditchling Common. Unless my mother's secretary at that time, called Marjorie, was free to drive me, I walked up to the bus stop at Handcross, changed buses in Haywards Heath and caught a connection to Ditchling. Because of the time this took, I usually stayed the night; and likewise, when Margaret came to stay with me, she stayed overnight.

I did not consider her visits anything like as much fun, as there was nothing exciting to do where I lived, whereas at her house when the weather permitted, we would go riding on the South Downs, taking a picnic lunch with us. Not that either of us had ever had a lesson. We rode bicycles down to the livery stables in Ditchling, hired ponies and rode through the village and up to Ditchling Beacon. We were left entirely to our own devices, which, in retrospect, seems unbelievable seeing how young we were and what inexperienced riders!

Margaret was a wonderful friend, not least because she always liked my good ideas – or most of the time. On one occasion I thought it might be exciting to go after dark to the little churchyard across the Common, about half a mile distant and wait for the clock to strike midnight to see if any ghosts came out of the graves. We decided to include Margaret's local friend, Winnie, in this escapade (safety in numbers?) but whilst we were easily able to slip out of Margaret's large house by a back staircase, Winnie lived in a two up two down. Undaunted, she agreed with my suggestion that she make a rope of her sheets and escape by her bedroom window.

In due course, we left the house carrying candles – Margaret's house had no electricity – and with beating hearts, made our way to Winnie's. She had been waiting for us and duly appeared down her rope of sheets. The church was not far off but the friendly moon suddenly disappeared and we were plunged into inky darkness. Somewhere nearby, a vixen shrieked and our nerves, already very much on edge, gave in to terror. No sooner had we reached the graveyard, by an unspoken agreement, we turned and ran back to Winnie's house. We stood beneath her window where the sheet rope still hung limply in the faint glimmer of returned moonlight – and looked at one another in horror. The clock now struck midnight and we were terrified that the ghosts had followed us from the graveyard and were about to appear, but . . . and it was a very big 'but', whilst Winnie had slid DOWN the rope with no difficulty, climbing UP it was proving impossible. There was nothing for it but to wake her parents.

To Margaret's and my everlasting shame – and even today I'm embarrassed to admit this – we left Winnie to her inevitable punishment and ran!

On another occasion, we were playing on Ditchling Common near a small pond. It was midsummer and we were extremely hot. The idea came to me that as there was no one else to be seen, we should have a swim. Margaret pointed out that we could neither get our clothes wet as the grownups would guess what we'd been up to when we went home, nor could we swim with nothing on. Not to be daunted I suggested we make ourselves 'grass' skirts with the reeds, which were growing in abundance round the pond. If a little anxiously Margaret, as always, agreed that it was a good idea.

We proceeded to make the skirts; not very successfully as so many reeds were needed to ensure they were not see-through. Too hot to do any more work, we stripped off our summer frocks and removed our sandals but decided after consultation that perhaps we should keep on our knickers. As I was not told until some years later of my near expulsion from the convent for dancing bare-chested, we were happy to leave our top halves bare.

The water was somewhat disappointing because although it was cold compared to the shimmering heat outside, the pond was clogged with weeds and our feet were squelching in unpleasantly slimy mud. Moreover, when we tried to swim on the surface, our knickers came off. We climbed back on to dry land and having pulled our dresses back over our damp bodies, we tried for the next half hour to get the duckweed off our knickers. As neither of us had ever had to wash our clothes, it didn't occur to us to go home and rinse them in the bath. Perhaps we were afraid we'd be detected doing so.

I wasn't conscious of the fact that this was yet another of my 'good ideas' gone wrong. Today, such an escapade is unimaginable, for who would allow two eight-year-old little girls to play on a common alone? It wasn't as if anyone even knew where we were. Or perhaps, as Margaret was the youngest of six children, her parents had given up worrying where they all were.

I'm glad to say our activities were not always naughty. Margaret's mother was a sweet, very quiet, patient person and she always made me welcome. Margaret's three elder brothers were all but grown up, her sisters older than her, so I imagine Mrs Pepler was pleased to have a companion for her youngest child. Margaret was not only pretty but also sweet natured and we never quarrelled, swearing undying love for one another. I admired her enormously because she was already showing her ability as the ballet dancer she was later to become and looked like a beautiful little fairy when she danced for my mother and me. We would have spent every day together had we lived nearer.

At the age of ten, I did have another close companion, Tony. He was the same age as me and filled the role of brother perfectly. Tony's father had recently died and his mother was often away, leaving him in his beautiful large home near Haywards Heath to the care of the household staff. Our mothers were friends and it suited both of them to leave us in the care of the servants to enjoy ourselves however we wished. This frequently consisted of climbing over the vast areas of roof, daring each other to jump from wall to wall or to balance on the edges. I wonder how we survived!

Tony had a pet white rat called Penelope and, somewhat to my surprise, my mother allowed me to get one, too. I called him Jeremy. We always took our rats with us when we visited each other and they were extremely tame – and intelligent. One day, however, when I arrived at Tony's house, he was close to tears. Penelope had died. As it tran-spired, her death very nearly resulted in mine!

The cold, stiff corpse of Tony's pet met my uneasy gaze as I got out of my mother's car and she drove away. I was glad that Jeremy, unlike the stiffened Penelope, was snug in my pocket, warm and vibrant. We could not make up our minds whether to bury her or whether, as I now suggested, we skin and stuff her, so preserving at least her likeness for always.

Tony thought my taxidermy idea was a good one. The difficulty lay in deciding which of us was to perform this tricky operation. Tony sharpened his penknife several times but neither of us could stomach the role of surgeon.

I loved Tony with all the passion of a brother-less ten-year-old and until this moment I believed I would do anything in the world for him. But sticking a penknife into that small white corpse was more than I could bring myself to do. I was deeply disappointed in myself but although Tony likewise could not do the job, I made allowances for him, as Penelope was his much loved pet.

I suggested tentatively making a coffin and having a real burial ceremony. Tony cheered at this suggestion and we went in search of a suitable box. We used Jeremy for sizing up the coffin and found a Havana cigar box in which Penelope fitted perfectly. The name 'Havana', however, seemed inappropriate. Tony suggested we paint it, but we had no paint. All that was available was a can of green paint in the potting shed. Tony had been forbidden to touch it because, so the gardener had told him, it contained arsenic, which was a deadly poison.

Having shown myself to be too squeamish to skin Penelope, I now saw my chance to vindicate myself in Tony's eyes. *I* had not been forbidden to use the paint, I pointed out.

We finished the coffin as the lunch gong sounded. One minute I was surveying the attractive display of cold chicken and fruit salad with a mouth-watering appetite, the next, my stomach had curled into a knot and I knew I couldn't eat a thing. Fortunately Tony's mother was out and the maid who had charge of us was not supervising our meal. Tony, pleased with the prospective funeral, ate enough for two.

I was feeling too sick to watch him. I stood by the window staring at the green grass, the green leaves, the green hedges, remembering the green paint. Arsenic. Deadly poison. I followed Tony out into the garden. Somehow, I helped him place Penelope's body now wrapped in a handkerchief, into the green coffin. Somehow I stood upright while he dug a hole. Somehow I read the burial service from a prayer book. Dry-eyed, Tony filled in the hole and asked me what was the matter.

'You've gone green!' he said.

'I feel sick!' I told him as my legs buckled beneath me and I collapsed on the grass beside Penelope's grave. 'And I have a terrible pain.'

Tony regarded me anxiously. Perhaps it was the paint and I had been poisoned, he suggested, confirming my own suspicion. Then the thought struck him that he would be in big trouble if the grown ups found out we'd used the paint.

Waves of pain engulfed me but I managed to gasp out a promise that I wouldn't tell. He made me make our usual vow of 'Cut my throat and hope to die' – which was unfortunate in this instance as I had no doubt that I *was* going to die. The pain came in regular spasms increasing each time in intensity. Every so often I vomited on the lawn. Tony informed me, but without much hope, that there was no sign of green paint in it.

Slowly, inexorably, the afternoon wore on and the rays of the sun cooled but I was burning hot. At six o'clock my mother came to collect me. I don't remember the drive home. My next recollection was of the doctor saying:

'Acute appendicitis . . . into hospital . . . operate tonight!'

I knew his diagnosis was wrong. I wanted desperately to shout out that I was dying from arsenic poisoning, and that taking my appendix out couldn't possibly save my life. But I had promised . . . I would die rather than let Tony down. Today I can still recall the surgeon's voice telling me to count up to twenty, to breathe deeply and not be frightened.

I came round some hours later in a room in the cottage hospital in Haywards Heath. The nurse told me my appendix had been safely removed and that I was going to be just fine. Although I felt all right, I didn't believe her.

Next morning I saw my scar. I no longer had any pain. I no longer felt sick. I lay waiting for my mother's promised visit wondering if the arsenic had drained out of me along with my appendix. Arsenic was green. So the surgeon must have noticed it. My mother told me there had been nothing unusual about my operation – only that my condition had flared up so suddenly. I asked to see Tony.

He came next day and I showed him my scar. He was impressed by the two tiny metal clamps, which had been used instead of stitches. He then told me I was stupid not to have asked the doctors to keep my appendix in a bottle where we could have looked at it to see if it was green. He was not very pleased with me but then he asked the one question that had brought him to my bedside. Had I told? I informed him proudly that I hadn't broken my vow.

He picked a bit of fluff off the red blanket of my bed and screwed it into a tiny ball which he flicked at me.

'I didn't think you'd sneak,' he said. 'I told my friends at school that you were as good as any boy.'

He was soon bored with the sick room visit and left me to make the best of my convalescence. I lay in bed remembering '. . . as good as any boy.' It was the highest accolade he had ever awarded me and I hugged my sore stomach feeling on top of the world.

Unfortunately our two mothers quarrelled so my visits to Tony ceased, and not long after, my mother decided that it was time for her three daughters to go to boarding school. Because of my disruptive behaviour, she decided to send me to a different school from the one she chose for Eve and Anne. It had only sixty pupils and like so many private girls schools on the Sussex coast, supplied a reasonable education, outdoor games, indoor dancing lessons and needlework (which I hated) – in other words, it prepared us for our future lives as wives to young men from similar backgrounds, and mothers of future generations of the upper classes! Not that there was any class distinction in my school. There was no need because we were all of the same ilk.

I loved my life at school. I made friends easily and readily accepted school discipline which I quickly realised applied strictly to all of us, unlike the situation at home where I felt there was one rule for Eve and one for me! I was good at games, good at ballroom dancing, bad at needlework and an average academic student. However, I had not been at the school very long before I was at odds with the History/English teacher who I now don't intend to give her real name. I had written a story about three pet rabbits which escaped, got lost and had sundry adventures. It was the kind of story I made up for Anne. Doubtless to ingratiate themselves with my now famous mother, her publishers had produced it. I, myself, did not think much of it but it had a large number of reviews, one of which, the *New Statesman* no less, said in their review that 'Miss Robins should go far'. I was quite delighted with the title he had given me which made me feel extremely grown up. As a consequence, I decided I would be an author when I grew up and when we were asked to write essays, I put my heart and soul into them.

They were not meant to be funny but Miss Stewart decided to ridicule my efforts. She would read them aloud managing to make them ridiculous to the point where the entire class would be in fits of laughter. Gradually, I ceased to pay more than a bare minimum of attention to her lessons and I sat at my desk wondering if there was any way I could kill her without being found out!

Perhaps because I was an exuberant, lively child, the teacher was unaware of my inner turmoil. At a very young age, I developed warts on my hands (I believe they were of nervous origin). I was taken regularly by my mother to Brighton to have them 'frozen' – a treatment which had no results and the numbers increased. Such was my shame at this deformity, my hands would break into a sweat whenever I was required to 'shake hands politely' with visitors. It soon followed that whenever I had to use my hands in public, my palms would become dripping wet.

Curiously, all the warts disappeared overnight after an occasion when I'd had grease paint put on them for a fancy dress party where I went as a Red Indian. They never returned, but the nervous reaction to my hands remained into adulthood and my boyfriends failed to understand why I would never hold hands.

Now, at my new school, I had managed to hide my 'deformity' – or at least until Miss Stewart decided to entertain my classmates with my essays. Knowing I would eventually be required to collect my exercise book from her and that I could not hope to wipe my hands dry, I really did suffer. Although that affliction has all but left me in my old age, my palms still become damp as I recount the embarrassment of those readings.

However, it was not long before I had one of my brainwaves. Miss Stewart wore glasses. Her desk, raised on a small dais, faced the afternoon sun. At certain times in the afternoon, as the sun moved round, it reflected on her glasses sufficiently to oblige her to move her chair a little to one side. All I needed to fulfil my murderous intent, was to find a method of keeping the sun on her face long enough for her to move her chair so far that it toppled her off the dais and hopefully killed her.

I had the means to achieve my objective on my desk – a Smarts toffee tin lid, gold on the outside and with a silver lining, which I used as a pencil box. When the sun's rays touched it, a dancing light would appear on the wall opposite. By adjusting the lid, I could move the light more or less where I wanted. I had only to sit quietly through one of Miss Stewart's lessons until the sun had moved round far enough for me to guide the reflected light on to her spectacles.

I am ashamed to recall that this particular idea worked perfectly. However, as I saw my victim tipping backwards off the dais, I was frightened to death. Much as I hated her, I didn't really want to be a murderess. Fortunately for me, my many past prayers at the convent to be forgiven my sins, must have paid dividends because Miss Stewart only suffered a big bruise on the back of her head and another on her hip. She never knew it was my fault.

Reflecting on this vengeful side of my nature, I cannot recall any time, past or future, when I felt the same desire to get rid of an enemy – and an enemy Miss Stewart most certainly was. I came to the more charitable conclusion when I was older that she was, in fact, a bitter, frustrated woman. A university graduate of some distinction, she had doubtless hoped for an academic future, instead of which she was spending her days in a minor girls' boarding school as a teacher with no prospects for advancement. A spinster, childless, she must have become embittered, most especially when considering my mother's success as a writer. Moreover, my mother was beautiful, married with children, and comparatively wealthy, yet without one academic qualification. Whilst eminently readable, her books were far from being literary masterpieces. In fact, years later my mother said to me: 'I'm not a literary writer but I am a first-class story teller!' Those words were no idle boast. Today in 2006, twenty-one years after her death, her books are still being widely read every year by not only hundreds but thousands.

Sometimes today when I am asked to talk to a group of women, there are always one or two who tell me they would love to write a book but have no qualifications. Unless they are aiming for the Booker Prize for literature, I tell them, all they need is a good plot, a good imagination, an understanding of human emotions and the ability to express them.

Apart from my unhappy relationship with Miss Stewart, I was entirely happy at my school. I had many friends, was good at games and got on well with my other teachers. My two sisters, however, were far from happy at their school. Eve, as always, hated being parted from my mother and was terribly homesick. Anne, too, was homesick but was missing Joan, and her much-loved rabbits! Eve excelled at sports and did well in class, whilst Anne showed all the signs of a budding musician. This was not surprising as the gene was undoubtedly in our maternal family line.

Our maternal grandfather, a gentleman from Alsace by the name of Herman Klein, was a musician of some distinction. He could not only play the piano, sing and act but he was also a composer and author, and at the tender age of twenty-two was music critic on the *Sunday Times*. Alas, we children never knew him. My mother could play the piano beautifully entirely by ear but although she had been considered a talented musician at her convent, after hearing her sing one verse of a song with which she had hoped to impress him, her father told her never to sing in his presence again! It would have been a very different state of affairs had he lived to hear his granddaughter, Anne, who had a voice like a choirboy and she sang in the Bach Choir at the Albert Hall.

Our grandfather was the eldest of eight sons all of whom played some kind of musical instrument. Herman's wife, their mother, also from the Alsace, spoke and taught seven languages. Grandfather studied singing under the famous teacher of the day, named Manuel Garcia. He could not only play the violin, the piano, sing and act, but he was also a composer. When he was only twenty-two, he composed a Grand March for the opening of the Paris Exhibition, which started his rise to fame. He held musical soirées at his home attended by the famous and talented musicians of the day, and also arranged several soirées at Buckingham Palace for Queen Victoria's Jubilee celebrations.

As well as being musically talented, my grandfather was an excellent cricketer and tennis player, and, not least, an author. Between the turn of the last century and 1935, he wrote learned books about the development of operatic and musical life in England since the 1800s. As music critic for the *Sunday Times*, a position he held for twenty years, he knew all the great singers and composers of the day. Several of his books contain pictures of such noteworthies as Wagner, Jenny Lind, Verdi, Brahms, Adelina Pati, Melba, Paderewski, Puccini, Elgar and so on. During his career he was also Professor of Singing at the Guildhall School of Music and music critic for the *Gramophone*.

Small wonder, therefore, that my mother had such a perfect musical ear that if she heard a pleasant melody, she could sit down at her piano and reproduce it entirely by ear.

As for me, my piano teacher told my mother after a few terms that she was wasting her money having me taught! Nevertheless, I am not entirely tone deaf as I have always been able to detect if someone else is even fractionally off key. I also have a good sense of rhythm and was considered one of the best dancers when we had our ballroom dancing lessons at school. I just wish that I could at least sing the National Anthem in tune!

Unfortunately, none of us ever knew our grandfather who had remarried and, in any event, was not interested in children. He had divorced my grandmother when, after giving him three children, she eloped with a dashing young army officer called Berkeley. He was promptly cashiered, divorce being a serious disgrace in those days. My two uncles, Adrian and Daryl, remained with him, and my mother, Denise, went to America with Granny and her new husband, where he tried to make a living picking oranges in Los Angeles, in those days a small sleepy town. Hollywood did not exist. He then joined an estate agency and sold land round Ocean Beach, which was then a lonely place with only a few bungalows dotted along the dunes.

Berkeley was the second of Granny's three husbands. She was an Australian by birth. With her petite features and enormous blue eyes she was always attractive to the opposite sex and even in her eighties flirted unashamedly with all our boyfriends when we visited her.

My grandmother, Berkeley and my mother were in California in 1906, the year the earthquake flattened San Francisco in the month of April. My mother wrote in her autobiography that the quake was near enough to where they lived to shake the house, which soon became a refuge for the homeless. It was impossible for Berkeley to sell land in an 'earthquake' area and so they returned to England. It was then that my grandmother decided to try to earn money to support them by writing stories for what were known as 'penny-dreadfuls'. Berkeley hired a typewriter and typed her handwritten manuscripts.

The stories were about poor waifs or servant girls who were rescued from poverty by well-to-do (sometimes titled) husbands-to-be. D.C. Thompson of Dundee published them and asked my grandmother for serials, which she promptly produced. She was paid five or six pounds a week for these instalments. Thus it was that she decided that when my mother finished her education at the convent in England, her seventeen-year-old daughter should go up to Dundee to work on one of D.C. Thompson's magazines. This was a highly unusual thing to do considering how sheltered girls of that age and class were, not to mention that she knew no one in Dundee other than the publishers, who could hardly be considered adequate chaperones.

When I am asked whether I think there is a 'writing' gene which a child inherits, I often question whether such a thing exists or whether it is the environmental influence that affects them. My mother grew up seeing her mother typing her stories and managing to earn a living, and she did the same when her own family finances were in poor straits. I, too, grew up watching my mother at her typewriter. She wrote every morning of her life from nine to one unless she was on holiday. Sometimes, if her secretary went with her, she even continued to write when she was abroad.

So, I, too, turned to writing, but thanks to my portable typewriter, I began at a somewhat earlier age! That Remington accompanied me all through the war and remained a faithful friend throughout hundreds of stories, serials, articles and over fifty novels before I was finally persuaded to allow it to retire in favour of an electric typewriter. That eventually gave way to a word processor. I now struggle with a computer whose technology frequently defeats me, at which point I think secretly of my faithful Remington who never wiped a chapter; caught a virus; asked me questions or told me what next I should do. This

I dare not tell my grandchildren, who have been computer literate practically since birth!

There were 'genes', if such exist, on both sides of my mother's family. Her cousin, Sydney Carroll, became a journalist and theatrical producer; another was George Hutchinson who founded the publishing house, and my Great Aunt Alice, who became the proprietor of the *Sunday Times*. It was she who employed Herman Klein.

My father, Arthur, on the other hand, was very much a typical Englishman, not artistic but an excellent sportsman, although his activities were curtailed by the severe leg wound he received in the First World War. There were Huguenots in his family so his three daughters – 'the three little works of art', as Roland Pertwee liked to call us – had a somewhat mixed heritage. He was a quiet, reserved man who was seldom involved in our upbringing, which he left to my mother; however, we deeply respected him and as I grew up, I realised what immense courage he had. He was intensely patriotic and a man of principle.

Subsequently, in the year or so before he died at the early age of sixty-three, he became something of an eccentric, but to my knowledge, I never heard a word spoken in his disfavour. I wish he had lived long enough for my sons and grandsons to have known him and learned the many skills he could have taught them.

Eve showed no inclination to follow in our mother's footsteps and become a writer. She preferred more homely pursuits. When a plan was devised for her to go to a Swiss international school near Vevey, she was horrified. She had hated being away at boarding school and was hoping now to be able to remain at home with our mother. After a great deal of persuasion, she finally agreed to go – but only if I could go with her. I was thrilled. Much as I had enjoyed my school, most especially playing tennis and hockey matches in which I was in the first teams, I loved the thought of the proposed adventure. Not yet fifteen, I had not been required to take any exams, so my father voiced one of his rare objections to my leaving my school. He was over-ruled, however, and off went Eve and I to what seemed like another world.

CHAPTER 3

The *Institut Préalpin* was perched on the side of a mountain overlooking Lake Geneva in the village of Chexbres, above Vevey. It was run by a Monsieur Buser and his wife who took in pupils up to the age of eighteen. By normal standards, the building was small for a boarding school but this contributed to the family atmosphere. For the most part, bedrooms were each shared by three girls. We were of different nationalities so even were you able to master a few words of Spanish, for example, these would not enable you to speak to a Dutch or Polish girl who shared your room, nor at mealtimes to converse with the Belgian girl sitting next to you. All lessons were in French and thus it was that in a very short time we all became bilingual.

The regime was tailored to an individual girl's requirements. Domestic science was mostly for the older girls; any child could join art lessons and there was a choice of languages, so apart from French, I learned the basics of Italian.

Physical training was compulsory and took place out of doors. We were taught how to throw a javelin and those who wished could play tennis. Keen players as Eve and I were, we asked M. Buser if we could weed and roll the school's old red hard court to improve its surface; and having done so whether we could play tennis matches against the several English girls' finishing schools around Lausanne. We looked on them as being very 'stuck-up' and M. Buser was absolutely delighted when we finally got a team of six together and beat all the schools we challenged.

Apart from the pleasures of lessons in the garden in the summer and educational visits to concerts and the theatre in Lausanne, we enjoyed a lot of freedom. We were allowed to walk in the surrounding mountainside with its beautiful wild flowers and streams in the summer, go into the little village of Chexbres to buy cakes and sweets in the *patisserie*. The big thrill for me was skiing. As a new girl, I had never been on skis but struggled on the hill outside the school grounds as soon as the first snow fell. I could just about stand up by the weekend when a notice went up (as I later discovered was customary) for girls to put their names down on the list if they wished to join the weekend skiing trip to Crans-sur-Sierre. We were to stay the night in disused army barracks so as to allow us two whole days skiing. It sounded enormous fun and I immediately put my name down. Nobody questioned my ability – or otherwise – to ski, presuming as my name was on the list, I was fully competent.

At four o'clock on Saturday morning, the eight other girls and I collected our packed lunches, shouldered our skis and proceeded to walk down in the dark through the vineyards to the railway station at Vevey. There we caught the train to Sierre and a funicular up the mountain to Crans. By this time, the sun was just beginning to turn the snow pink on the mountaintops. Everywhere was sparkling in the sunlight and, suddenly remembering dull old school walks in a crocodile along the seafront promenade on winter days, I felt as if I had been transported to Heaven.

After I'd had breakfast and limbered up on the slopes, we were told to put on the sealskin covers for our skis as we were going to climb the mountain stretching above us in order to have the enjoyable run down. At this point, I still had no fear, as, although tiring, I was able to manage the uphill climb. It took several hours before we stopped for lunch. The view was now quite breathtaking and I

looked forward to the run down to the village. For those
who have been to Crans in recent times, I should point out
that there was one hotel only in the tiny village; no T-bars,
or ski lifts of any kind. If you wished to ski down a mountain, you had first to climb it.

This, however, was all new to me and when M. Buser,
who was in charge of us, set off down the mountain at
great speed, the other girls quickly following him, I suddenly
realised that mastering the gentle slide down the hill outside
the school when I had managed to remain upright, in no
way equipped me to ski down a steep mountain. Neither
could I remain where I was since I was unlikely to be
missed until the group reached base. At best, it would be
at least four hours before someone could climb up and
rescue me when they found I was missing. Even then I
would still have to get down the mountain which in deep
snow would be unwalkable.

There was no alternative but to ski down as best I could.
It was a good thing no one was behind to see me. My legs
were wide apart to assist my balance and when I couldn't
bring myself to a stop in front of a tree, I sat down. My
momentum invariably stirred the overhanging fir branches
and a shower of snow would float down and cover me.
The waterproof material of the ski suits we all wore in
those days, was inadequate to keep out this persistent
drenching so I was soon not only breathless but also uncomfortably damp.

Although undoubtedly I was anxious about the time it
was taking me to get to the bottom of the mountain, I
never doubted that I would eventually find my companions
as I could see the tracks of their skis in the snow. Besides,
there was a certain magic about the perfect stillness as I
lay in my deep snow beds. It was as if I was alone in the
world, but not a threatening one, with pools of bright
sunshine sparkling on the white snow between the gaps in

the branches. But all too aware of time passing, I knew I must struggle to my feet and continue my perilous descent as best I could. It is with some pride I relate that I reached the village without any broken limbs. There and then I resolved to learn to ski properly as soon as I could. In those days we had extremely long, wooden skis which, if stood upright, reached from the ground to the tip of one's fingers when the arm was held aloft above the head. The bindings were coiled metal springs which, once snapped shut, could only be opened by hand. Thus a nasty fall resulted either in a broken ski or a broken leg. Skiing in icy conditions could be frightening but it was also exhilarating and gradually during my two years at school, I learned, if not to ski elegantly, at least to stay upright and get down what today are called black runs. Pistes did not exist and there were no such people as ski instructors.

Many years later, when I was in my fifties, a ski guide watched me descend a steepish piste and stood laughing his head off at my ungainly stance.

'You are too old now for me to teach you to be good skier,' he told me bluntly, adding to my disbelief that as at least I remained upright, I could accompany him to the top of the most difficult run in the resort. I was instructed to follow him down, turning in the same spot he did and stopping only when he did. He only stopped twice and went at a speed I would never have dared to go by myself. It was terrifying and yet the most exciting ski run I have ever done before or since. Still laughing, he told me that I may not have the grace but, as I had not fallen, 'I 'ad ze balance; ze rhythm; ze courage!'

Eve did not greatly care for skiing but she was moderately happy at the *Institut*, although she still would have preferred to be at home. After our first year there, she was allowed to leave and return to England in order to attend daily a domestic college instead. I was allowed to spend

another year as well as the Easter holidays (for skiing) at
the *Institut*. I was now fifteen, rising sixteen and I have a
photograph of myself sitting in the garden with my faithful
portable typewriter on my knee, on which I would write
long letters home. One of these contained a graphic account
of the radio broadcast the then King Edward VIII made
on his abdication. Because M. Buser deemed it a matter
of national importance, I and one other English girl, Valerie,
were allowed to go to his private salon to listen to the
broadcast.

Edward VIII was very much a hero to us. He had acceded
to the throne when the elderly George V died, was young,
good-looking and fashionable. News of his on-going affair
with the divorcee Mrs. Simpson had not reached us and
so the possibility of him having to give up the throne to
marry her had never crossed our minds, nor indeed the
minds of most of the population of the country. We were
quite saddened by the news of his departure and I think
we were in tears. I was more concerned about his brother,
now King George VI, who had to struggle through a
follow-up broadcast despite a very debilitating stutter. A
few days after the broadcast, we received cuttings from the
English papers showing photographs of the new King and
Queen Elizabeth with the two little princesses, Elizabeth
and Margaret. They were quickly forgotten whilst I got on
with my enjoyable life.

Unbeknown to me – and I have to say, I would not have
been interested in the knowledge – other events of note
had taken place. In England, Neville Chamberlain had
replaced Stanley Baldwin as Prime Minister, Italy had
invaded Abyssinia, and Germany had been rearming its
navy to an alarming degree. Adolf Hitler had become the
German Chancellor and the National Socialists were now
in control. One of the girls at school, called Ingeborg, was
a Hitler *mädchen* – a staunch member of the Hitler Youth

organisation, and she had posters of him stuck all round her bedroom walls. I don't remember her trying to convert anyone to the Nazi ideals, but she looked very Germanic – a tall strong girl with very blonde hair which she wore in a thick pigtail.

Among my friends was an American girl who, though I wasn't aware of it, was Jewish. We were so politically ignorant that none of us could have conceived what horrors Inge might one day inflict on Carol. I don't doubt, however, that both sets of parents were well aware of the anti-Jewish regime developing in Germany, and their daughters' presence in this international environment may have been deliberate. I also had a German friend called Hannalore who invited me to stay with her at her parents' house in Frankfurt for two weeks during one of the school holidays. I wrote home to my parents remarking how very heavily we were chaperoned. There was always someone with us even if we were playing tennis on the local tennis courts. If we went to a cinema or the theatre, both her mother and father went with us.

I had the feeling that wherever we went, Hannalore's father and mother wanted people to see me. We spoke English at all times and I was always introduced as 'Hannalore's English friend'. It was somehow a sinister atmosphere and I did not really enjoy my visit despite their obvious wish to ensure I never lacked for entertainment or activity.

At that time, I supposed her parents to be unnaturally strict. However, a year later, when my mother was in her flat in Sloane Street, late one night there was a knock on the door and Hannalore and her parents stood there. They had only what they were carrying and they had come to ask my mother to lend them some money. They had managed to get out of Germany secretly, only by leaving everything they owned behind them. They were on their way to

Australia, thankful not to be amongst their Jewish coun-
terparts being rounded up and sent to labour camps.

Was it possible, I ask myself now, that my mother really
knew nothing of Hitler's intention to exterminate the Jewish
race? This was 1937 and yet I was not only allowed to
visit Hannalore's Jewish family in Frankfurt that holiday,
but I was to be allowed a year later to go to Germany for
another year.

But now in the carefree environment of my Swiss school,
we all had lessons together, went to the theatre, skied, were
taken for picnics up the mountains in spring to pick bunches
of the narcissi growing wild to put in special boxes to send
home to our families; and were all, including Hannalore
and Carol, without any fears for the future.

M. Buser's second in command was a short, thin, highly
motivated Swiss woman called Mademoiselle Traveletti.
Every morning, she would make a tour of our rooms and
woe-betide us if we left so much as a single hair in our
hairbrushes or a smeared washbasin. Offences were read
out in detail after lunch whilst we sat shame-faced at our
tables. Even now, almost seventy years later, I still feel guilty
when I see any stray hairs in my hairbrush! I don't recall
what punishments there were – perhaps publicly shaming
us was sufficient.

Rumour circulated that one of the girls who'd been
missing for a few days, had in fact been expelled. Eve,
senior to me, confirmed that the rumour was true, and
added that it was because she had been found in another
girl's bed. Knowing nothing of lesbianism, we none of us
understood why this should be a crime worthy of banish-
ment. She was soon forgotten in the excitement of a more
recognisable crime – that of a senior girl not only smoking
but also on hearing Mlle. Traveletti's footsteps outside the
room, had tossed her cigarette out of the window where
it had landed on M. Buser's sun canopy below and burnt

a dinnerplate-sized hole in it. To our surprise, she wasn't expelled.

I cannot recall a moment's unhappiness there and I was loath to leave school at the end of my last term.

My mother had then just finished her thirty-ninth novel called *Climb to the Stars*. There were now regular weekend parties at Furnace Pond Cottage which included many V.I.P.s – actors, editors, authors, composers, producers, and musicians. One of the many was an actor, then moderately unknown, called George Sanders. He had been chosen to play the lead opposite Edna Best, the star at that time, in the play, *Further Outlook Unsettled*, which my mother and Roland Pertwee had jointly written. Edna Best decided during rehearsals that George was not up to the standard of acting she required, and to his chagrin he was subsequently replaced.

He did not take this rebuff lying down. When the first night dinner party was arranged at the Savoy and he found he had not been invited, he booked a single table for himself positioned as near as was possible to the party and remained silent but steadfast throughout the evening – needless to say to everyone's acute embarrassment. I think my mother, who thought he should have been invited, was the only person who went over to speak to him as he had been a frequent visitor to our house.

Determined nonetheless to prove himself, he went out to Hollywood and before long became one of the top British film stars of the time. For thirty years he played the villain in such films as *All About Eve*, for which he was awarded an Oscar.

On one of the frequent visits he made to our house at the time of the rehearsals, he fell in love with my sister, Eve. He would serenade her with his guitar, singing the love songs of the day in his beautiful voice. Eve was only sixteen and found his interest in her embarrassing but flattering. My father thought her far too young for such attentions and most unusually put his foot down and said my mother was not to invite him to the house again.

Many years later, after Eve and I were married, George came over to England from America and got in touch with Eve, asking if they could meet. She was somewhat reluctant to do so being now a happily married woman and consulted me. We jointly decided it might be quite interesting to see how fame had changed the George we'd known. It was a big mistake. Although he was as handsome as ever, the life he had led and his two unhappy marriages to Susan Larson and then to Zsa Zsa Gabor, had turned the ambitious young man into a disillusioned middle-aged one.

He produced some singularly unpleasant pornographic postcards which he seemed to think would amuse us. Eve, to whom he first showed them, blushed a fiery red and quickly handed them to me. Although both of us were still ridiculously ignorant of homosexual activities, we were both married and there was no mistaking what the men were doing! I supposed that George must be trying to shock us (which, indeed, he did) and wondered how best we could extricate ourselves from this embarrassing situation. I handed the postcards back to George without looking at him and turning to Eve, told her she had overlooked the fact that we were meeting her husband in ten minutes and we were going to be very late if we didn't leave immediately.

As we had invited George to come for a drink and we had not as yet offered him one, it must have been pretty obvious that we hadn't found his postcards entertaining. However, with Eve grasping eagerly at the straw I'd offered her, we were able to get rid of our unwanted guest. Discussing him later, we decided that he had become debauched by his riches and was probably more to be pitied than condemned! On the other hand he may still have been in love with Eve. In any event, in 1972 we read in the paper that he had taken a drug overdose alone in a hotel near Barcelona. The note he left blamed boredom for his suicide, but his third marriage to Benita Hume had also ended in divorce as, too, had his final marriage to Zsa Zsa Gabor's sister, Magda, so Eve and I thought it more likely to have been depression. It seemed sad to think of such an end to the life of the handsome young man with the beautiful voice we recalled from all those years ago.

Now, in 1937, my mother's career was still in the ascendant. She was billed all over the London buses and Underground stations with posters saying 'ROBINS FOR ROMANCE'; this, long before Barbara Cartland, who was a friend of hers, took over her role as 'the Queen of Romance'. I imagine the last thing my mother then wanted was to have to cope with her difficult adolescent middle daughter. Whatever the reason, my plea to go to Germany to learn German was granted and I was packed off to Munich to a Professor Herr von Zwehl where I was one of three paying guests.

I had a number of lessons on a daily basis with Herr von Zwehl and was enrolled in the University for some of my studies. To be truthful, I don't think I took any of them very seriously. It was 1938 and Munich was full of students of all nationalities. We had the greatest fun. There was ice-skating on a floodlit rink at night, fancy dress dances, and operatic performances at student rates in the magnificent *Opernhaus*. There was the festival known at the *Oktober Fest* with dancing, singing, and tents full of people at long tables drinking the local beer from tall steins. There were trips in the summer to the lakes at Tegensee, skiing in the winter and spring at Garmisch.

Before I had been very long in Munich, I met a girl two years older than myself called Pam Johnsen who, coincidentally, came from a large family living not twenty minutes from my own home in Slaugham. Pam was the eldest girl of a family of eight and she was a lot more sophisticated than I was. Before long, we had a whole group of friends, many of them boys because Pam was both attractive and good fun. Swedish, Norwegian, German, and Swiss – we were one large group of young students enjoying ourselves.

Certainly I, if not all of the group, were very much still 'children'. As far as I know, although there was plenty of friendly kissing, sex did not complicate our relationships. I had an eighteen-year-old Norwegian boyfriend called Knut, and Pam was friendly with a Swedish boy called Eddie. We did exchange kisses from time to time but it never got what is now called 'heavy'. Very many years later, I wrote a book in which I needed a Christian name for a Norwegian and remembering my friend, I called this character Knut. I won't embarrass the editor/publisher responsible for the ensuing mistake which had NOT shown up in the proofs. Or did the printers change the order of the letters deliberately? With so few possible computations, I wonder how many readers tut-tutted when they read my character's name!

When we went skiing at weekends to Hochalm, our favourite venue, we stayed overnight in the only tiny mountain hut, where we all slept on a straw-covered dais, sexes side by side. As far as I was aware, there was no overt sexual activity. It was primitive with only a cold-water tap outside to wash under and an outside privy. In the evenings, we sat in a large group round a central stove in a communal room where an old Bavarian called Sepp with a zither would sing songs. These were in a dialect quite beyond our understanding but, when I enquired why everyone kept laughing, I was told they were about a house painter called Adolf Hitler. I often wondered what happened to poor old Sepp when dissidents were packed off to concentration camps like Dachau.

Although we knew nothing of it, the forced labour camp, Dachau, had already been built. It seems impossible looking

back that we saw nothing of the anti-Jewish demonstrations
that were even then taking place. There were uniformed
blackshirts everywhere but they were always very polite
and friendly to us foreigners. Sometimes there were torch-
light parades when we would all join our German friends
in the crowds cheering Hitler as he was driven down the
main roads. We saw only what we were supposed to see
– happy young people laughing, cheering, the boys and
girls singing as they went off to picnics in the mountains
in their uniforms waving their Swastika flags.

Retrospectively, I realise that without knowing it I did
step close to the fringe of the Jewish purge. Herr von Zwehl
sent me to have oral German lessons with an elderly woman
living alone in a huge house where she seemed to frequent
only one room. She was a totally inadequate teacher and
having given me a book to read, she did little other than
stare out of the window or listen at the door of her apartment which she kept locked. I did realise that she was a
hopeless bundle of nerves but having no understanding of
her situation, I imagined it was because she was old. She
hated me leaving when my 'lesson' was finished. I was
aware of this and felt sorry for her because I thought she
was lonely. In fact, she was an old Jewish friend of Herr
von Zwehl and he'd sent me to her knowing that the Nazis
would not come to take her away whilst a foreigner was
likely to report what was happening.

Although my father, having suffered dreadfully in the
war, used to say on occasions: 'There's no such thing as a
good German', the fact was I made many friends among
them – not least with young men in the German Luftwaffe!
Part of the training for officer cadets in those days was to
learn the social niceties, which included weekly ballroom
dancing lessons. They needed partners, and female foreign
students were invited to be their guests. I had always loved
dancing, even more than skiing, and so I and some of my

friends attended these lessons which were great fun. I still have an invitation from the Officer Corps of the Combat Squadron 255, 'respectfully' inviting me to a Christmas tea dance at the Landsberg/Lech Airbase. Interestingly, when I joined the Royal Air Force in 1940, I still had an address book full of names of the young German air force cadets who were now my enemies. I wonder how many survived.

On one memorable occasion, Pam and I came face to face with Adolf Hitler. We were on our way out of Munich in the little Austin Seven Pam had bought for ten pounds heading for our skiing base in Garmisch. Hitler's car was coming in the opposite direction. Obviously we should not have been on that particular road along which were gathered the usual cheering crowds. As Hitler's car approached, he standing as always waving to the people, there was a surge forward and we were brought to a halt directly alongside him. His attendant blackshirts immediately surrounded his car and freed a way forward for him but not before Pam and I had both stared into his quite extraordinary blue eyes. I am convinced his expression was one of fear, and small wonder when, had Pam or I had a gun and used it, the lives of millions of people would have been different and Europe if not the United States, altered in incalculable ways. Strange to think we could have had such an extraordinary effect upon the state of the world! As it was, no one stopped to apprehend us and as Hitler's car moved on we proceeded on our innocent way, our long skis wobbling insecurely on the little roof of our car.

Back at home, my parents were very aware of the threat of another war. When Germany annexed Austria, telegrams were sent by my mother and Pam's father instructing us to return home immediately. We viewed these instructions with disbelief. As far as we could see there was no sign of a war – in fact everyone seemed in a jubilant mood, besides which, we were due to go skiing at the weekend! Pam had saved up (her parents were very wealthy and she had more pocket money than I had) and her purchase of the old Austin Seven meant that by driving to Garmisch instead of using the train, we could save more money for future escapades. We reached the conclusion – I honestly don't think that this time it was one of MY good ideas – that we would not 'receive' our parents' telegrams until at least a day or two after we came back from skiing. By then, hopefully, the IMMINENT threat of the outbreak of war our parents had forecast would have blown over.

Everything settled down once more but because of our skiing expeditions we were always short of money. Payment from our homes to our respective guardians came directly to our bank from which source we paid our dues. Pam now found a couple of rooms in a house where the German owner was willing to part-board us – she already had a French girl staying – with breakfast but no other meals or tuition – this at a fraction of the cost of our present establishments. I don't know what Pam said to her parents about this new, highly desirable swap but they must have okayed the change with my parents as a few weeks later, we had permission to move.

Everyday we bought fresh baguettes which we ate with butter and anchovy paste because both were really cheap. I suppose we must have varied this diet but I can't remember what with. I do remember that we saved lots of the money we needed to buy petrol and to pay for the funicular which took us half way up the mountain from Garmisch to Hochalm. After that, we had to climb for an hour to the top on our skis. If we had travelled after our lessons at university on a Friday, the last part of our journey was frequently in the dark. Thinking back to the freedom we had then when I was only just sixteen, I realise what a safe world we lived in compared with today. We never came to any harm.

Alas, my happy student life came to an end at the end of the year. I was now fairly fluent in German but doubt if I could have passed even a simple written test. However, my mother and I were for once agreed – that I should have a career in journalism. Not so agreeable was her insistence that I should first go daily to a secretarial college in Brighton to learn shorthand – I could already type (albeit two fingered) as fast as I could think, having used a typewriter for the last ten years. I did learn shorthand – after a fashion. I hated it, hated the college and missed my life in Munich and all my friends, and I was overjoyed when my mother informed me that she had got me a job on a magazine. I was to be a junior editor on *Woman's Illustrated* and would be paid the princely sum of three pounds ten shillings a week, I couldn't wait to begin.

CHAPTER 4

My friend Pam had also returned from Germany. Her family lived in Gravetye Manor – now no longer a private house but a hotel and country club. They had a retinue of servants and as Pam's mother had recently produced yet another son to add to the seven children she already had, there was also a nanny and a nursery maid. Roy was the eldest son, followed by Pam, then her sister, Sheila, then John, Peter, Dick, Graham and the new baby, Robin. Their father was Norwegian, their mother a member of the Bowater family. Pam had inherited her father's Nordic fair hair and dark brown eyes, and with her ebullient personality, already had a number of admirers, among them a steady boyfriend, a medical student called Richard. I was very envious of her as he was extraordinarily handsome, a double of my cinema-screen heart-throb Gary Cooper.

I did, however, have one admirer; Pam's eldest brother, Roy. He had just left Eton and was very quiet and shy. His younger brother, John, fair haired and brown eyed like Pam, was really a great deal more fun as well as better looking but he was still at school and two years younger than me, so there was no budding romance. The four eldest children, Pam's boyfriend, Richard, and I spent a great deal of time together, mostly at Gravetye Manor. My mother was happy with my choice of friends and would have liked one of her daughters ultimately to marry Roy who, as the eldest son, was destined to join his father in their affluent family firm.

Whilst we were all enjoying the innocent pursuits of country life in Sussex, the threat of war had come closer. Overshadowing this dark cloud was the impending separation of my parents. They had always been totally incompatible and now my mother, ever the romantic, had met an army officer younger than herself (a repetition of Granny's life). It was decided we would sell our lakeside home, and my father moved into the cottage overlooking Slaugham village green, which he had been restoring as a hobby; and my mother moved from her flat in Sloane Street into a house in Eaton Terrace.

It was whilst we were staying there one holiday that she told Eve and me she intended to marry her army officer, Neill. We had already met him as he had been a visitor to our house in the country and joined us in tennis games earlier that year. He was good-looking, a keen sportsman and easy to get along with. A regular army officer, he was in no way artistic nor in any way that I could see, more compatible with my mother than my father had been.

As I discovered many years later, he was even less erudite than my father. Although an excellent mathematician, Neill found it difficult to contribute conversationally with my mother's celebrity friends. On one memorable occasion my mother was about to entertain ten guests at a lunch party: Nancy Spain and Godfrey Winn, both journalists; Sheila Van Damme, the noted rally driver and owner of the Windmill Theatre; Michael and Roland Pertwee, both playwrights; Christina Foyle, whose literary lunches were famous; Harold Huth, the film director; Phyllis Panting, the editress of *Woman & Beauty*; Raymond Massey, the actor and Donald Gray, a film star. Aware that Neill, being an army officer, might be out of his depth, my mother begged him to do his best to take part in the conversation whenever an opportunity arose. At one point there was a discussion between Michael and Harold about the upbringing of recently purchased puppies. Having not spoken for quite some time, and with his mind obviously elsewhere, Neill recalled my mother's recent request for him to contribute to the conversation. Only vaguely aware of the current discussion he turned to Michael and said:

'I say, Michael, have you got a dog?'

My mother was mortified. But Neill had such charm everyone forgave him.

This, of course, was some years after they were married. Ultimately I grew very fond of him despite his Peter Pan limitations, but even in those days I quite liked him but Eve was deeply affected by the fact that our mother was about to leave home to go to Egypt (where Neill was stationed) after they were married.

To my shame, I have to admit that I saw only the advantages to myself in the divorce. I would no longer be under my mother's jurisdiction but would be as free as I had been in Germany to run my life as I pleased. Although I was not close to my father, we did not seem to rub one another up the wrong way and he was a very fair disciplinarian. Our parents never quarrelled in front of us but I was aware that my mother was restless and needed a very different way of life to the quiet country pursuits my father enjoyed. There was no sign of the passionate demonstrative love depicted in my mother's books.

Obviously, my father was not 'Mr. Right' as far as she was concerned and I hoped this mysterious 'Mr. Right' would appear in my own life at some future date. I vowed not to be silly enough to marry someone I did not get along with. I thought I might like a husband to be a cross between my cousin Buzz, Tony, because he liked animals, Knut, because he liked skiing, a boy called Dennis who I played in tennis tournaments with, because he played better than I did, and my father who liked outdoor activities and gardens. As far as looks were concerned I remembered the

man I had fallen in love with in my childhood – the man
who came to repair our radiogram. He had dark hair and
very deep brown smiling eyes. I now presumed my 'Mr.
Right' would also have dark hair and brown eyes. But
having just started my career, I was in no hurry to find this
paragon!

My cousin, Buzz, who had just returned from Spain
(where he had been fighting Franco's fascist troops on the
side of the Republican army in the civil war) told me he
did not think my mother's marriage to Neill would last.
I hoped for her sake it would and I waved her goodbye
without a tear, unlike Eve who cried for weeks and did
not forgive my mother for several years. Joan, our
governess, was still at home acting now as housekeeper
and she looked after Anne when she was on holiday from
her boarding school. Eve spent as much time as possible
with my father and I tried not to notice how sad and
withdrawn he became.

At the age of eighteen, my elder sister had acquired a
beautiful figure as well as her blonde good looks and she
had more than one admirer. One such was a refugee from
Germany called Rudolf who bore a striking resemblance
to the actor Herbert Blom. Another was the music composer
Herbert Menges who had written the musical score for the
play *Richard of Bordeaux* in which John Gielgud starred.
A year or two previously, we had been taken to the actor's
dressing room after the performance but I'm ashamed to
say I was not particularly impressed, brilliant actor though
he undoubtedly was. I was too young and inexperienced
to appreciate his talent.

Eve became engaged to a young tea planter home on
leave from Ceylon. He was quite good-looking but extremely
pompous, and after Anne and I had nicknamed him 'the
pound of tea' and giggled about him often enough, Eve
broke off the engagement.

My father now bought a house in Smith Street* where we lived during the week, with Joan acting as our house-keeper. At weekends, we all went down to Jenners, the cottage in Slaugham. Very often in the evenings in London after work, Eve and I would double date, she with Rudolf as a partner and I with our second cousin, Maule, who was brother to Cecilia College, the British skating champion. Maule was quite mad. He had been greatly indulged by his parents. His father was a busy, eminent surgeon and his mother devoted herself entirely to her daughter's career. As a consequence, Maule had been looked after by his father's valet and given anything he wanted. Now that he was old enough to drive, he had his own car and a small Moth aeroplane in which he took me flying down at Shoreham in Sussex. There he 'buzzed' Brighton and other coastal towns to impress me and performed sundry aerobatics without a whisper of fear.

Needless to say, when war broke out and pilots were desperately needed for what was to become the Battle of Britain, Maule joined the RAF at once. He only survived a few months. Buzz, too, joined the RAF and was killed, although not until a year later.

Both Maule and I were very immature for our ages. As a not-long-distant pupil of an all-girls boarding school and with no brothers, I was entirely ignorant where sex was concerned. Maule, in his turn, had been at an all-boys school and I was his first girlfriend, if such I could be called. We were not in the least romantically interested in one another, but after one of our foursome visits to a cinema or theatre, Maule always stopped the car before we reached my home and kissed me goodnight. I think we both thought this was expected of us. The kisses were long lasting, the reason being that we both counted how long we could maintain a kiss holding our breath before having to exhale.

---

* *Only a few weeks after my father had sold our house in Smith Street when war broke out, it was completely flattened by a bomb in the Blitz.*

Maule in particular was delighted when we could create a new record. By taking really deep breaths before our lips met, we managed some spectacular figures – but never the century Maule was aiming at!

Such was the innocence of most of the girls of my age and background. Obviously there were exceptions but reminiscing with my contemporaries, we are agreed that many of us had no idea what men and women did to conceive a baby, or whether a French kiss could get you pregnant, or even, once a baby had got inside the mother's body, how it ever got out! Those of us who lived in the country, had seen dogs or cats or farm animals give birth, but we did not relate these events to ourselves. We were, after all, human beings, not animals!

It was from our house in Smith Street that I set off each day for work. Although IPC, the huge building which today still houses a great many magazines, was not actually in Fleet Street but in Farringdon Street near St Paul's, when I walked to work from Blackfriars underground that first morning, I was really excited. My life as a journalist had actually begun! My enthusiasm was not mirrored by the rest of the staff on *Women's Illustrated* magazine. They were aware that I was the daughter of Denise Robins, their most prestigious contributor, and they assumed I would be useless, uppity and self-important. Far from it, I was shy enough to blush very easily and was very self-effacing with strangers.

The girls now gave me every lowly job they could think of – tea making, floor sweeping, taking galleys to the printers, collecting information from the communal library, sticking on stamps and so on. Unaware I was being treated as their skivvy, I rushed enthusiastically to fulfil my tasks and eagerly awaited more. Like a new girl at school, I respected my seniors and happily accepted my 'junior' status. Their denigration went over my head because, as far as I was concerned,

I was actually helping to produce a magazine, and I was on top of the world.

Came the day when my colleagues realised that they had misjudged me and they started to initiate me into the more difficult tasks of a junior sub-editor. I had to try my hand at writing captions for illustrations; writing subtitles and synopses. I learned how to cut copy on galleys up from the printers so that it would fit into the allotted space in the paste-up – the dummy of the magazine which would go down to the printers on press night. The number of pages we could fill each week depended upon the number and size of the advertisements sold. On occasions there could be quite a lot of cutting of material to be done.

Among other duties was the need to read and précis the stories, articles and serials that were sent in by contributors. On one occasion, I was given one of my mother's manuscripts to read and cut! I loved everything I had to do and before long became fairly proficient at my tasks. I didn't mind how late I worked on the night we went to press, nor how much reading I was given to take home. Happy as I was, I would have stayed there indefinitely had it not been for the outbreak of war. Hitler had annexed Bohemia and Moravia and although the Prime Minister, Neville Chamberlain, had obtained a pact from Hitler that he did not intend to make any further inroads into Europe, he now swept into Poland. An ultimatum was issued but remained unanswered and at eleven o'clock on the 3rd September, 1939, we were at war with Germany.

I don't think the true seriousness of the situation hit me until the news reached us on the wireless, as the radio was then known, (we had no television in those days) that the British Expeditionary Force and French army were on the retreat. My father was too old for active duty and I had no brothers so, somewhat selfishly, I didn't see this new war affecting me greatly. In any event, we never imagined it was going to last very long. In retrospect, this ignorance seems hard to believe. However, the true horrors and dangers were brought home in no uncertain terms when in the June of 1940 there was the nightmarish evacuation of our retreating armies from Dunkirk.

My father now made me see the realities of the situation we were all in. Our country was totally unprepared for the kind of war Hitler was waging with his vast air force and well-trained army. France surrendered and with Italy now Hitler's ally, it was only a matter of time before, having annexed the whole of the rest of Europe, he would want to add Great Britain to his empire.

Gas masks were issued to everyone, including the children; bomb shelters were built in people's back gardens and thousands of children living in London were evacuated to the country. Our new Prime Minister, Winston Churchill, made a stirring speech on the wireless, telling us we must all stand firm against the evils of Hitler. Roy, a Territorial Army cadet, had already been called up. Maule and Buzz had enlisted in the RAF. I decided that I must volunteer my services.

I thought I would prefer to join the army. Brought up on my mother's romantic novels, I fancied the idea of driving an ambulance to the trenches and rescuing wounded officers. Why other ranks were not included I can only assume was because during my entire childhood, I had never had anything to do with the working classes other than our own and our friends' servants. I was particularly fond of old Longhurst, our gardener, and I'm sure if I'd seen him lying wounded on the battlefield, I would have stopped to pick him up! Having just recently passed my driving test and being keen to drive whenever I could, I set my heart on a driving job.

Added to this wish was another salient reason for me to enlist. My editor had recently brought in a new junior sub-editor and I had been asked to show her the ropes. I was delighted to do this until I found out that her salary was nearly double my own. I went to see my editor to protest very strongly against this injustice.

It was a matter of union rules, he told me. I was only eighteen and the other girl, who was over twenty-one, qualified for an adult wage. No amount of protests that this was highly unfair moved him to break the rules. I told him that in that case, I would resign and go off and join the army. It was now his turn to protest. I was told I had shown great promise; that I had a wonderful future ahead of me; that although he had originally taken me on to please my mother, I had proved my worth over and over again. And so on. But I was not to be coerced. I announced that I would use my lunch hour to find an army-recruiting centre.

Three-quarters of an hour later, I had seen no sign of one. Realising that I was not now going to be able to return to the office triumphant as I had planned, I walked slowly back towards the beautiful landmark of St Paul's Cathedral. Suddenly, I came upon Adastral House, miraculously a recruiting centre, but for the RAF. With a beating heart, I realised that I could just as easily rescue wounded RAF officers as army ones, and still be driving an ambulance.

Inside the building, I found myself in a large rectangular room. At the far end was a platform on either side of which stood a man in air force uniform. Beside each of them was the kind of four-sided figured board you see in opticians, the letters graduating from very large at the top to very small at the bottom. There were benches along the walls leading up to the platform, on which sat queues of people of both sexes. I sat down and watched. The head of a queue would be called up to read the letters off the board, and then have his or her name taken down, or else they'd be dismissed. Then it was the next person's turn.

I moved speedily up the line, confident that I would soon have my name taken and could return to my editor telling him what I had done. I read the first four lines without much trouble but when it came to the last line, I was lost. There was no arguing with the RAF sergeant; I was dismissed. Glasses were not permitted.

Walking back to the door, my mind worked furiously trying to find a way round the problem. It was true I had always had severe astigmatism in my left eye, but with glasses I could read even the tiny print on medicine bottles. My glasses were in my pocket. Time for a 'good idea' to save the day! Quickly, I joined the end of the queue on the opposite side of the room. The conveyor belt speed with which the two men were working gave me hope that the one who had dismissed me would not notice me appearing again on the other side of the platform.

Whilst moving up the queue, I memorised all four bottom lines. It wasn't difficult but I had to be careful to note which of the four sides of the board would be offered to me when my turn came. As the tester turned them systematically one after the other, I counted my board coming up after every third person in the queue. At last my turn came and having removed my glasses, I passed with flying colours. The previous June, 1939, the Women's Royal Air Force had become the Women's Auxiliary Air Force, so I would henceforth be known as a Waaf, my rank that of an ACW – an Aircraft Woman – the bottom of the pile!

My editor was surprised, angry, upset and finally when he knew there was nothing more to be said, he called me in and told me that although I would soon no longer be on the staff of *Woman's Illustrated*, I could still be a contributor. He said that if ever I wrote a story or an article about, for example, my experiences as a Waaf, he would be more than happy to consider it for publication. I didn't see how there would be much time if I was busy driving my ambulance to and from hospitals but I thanked him especially warmly when he pointed out that a story could earn me a great deal more than the weekly wage I had complained about, since there was no union control over what was paid to contributors.

Although there had never been an occasion during my childhood when my parents could not have afforded to give me unlimited pocket money, we were only given relatively small amounts so we learned that if we wanted more, we could earn it. I recall in those childhood summers picking up bucketfuls of stones from the rose beds, weeds off the grass tennis court, leaves off the lawn, to enable me to buy whatever was the latest craze. It was a lesson which served all of us in good stead as none of the three of us married wealthy husbands!

It was several months before my call-up on 1st July 1940 and during that time, my editor gave me the children's page to write – a job I really enjoyed as I loved small children and had made up my mind to have twelve of my own when I got married. After the war, I wrote the children's page for the magazine *Woman's Day* and later, a regular article for the children's magazine *Princess*. But now, there were far more pressing things to consider. Invasion was imminent. Our house in Slaugham was only fifteen miles from the south coast where it was expected the Germans would land. My father dug a trench at the bottom of the garden, polished all his shooting guns, collected as much ammunition as he could, and like the rest of the population, waited for the worst to happen.

The Battle of Britain was now raging in the skies and when we went home for weekends, the dogfights were more or less continuous in the skies overhead. Sometimes stray bombs fell in the fields. Sometimes an RAF or German aeroplane crashed in a field where men were harvesting in the beautiful sunny weather. The newspapers were full of statistics as to the number of enemy planes shot down each day and I did quite often wonder if the pilots were one of my former Luftwaffe dancing partners or one of the young men with whom I had skated, danced and skied. My address book was full of names of German boys and girl students who I still couldn't believe would want to kill me or anyone else.

Eve had decided to become a VAD (Voluntary Aid Detachment), as was our mother during the last war. It was a voluntary organisation and in fact she only remained with it a short while before enlisting in the ATS, the Auxiliary Territorial Service. So our father now had two of his daughters in different uniforms who had left home to 'do their bit', as it was called. He himself offered his services despite his still troublesome leg wound but was obviously not fit for active duties. My mother was in Edinburgh where Neill was now stationed, and was still writing. She had recently published her fifty-ninth book, *Island of Flowers,* and was now including the war in the background to her stories. Anne was at Downe House, a school with particular emphasis on music, where she was happily settled and becoming an accomplished pianist destined, when she had completed her education, to go to Trinity College of Music.

As for me, I was on my way to West Drayton to be kitted out and evaluated for my future in the WAAF.

CHAPTER FIVE

As instructed in my call-up papers, I travelled by tube to the enrolment centre at West Drayton where, amongst what seemed like thousands of other recruits, I was kitted out with the requisite uniform. The uniform itself was not unattractive but the same cannot be said for the grey lisle stockings and voluminous knickers which were known as 'blackouts'! For a week or so, I had trouble managing the collar stud that kept the loose collars attached to our light-blue shirts. I was duly weighed and was horrified when I stood on the scales and was shown to be twelve stone.

During my employment at the IPC, I used to go in my lunch hour to Joe's café in Fleet Street. There I had enjoyed daily as my staple lunch two large sandwiches and a glass of Horlicks with lots of sugar in it. My life was a sedentary one and consequently, without realising it, I had put on weight.

Owing to the fact that throughout my boarding school days we were only allowed two sweets on Wednesdays, Saturdays and Sundays, I had acquired a very sweet tooth. But at school, dieting was unheard of and no one had ever heard of anorexia, so we were not figure conscious other than for our concerns about breasts. Those who hadn't yet grown any watched anxiously for signs that they were not deformed. The older girls who had developing breasts wore Kestos bras, known to us as bust bodices (or b.b.s or b-squared) that did little to conceal their contents. If these were large, they caused considerable embarrassment to the owner and hunched shoulders were one way of helping to conceal them. Unfortunately, the girdles tied round the waist over our regulation pleated tunics, exaggerated the protuberances above, and those less well developed felt sorry for them.

Unconcerned as I had been in the past about my weight, I was now uncomfortably aware that my smart new airforce-blue tunic looked a lot less smart on my portly figure than on the thinner girl standing beside me.

Amongst the equipment issued to us was a metal knife, fork and spoon and a mug, all of which we took with us for use at mealtimes; a housewife (pronounced 'huzif') consisting of a small cloth purse containing needles, threads etc., a shoe-cleaning kit and a button-cleaning kit. The brass buttons and cap badge slid up a forked metal plate which protected the tunic cloth beneath when Brasso was rubbed on to them. Like our black lace-up leather walking shoes, buttons had to be kept shining at all times and there were regular kit inspections.

We were housed in long Nissen huts containing iron bedsteads on which were heaped the three straw-filled square pallets (known as biscuits) serving as a mattress. The corporal in charge of our hut demonstrated how these must be stacked and our bedding folded each morning and placed at the foot of the bed. It was all relatively primitive but having spent a large number of years in an English boarding school where we had, quite literally, to break the ice in our water jugs in winter, the privations did not particularly worry me or girls with similar backgrounds to mine. Those, however, who had never left home where they had been cosseted, moaned about the privations. I quickly made friends with three other girls who had had the same upbringing as myself. We went together to meals and on parades where we were taught to march, salute and so on. We giggled a lot and no wonder, as the female shape is not really conducive to marching. We also had rifle practice which I enjoyed as I had not been allowed even to touch my father's sporting guns at home.

We'd not been at the camp long before a notice was put up, as all directives were, on the entrance door to our hut. We were to report to an assembly hut for nit inspection. My friends and I had never heard of a nit and assuming it to be a mis-type, at my suggestion we prepared for one of the usual kit inspections and duly laid out our kit on our beds as was required. The other girls disappeared giggling when they realised what we were doing. We were given a verbal roasting by our corporal who called us names, some of which like 'nits' – but much ruder! – we had never heard of, and were packed off belatedly to have our hair searched by the M.O. (Medical Officer). This we considered somewhat humiliating to say the least, but we made no complaint, accepting the indignity as part of our war effort.

One might suppose that I would have learned my lesson and not repeated the mistake of jumping to conclusions, but several months later, when I was at No. 10 group – Rudloe Manor, near Bath – I did just that. The authorities were trying desperately to adjust their accommodations to include the revolutionary influx of females into a former all-male RAF establishment. The huge shortage of manpower had necessitated the enrolment of women although there were still a great many who felt the 'weaker' sex were incapable of replacing men in non-domestic tasks. But there we all were, and on my camp the Works Department was constantly having problems with the plumbing, which was continually becoming blocked. The reason for this was because the girls were putting their sanitary towels down the toilets, there being no other receptacle provided for the purpose. Disposable towels and tampons had not yet been invented, and the variety of S.T.s issued by the medical centre was large and cumbersome. We had been informed that efforts to remedy this problem were currently being made by the overworked Works Department and meanwhile, we were to walk across camp to the incinerators – something no one liked doing because the airmen knew exactly why we were going to such an unlikely venue and we were embarrassed by their grins.

We were not therefore in the least surprised when a notice went up saying we were to report to the Assembly Hut for a lecture on VD. I now made the mistake again of assuming this was a typing error and should have been WD the usual identification for the Works Department. I should add here that neither I nor my friends had ever heard of venereal disease. Arriving a little late for the lecture, we crept in at the back of the room. At the far end, an officer stood pointing to a large diagram on a blackboard beside him. We presumed at once that our suspicions were right – this was the camp plumbing system at fault again.

On the board in different coloured chalks was a diagram of – we supposed – the camp sewage system: two blue circles from which led two yellow pipes emptying into a large container resembling an upside down pear. It had an opening at the base to which he was pointing. This seemed to be the area that was most concerning him. Unable to interpret half he was saying and not having the least interest in plumbing, we left the hall at the end of the lecture as ignorant as we had entered it.

When I related this story to my grandchildren, they were hard put to believe that I was not making it up. Sexual knowledge may be desirable for the young these days but in those early years our total innocence was quickly recognised and respected by the men who asked us out, and we were almost never bothered by unwelcome attentions.

Certainly the exciting mystery surrounding our conception which intrigued us as children has now vanished for ever. The following conversation which took place recently, between two children in their parents' presence, shows how times have changed. To save the children's embarrassment I have not given their names.

Child A (aged eleven) following a sex lesson before leaving Junior school and child B (two years younger):

B: 'So what did they tell you?'

A: 'I'm not going to tell you – you're too young.'

B: 'No, I'm not. Go on, tell me.'

A, longing to air her knowledge, describes the sex act.

B: 'I don't believe you. If Mum and Dad did that, we'd have seen them.'

A: 'Don't be silly. They do it at night when we've all gone to bed.'

B: 'But I've often gone into their room when I've had a bad dream or I'm feeling sick, and I've never seen them.'

A, for the second time: 'Don't be silly. Mum would hear you coming and she'd say: "Quick, get off me, darling, one of the children is coming!"'

On hearing the story I could applaud the fact that the parents' presence did not inhibit this interchange in these modern times but at the same time I regretted the early loss of innocence. Perhaps I should not consider it 'early' when my daily paper informed me last week that the government is planning to introduce sex lessons at the age of five.

Back at West Drayton came the day for interviews so that we could be given our postings to appropriate jobs. What did I want to do, asked the Waaf Officer who had my CV in front of her. 'Drive an ambulance!' I told her without any hesitation. She noted I was still in my teens, realised I had not long passed my test and told me she considered it more appropriate if she put me down for Special Duties. I was disappointed about the driving but intrigued to know what Special Duties entailed. It sounded important. I could not be told, she said, until I had signed the Official Secrets Act.

My heart soared. It was on my CV that I spoke fluent French and moderately fluent German. If the work I was to do was secret then it must mean I was going to be a spy and be dropped behind enemy lines. I was so excited I couldn't sleep that night and all thoughts of ambulance driving were happily discarded.

A short while later, my posting came through. Together with three of the friends I had made, Joan Bishop, Audrey Prentiss and Jill Hudson, we said farewell to the other girls in our hut and with the use of our railway warrants, set off for Leighton Buzzard. Here, to our surprise, we discovered our accommodation was in the workhouse, which we first had to scrub with soap and water before we moved in. The sexes were segregated, Waafs upstairs on the left-hand side of the courtyard and airmen on the right! The courtyard was not very large and as each set of rooms had a balcony along their length, it was not long before the men were out on their side, trying to get our attention. This segregation did seem strange, especially as we were all to meet up the morning after our arrival in the rooms below where we would be told what Special Duties entailed.

To say I was disappointed when I saw the large table with the map of the western half of southern England painted on it and the heaps of little coloured counters lying at intervals along the edge, is to belittle my initial distress. Whatever we were to do with the counters, it could not entail the work of a spy! However, it was not very long before my interest was aroused. After signing the Official Secrets Act, our RAF instructor told us that we were to be trained as radar plotters in order to release as many men as possible for more active service.

Sited at different points along the coast, we were told, was a chain of radar stations (CH – Chain Home – stations) which could detect approaching aircraft in their range. The operator of each of these was in contact with a plotter in a Filter Room (i.e. us), to whom they would relay a grid reference as to the position of an aircraft. Plotters placed a coloured counter in the appropriate grid reference on the large table around which we would be seated wearing earphones. Each plotter had a different coloured counter.

Whilst a radar station's grid reference was accurate regarding the distance the plane was from them, the actual direction could not be relied on. Neighbouring stations could position the plane the correct distance from themselves but which would be at different grid references from each other. There was therefore an officer, known as a Filter Officer, who could move freely around the table placing an arrow where the different coloured plots intersected.

The CH stations are perhaps most easily understood by likening their radar screens to those far more sophisticated ones used by today's air traffic control centres where dots of light appear on a screen indicating the movements of aeroplanes. Waafs as well as airmen were now manning these stations.

Our instructor now told us that in the Filter Rooms there would be a balcony overlooking the table on which there was a map depicting our area of the coast, depending upon which part of the country we were posted to. Each new line of arrows placed by the Filter Officer would be given a designation on a plaque, i.e. 'H' for Hostile, and its estimated speed and height. A 'teller' would then relay this information by telephone through to the Operations Room, where the movements and identity of the planes were duplicated on a similar table to ours. On the balcony above, the officer in charge decided which squadron or squadrons of our aircraft he would order to be scrambled to intercept the enemy.

This early detection of the approaching planes obviously gave the British a huge advantage over our enemy who had not yet discovered radar. In the films and on television pictures have often been shown of the girls in the Ops (Operations) Room pushing plaques around with long handled rods. Our work as 'plotters' and 'filterers' in the Filter Room has not, to my knowledge, been portrayed despite the fact that the Ops Room could not have functioned so efficiently without us!

During the time of heavy German bombing raids on London, the table would be a mass of coloured counters and arrows, and we had to work extremely fast. Whilst these really big raids were taking place, it was only possible to mark the squared outline of the area which would be given an estimated so many hundred planes plus identification. In these busy times, plots were relayed to us as fast as the operator could talk until such time as the operator could not separate one echo from another.

Plotting was what we now learned to do. Needless to say, we were faster than the men with our smaller fingers and it was not long before nearly all of the men were replaced by Waafs. Plotting enemy aircraft sounded more important war work than, as I had feared, playing around with coloured tiddlywinks, and as we'd had to sign the Official Secrets Act before our training began, I was eager to learn the ropes. Radar, we were told, was unknown to the Germans and therefore this early detection of their planes gave our fighters a very big advantage; badly needed as Britain had only a fraction of the numbers of their planes at our disposal.

Whenever the wartime work of Waaf plotters is pictured on film, television or in newspapers, it is always the Ops Room that is depicted. As they received the vast majority of their information about approaching enemy planes from us, it seems a pity the Filter Rooms have not been illustrated, too.

This preliminary, very basic explanation of our work was sufficient to enable us trainee plotters to sit down at the table, put on our earphones and attempt to master the grid positions. All this required was practice, more practice and still more, until we could find a grid reference so speedily that we could keep up when plots were coming through as fast as the radar operator could speak.

At the workhouse, we ate our meals in a communal dining room that we shared with the airmen. It sounds very strange but many of us had never had any contact socially with each other's classes which were very much more clearly defined than they are these days. We were not sure quite how to behave with the airmen or they with us. In civilian life, they would have been calling us 'Miss This or That' and now we were on Christian-name terms. However, by the end of the first week, relationships of a kind were established. I had an admirer called Len who I quite liked until he told me he had false teeth! I was horrified, not just by the teeth, which I now couldn't stop looking at never having seen any before, but by the fact that he had admitted to having them. I now saw that they were unnaturally white and the gums a bright shiny pink. There was absolutely no way I could let him kiss me as he wanted when, on our last day at the workhouse, we were allowed to have a farewell dance in what was called the mess.

Poor old Len! I was left wondering if all people from his background had false teeth. I knew from books I had read that poor children had rickets through malnutrition. It seemed probable therefore that if their parents couldn't afford doctors, nor could they pay for dentists and so their teeth would fall out. I felt sorry for Len but forgot him in the excitement of my first real posting which was to No. 10 Group, a Fighter Command non-operational Headquarters just outside the beautiful city of Bath.

We were billeted in a relatively small house in the village of Corsham, as they had not yet built accommodation on the camp for us new arrivals at our H.Q., Rudloe Manor.

We slept four to each room and all twelve of us shared the one bathroom. In true boarding school spirit, we somehow managed without disputes to share the use of this bathroom where hot water was strictly limited. This was made easier by the fact that some of us were on day shifts and some on night shifts. However, there was nearly always a queue. We did have a fairly senior Waaf Admin Officer supposedly in charge of us, but as we worked shifts and were under the same orders as the airmen, I don't think she had much control of our activities except on one of the rare occasions we were put on a charge for some misdemeanour. I can't recall this happening very often as we were all dedicated to our jobs. In those early years those of us on Special Duties were not available, as were the ordinary Waafs, for route marches, church parades or even kit inspections, as we were either on duty, or sleeping after a night duty, and were therefore only around at odd times between day shifts.

Our place of work at Rudloe was a converted cowshed that had to fit the bill whilst a new underground room was hurriedly being built a short distance from Rudloe Manor. The table and our chairs around it filled what little space there was on the floor. The officers and teller were on the makeshift balcony that had not long since been a granary. The electric light frequently failed and we operated by candlelight. As far as I can recall, there was only one outside lavatory which had to serve all of us. Despite attempts to heat the place in the winter, it was often extremely cold. We were allowed to wear our greatcoats and mittens and were frequently replaced by a relief plotter so we could go and get a hot drink.

Our officers were a mixed bunch – many were professionals such as business managers, schoolmasters, even barristers, and were all volunteers unfit for more active duty. Our more senior officer, a squadron leader, had been promoted from the ranks, having a particular knowledge

of radar as he had worked with the renowned Scots phys-
icist Robert Watson Watt*.

I was vaguely aware that he paid an unusual amount of
attention to me but I neither found him particularly attractive
nor liked him. He had an extremely unpleasant way of
leaning over the balcony and reprimanding one of the filter
officers for some mistake or other, his voice that of a sergeant
major on parade. One Christmas Eve, there was no flying
activity and we were all sitting round the table relaxed and
talking to one another. I was suddenly interrupted by a
voice on my headphones asking me if I would like to go
upstairs for a change. Realising who was addressing me, I
politely declined the invitation. He came on the phone
again, this time ordering me to go up. I had no choice but
to obey. Why, he enquired, was I not willing to be more
friendly? After all, it was Christmas.

As he had invited my comment, I decided to be honest.
I told him I was frequently embarrassed by his behaviour
when he reprimanded his junior officers in front of the
other ranks. (My father had once given me a lecture on
the subject of etiquette where 'inferiors' were concerned
after having taken a hairbrush to me for being rude to our
cook who, he said, was in no position to be rude back.
He'd told me about army life and how senior officers must
never undermine their juniors in front of the troops who
would lose respect for them. Being a man of very few words,
those my father spoke were noted and remembered by all
of us. Even in our old age when my sisters and I were
together, we found ourselves quoting something he said
which we had never forgotten. I now quoted him to the
squadron leader.)

I suppose I took an awful chance – me a mere ACW

---

* Robert Watson Watt was superintendent of the Radio Department at the
National Physical Laboratory. In 1935 he proposed the first experimental
radar system which came into effect in 1938 with 5 early-warning stations.

telling a squadron officer how to behave! It was on the
impulse of the moment and I knew it was wrong of me.
However, far from reproaching me, the squadron leader
invited me to sit down and tell him about my father and
his experiences in the First World War. He also admitted
that what my father told me made excellent sense. I immediately changed my mind about him and to his immense
credit he never did shout at the filter officers on duty again
– or not to my knowledge. After I was commissioned, I
often met him in the officers' mess and we ended up
becoming good friends.

A tarpaulin-covered lorry collected us from our billet
and drove us to and from work. In winter, it was bitingly
cold, especially if we were going on duty at night. Our
shifts were either from eight a.m. to one p.m., one p.m. to
five p.m., five p.m. to eleven p.m., or the long night shift
from eleven p.m. to eight a.m. We were now given the
unprecedented permission to wear trousers instead of skirts.

At first, there was very little night-time activity. We were
allowed to do whatever we liked so long as we remained
attached to the table by our earphones in case a sudden
plot came through. Out came knitting, embroidery, writing
paper or books to read. Domestic pursuits were not to my
taste but I did see an opportunity to augment the very
meagre fifteen shillings and two pence a week we received
by way of pay – 75p in today's money. My father had
allowed me to take the family Standard car with me when
I was posted to Bath. Petrol rationing was in force and he
preferred to keep his small Morris for his daily trips to
and from Haywards Heath station from which he commuted
to London. I had my ration of petrol coupons but not the
money to pay for the petrol. Remembering my editor's
suggestion that I should write stories for him, I decided to
do so.

Before long, I was receiving the princely sum of ten

pounds per submission which far, far exceeded my air force pay. This encouraged me to send in more contributions. There was no lack of material to write about. Everyone had a story to tell – fiancés who had been posted abroad before there'd been time to get married; whirlwind romances; lovers parted; bombing raids on the south coast radar stations, and so on. My editor loved them and my friends and I enjoyed the freedom the car gave us.

Now that my day-to-day life seemed to be relatively stable, I decided the time had come when I could have a dog. There were several on the camp, all with names of aeroplanes such as Spit for Spitfire, Beau for Beaufighter, and so on. I wanted to get a long-haired Dachshund which being a German breed meant I should christen him likewise with a German name. I decided upon Heinkel, the name of a German bomber. This, however, was before I had actually got a dog.

On my next leave in London, I passed a pet shop in the window of which were several puppies. They were Alsatian/Labrador crosses who would obviously grow too large for me. The woman who ran the shop assured me she knew a breeder of Dachshunds and would get in touch with me when the litter arrived.

I was prepared to wait. I had, after all, waited eight years to have a dog of my own. My mother had always had Cairn terriers and my father Labradors for shooting, but I desperately wanted a dog that belonged only to me. The white rat I'd had as a child was never the companion I envisaged. Came the day when I was about twelve years old when sadly my mother's Cairn Terrier, Mickey, was run over. We were all very upset and for some time, my mother did not feel ready to replace him. I then had one of my not very good ideas – *I* would replace him with a dog of my own.

Somewhat unusually, I had been saving my pocket money

as I wanted a new tennis racquet, and I had the princely sum of eleven shillings in my piggy bank. I knew this was insufficient to buy a pedigree dog but in any event, I had decided upon a mongrel. The best place to get one of them, my friend Longhurst, our gardener, told me, was from Brighton Lost Dogs' Home.

I went in search of my mother's secretary, Marjorie, who was sometimes employed to ferry us to the dentist or somewhere similar. Please would she drive me into Brighton, I pleaded. I was in luck, she told me. My mother was going out immediately after lunch and so she would be free to take me. It was only when we were actually on the way that I informed her where exactly I wanted to go. Later, as an adult, it's difficult to believe she did not turn round and drive me straight home – but she didn't.

It was distressing to see all the dogs looking hopefully at me as I walked with the attendant past the iron bars of their kennels. However, it was not long before I knew I need go no further. There was a bright-eyed, rough-coated terrier, ears pricked as he put his head on one side and wagged his tail furiously.

'That's the one I want!' I said, and almost speechless with excitement, handed over my ten shilling note. Romantic writers speak of women falling in love at first sight with a man. I don't think that could ever happen as instantly as I fell in love with Simon! I'm not sure where the name came from. I sat on the back seat of Marjorie's car with Simon in my arms, imagining the joy he would feel when we reached home and I could let him into the garden. It would be Heaven for him after his concrete kennel. I thought of all the walks we would go on together; how he'd sleep at the foot of my bed; how he could sit beside me when I went fishing on the bank of Furnace Pond, the lake opposite our house which had been named after it, Furnace Pond Cottage.

Marjorie made cautionary remarks from the front seat. I must prepare for the possibility that my mother might not be too happy with a mongrel that quite probably had fleas or worms. I said at once that I could quickly bath him; worm him with the medicine my father used for the two Labradors. Whatever she might find wrong, I would put right, I insisted. No one – but no one, would ever part me from the dog lying quietly in my arms.

It is questionable whether the fact that I was born on my mother's birthday meant we were destined at times to choose the same day to do the same things. Whilst I had been out finding Simon, she had been out buying a new Cairn Terrier puppy. It was in the garden when I arrived home. As I had expected, Simon went mad with delight. He tore round the garden in ever widening circles in a frenzy of freedom. Over went the tulips, the deck chair, the tray of tea on the garden table, the bird bath and then . . . then the very worst thing happened – over went the puppy rolling like a ball across the lawn with Simon prancing happily around it.

When I was told he'd have to go back where he came from, I thought my heart was broken. Such was my distress, I couldn't cry. All I could think of was that horrible concrete kennel, the iron bars and Simon now panting with exhaustion at my feet, having to be locked up there after his taste of freedom.

My mother would not change her mind but tried to console me with a compromise. She would ask Longhurst if he would have him if she paid for his keep. Longhurst lived in Handcross where the bus stopped. I could walk up to his house whenever I wanted and see him, take him for a walk, she said.

But I couldn't accept the compromise. Whilst I was pleased when Longhurst agreed to have Simon because I knew he'd be kind to him, I had envisaged having Simon with me day and night. If he couldn't be mine, I couldn't bear to see him again – and I never did. Longhurst used to tell me how well he'd settled; that his wife spoilt him; that he'd quietened down a lot and was a lovely dog but after a while, he stopped doing so, seeing that his bulletins always came close to reducing me to tears.

My choice of a Dachshund all these years later was, I imagine, because at least its coat would be similar to Simon's. I didn't expect to find a dog exactly like him. However, this was not to be. On telephoning the woman at the pet shop to enquire when I could expect my puppy, she told me that the two male dogs had been booked before I'd asked for one and the rest of the litter were bitches. I knew that it would be impossible to keep a bitch on the camp and told her so. She immediately offered me a Corgi puppy instead, but I didn't like the breed. The pet shop owner was nobody's fool.

'Let me send this puppy down by train to Bath where you can see him,' she said. 'If you don't like him, you can put him on the next train back.'

As two of my friends and I set off in my car to Bath station, the sun was shining and it was a beautiful day so the soft roof was down. We went to the shops first and then back to the station to meet the train. The guard handed me a large cardboard box with holes in it. We took the box out to the car and looked inside. There was no question whatever but that the puppy was the ugliest, most wretched looking bundle of wet fur I'd ever seen.

'That's it!' I said to my friends. 'Will one of you find out the time of the next train to London? This miserable-looking object has got to go back.'

It was three quarters of an hour before the train to London departed. We decided to leave the puppy in its box on the back seat whilst we went off to do some more shopping. The box was deep enough for the pathetic little thing not to be able to get out so we left it open to enable its fur to dry out in the sun.

Its fur did dry out and the 'pathetic little thing' had somehow managed to get out of the box. He had found a packet of potato crisps which he had been eating and the remains were now scattered around him. When he saw me staring at him, he looked up at me from two very dark, shining brown eyes and wagged the stump of his tail in welcome.

So he wasn't Simon's double, but I knew I would keep him despite the fact that he was so ugly. It was his fortitude, I think, which touched my heart. I found out he was only six weeks old – far too young to have been taken from his mother. He had had a long, frightening journey in a dark box all the way from London, left wet and miserable on the back seat of a car, but somehow found the courage to improve his lot, and still bore me no grudge for leaving him there.

'He's a Welsh dog!' said one of my Waaf friends, Muriel Braga, nicknamed Bragi. 'You can't call him Heinkel.'

We tried to find another name but we'd been talking about Heinkel too long. The name stuck and stayed with him for the next thirteen years.

CHAPTER 6

Throughout the summer of 1940, what came to be known as the Battle of Britain raged with continuous enemy bombing of the south coast and its airfields. The Germans knew that to invade England without certainty of air supremacy was to invite failure. But despite the damage they inflicted and the loss of civilian life as well as terrible losses of pilots and aircraft, we were still managing to fight off the daytime air attacks.

When Marshal Hermann Goering, in charge of the German air force, decided to start night-time bombing raids over the rest of the country, some bombers even reached as far north as South Shields, but it was London which now took the full force of the bombing which continued both day and night. In the Filter Room we were fully occupied throughout our shifts with only a few minutes' relief to dash to the loo and gulp a cup of tea or cocoa, or Horlicks which was humorously said to help us sleep after night-watch or keep us awake whilst on it!

When I went home to Sussex on leave, we could watch the bombers flying in huge clouds over the fields where the farmers were haymaking. Quite often there were dogfights overhead. At Slaugham, the bell ringers had ceased their customary evening practice and were detailed only to ring the bells to warn us that the expected invasion had begun. To all intents and purposes, we no longer thought 'if' but 'when'.

Names were taken off signposts, air raid wardens stood

ready with buckets of sand and water to deal with incendiary bombs. Nobody went outside without taking their gas masks with them. Indoors, blackout curtains now adorned the windows and a warden patrolled the village to ensure no light could be seen. My father still commuted to London, determined as all the population were, to carry on in spite of Hitler's threats. Everyone was inspired by Winston Churchill's speech, now famous, telling us to be prepared to fight the invaders even on the beaches, which in our case, were only fifteen miles away.

Back at Rudloe, down in the west of the country, we saw only the occasional overhead dogfight. But we were now plotting mass raids of German bombers on their way to London, Coventry, Bristol and other big cities. Having lost the initial battle for air supremacy for his invasion, Hitler was now trying to bomb the civilian population into submission. It never once crossed my mind that anyone would surrender. During the Battle of Britain, I worried about my father, only fifteen miles from the barbed wire beaches where my sisters and I had once built sandcastles and paddled. I knew if we were invaded he would not give in until he ran out of cartridges! Civilians who did not possess guns had armed themselves with pitchforks or garden rakes, old swords or ornamental Boer War weapons.

Although at the time we were aware of the very real likelihood of invasion, I don't think any of us actually envisaged it happening to the extent that we lived in fear. My friends and I were still in our teens, young enough to be enjoying the 'adventure' and were not too concerned about 'tomorrow'. The awfulness of war only touched me when my mother wrote to tell me both Maule and Buzz had been killed in the Battle of Britain. The war seemed suddenly very close and another boy, who I had partnered in a local tennis club tournament, had been killed on the beach at Dunkirk. Pam wrote and told me that Roy had been called up and was posted overseas to fight with the 8th Army in Africa. I minded most about Buzz who I had adored since childhood. Michael (Pertwee) enlisted in the army, Jon in the navy, and their stepbrother, Coby, was now a doctor. Pam's boyfriend, Richard, now a qualified doctor, joined the RAF Medical Corps. Pam, ever adventurous, learned to fly and joined the ATA (Air Transport Auxiliary) where she ferried planes alongside the world-famous woman pilot Amy Johnson.

I was not, admittedly, driving my ambulance to the trenches, but I was doing top-secret work and I felt a thrill every time I went on duty. I had several friends with whom in off duty times we walked, went to the cinema or had tea and a bun at the NAAFI. This was a Forces canteen in every camp run by volunteers – a place set up for services personnel. Occasionally there were dances in the NAAFI. Utterly unlike those I had enjoyed in Munich or at home, the first one we attended at the NAAFI was a revelation. At home, when a boy wished to take a girl to a dance, he collected her from her house, escorted her to the dance, probably gave her an orchid or camellia to wear on her dress and remained in attendance throughout the evening before taking her back home. In the NAAFI, we discovered, the girls stood in groups at one end of the room whilst the men stood in groups by the bar at the other. When the music started, the men went down the room, picked a girl – any girl they fancied – from the bunch, danced with her and then dumped her back amongst the group again.

It felt a bit like being at a cattle market, and being shy I was not alone in finding it somewhat embarrassing. Came a day, December 3rd, which although I would not have believed it had I been told then, was to have a huge impact on my life. There was to be a dance at the NAAFI that evening and some of the girls in our billet wanted to go. Living as we were in Corsham and with transport only available to get us to Rudloe Manor for work, they were reliant on me and my car to get to the dance. I agreed reluctantly to take them and two of my friends, Audrey and Jill, agreed to keep me company.

There was the usual grouping of men and women at either end of the room. Not capable of sending flirtatious glances towards the group of men, the three of us stood with our backs towards them. The music started up with Glenn Miller's wonderful signature tune 'Moonlight Serenade', and there was a surge of men down the room to select their chosen partners. Jill was by far the most attractive friend I had – slim, blonde, blue-eyed and with long nicely shaped legs which looked good even in our regulation grey lisle stockings. She was quickly snapped up and then I felt a hand on my shoulder. I turned round to see a nice-looking boy with dark hair and brown eyes looking at me expectantly as he said: 'Dance?'

It was not quite the polite, 'Can I have this dance?' that I was used to but I wasn't given time to refuse before I was pulled unceremoniously on to the dance floor.

It was some time later that my partner confessed he had not intended to ask me to dance. He had been aiming for Jill but another airman had got to her before him. In order not to have to walk back up the room empty handed, so to speak, he grabbed the girl with her back to him as being better than nothing. He could but hope that I would not fall over his feet.

One is not supposed to sing one's own praises, but the truth was, I had always been a really good dancer. At school, I was frequently selected by our dance teacher to demonstrate a step she was trying to show us. It was a question of timing and rhythm, a ski guide once told me when he crossed a very crowded dance floor at a ski resort to ask me to partner him in an old-fashioned waltz. It was, he said, why I stayed upright on the ski slopes despite my appalling stance!

At the end of the dance – my partner was a really good performer, too – instead of taking me back to the group, he asked me if I would have the next dance with him; he'd get me a drink while we waited for it to start. In one way, I was happy to fall in with his suggestion. I really did love dancing. Moreover, as I was obliged to remain at the NAAFI until the end of the evening in order to take the other girls home, it seemed sensible to stay with my good dance partner. His name, he told me, was Mel and he came from the market town of Melton Mowbray. This fitted with his accent which was very Midlands. He told me he was a crane driver stationed a few miles away at an airfield called Colerne. As he took me on to the floor for a waltz, holding me fractionally closer than need be, I wondered what on earth my parents would say if they could see me whirling round the floor in the arms of a good-looking crane driver. Hardly the titled husband material my mother had hoped to find for all her three daughters!

I was enjoying myself. I lost some of my shyness and we began joking as well as flirting. At the end of one dance, he asked me if I would like to go outside for a cigarette and some fresh air. I told him I didn't smoke but that I'd like some fresh air as the room was very hot. Once outside, he declined to smoke but took hold of my hands and drew me towards him obviously intending to kiss me. When I protested, he pointed out that I'd agreed to a kiss or two – that was what 'fresh air' meant. I was too naïve to disbelieve him, especially as he came from a different background to mine and there might be different codes of behaviour.

Although nervous, I enjoyed the kiss which was very circumspect. We talked for a while whilst he questioned me about my family and my work (it was always a thrill to say: 'I'm afraid I can't tell you – it's top secret'!) Then he lit a cigarette and held out the match for me to blow out. Immediately I did so, he told me that this meant the forfeit of another kiss.

I suspected I was being teased but I was having a lot of fun. Audrey, I saw, was having a smoochy dance with another airman not nearly so good-looking as mine! Mel and I continued to dance together until the evening ended when my new friend asked me if I would meet him in Bath to go to one of the dances held in the Assembly Rooms. I said I would think about it. There was no doubt that I would love to go dancing, but did I dare go with a crane driver? Audrey, it seemed when we got ready for bed that night, had had a similar invitation from the airman with whom she had danced. He was a fitter with a very Cockney accent. What on earth would our parents say if they knew, we asked each other? Did we dare trust these boys? We'd been safe enough in the environs of the NAAFI but we didn't know for sure they would actually take us to the Assembly Rooms. Their nice manners and polite behaviour at the dance could be a mask for whatever evil intentions they had. Neither of us knew what rape was but we knew from the newspapers that there were men who attacked women and did dreadful things to them. How could we tell if they were like this or were harmless people like Longhurst or my father's gamekeeper, Hutchens, or Maule's valet?

We sat up until the early hours yes-ing and no-ing until finally I said: 'I've got the car. I'll park it outside wherever they take us. If things go wrong, we'll make a dash for the car and drive off. They've only got bicycles so they will never catch up.'

For some reason this started us giggling until finally we went to sleep. Just before I did so, I realised that if I was honest, I'd meant to go despite the possible dangers, right from the start.

Thus began a singularly happy year for me. Whenever I

was not on duty, I would meet Mel to go dancing, to the cinema, for long walks with my friends, Bragi, Joan and Audrey and not least Heinkel. Mel was a wonderful companion for me – very much the non-existent brother with the added excitement as the months passed of hand holding and kisses, which on occasions became quite passionate. I was slightly concerned that some of the ardent kisses bestowed upon me might make me pregnant!

It must have been a frustrating relationship for Mel. He was six years older then me and because of his background, he was certainly street wise. One of eight children he had left school at fourteen and had had a number of different manual jobs. Because he was undoubtedly very good-looking, he'd had more than his fair share of girlfriends. I, of course, was as much a novelty to him as he was to me and soon realising how absurdly innocent I was, he never went beyond my limited boundaries. I wasn't in love with him although I did love being with him. He was so much more fun than the boys I'd known at home. He, Heinkel and I swam that summer in the weir; picnicked in the countryside, held hands through the Nelson Eddy/Jeanette Macdonald musicals, ate fish and chips wrapped in news-paper – a novelty for me – and necked, as smooching was called then, in the back of the car when I drove him back to his billet in Colerne.

I, for one, didn't think about tomorrow although Mel was aware that he had only been seconded to Colerne and might be recalled to his squadron at any time. We were, of course, cushioned from the horrors that were going on in London where the population were enduring terrible day and night bombing. By March that year, four thousand, two hundred civilian women and children had been killed. In the air force we ate reasonable meals whereas the civil-ians were now rationed to only a few ounces a week of bacon, butter, margarine, cheese, sugar and meat. They were allowed no more than three pints of milk, one egg and a tin of condensed milk once a month. Everyone had ration books with coupons for these allotted amounts. There was a black market for food but anyone using it was heavily fined. Later on in the war when I went home on leave, because of the shortage of meat, I would go to the kitchen in the Officers' Mess and ask for scraps for Heinkel. The cook's answer to that was to give me half a large block of spam! I gave this to my mother for her consumption and went down the Kings Road in Chelsea to buy horsemeat for my dog.

In the Filter Room at Rudloe we were now kept very busy but occasionally the weather was such that there was no flying at night, and then I was able to write articles, poems or a short story for *Woman's Illustrated*. Dreadful as it was for the people who were enduring the bombing raids in London, I have to admit it was a happy summer for me and my friends. My on-going friendship with Mel meant he was included in quite a few of our adventures – one such being a car journey using my last drops of petrol to drive to a saw mill at Yeovil owned by a relation of one of the girls. The owner was prepared to give us a few precious gallons of his fuel. We just about made it to the sawmill before we ran out and he filled up my tank and gave me a small can to put in the back of the car.

I invariably ran out of petrol before the next monthly issue of petrol coupons. On those occasions, we hitchhiked singly or in pairs. The latter was for company rather than for safety as in those days there was never a thought of any danger. I never heard of anyone being molested and the worst that could happen was for vehicles to ignore us or simply fail to go by, the amount of traffic on the roads (other than military transport) being minimal.

On one such night, three of us were trying to hitch a ride back to camp where we were due on duty that evening.

Dumped by one solitary van driver on a minor road, we walked anxiously in the right direction, aware that time was beginning to run out and that we could never walk the distance in time if another car did not pick us up very soon.

We were really desperate when we heard a noise behind us – a loud noise. It was a steamroller . . . hardly the kind of transport we needed. But it was travelling a lot quicker than we could walk. Moreover, it was getting dark and time was running out.

The steamroller driver stopped and much to his amusement, we clambered on board. By the time we reached camp there was no time to go to our billet and we rushed headlong into the Filter Room, conscious of the many stares – and grins – that were aimed at us. It was only when we stared at one another that we saw our faces were black – as black as that of the steamroller driver. In the darkness outside, we had not noticed the smoky changes to our complexions.

The lack of petrol for my car really was a deprivation for us all – not least Heinkel who was always perfectly happy to be left in it when I went on duty or into a cinema or café, provided I left some article of mine with him.

On one occasion, an airman on the neighbouring airfield offered me a can full of aviation fuel in exchange for my cigarette ration, which I gladly accepted. I have to say I never gave a thought at the time to the fact that the country desperately needed fuel which came, of course, from overseas as did so much of our food and other essentials. The newspapers ran stories of the frightening loss of ships sunk by the German U boats, some doubtless carrying the necessary fuel to sustain our defence. I suppose I didn't believe – if I thought at all – that a few gallons would make much difference to the war effort.

Equally thoughtless was my invitation to Mel that summer's

day to take a picnic and sleep out on the top of Box Hill the next night I was not on duty. We could take my portable gramophone, I suggested, and play my records. It would be a full moon (what was known as a bombers' moon) and I would buy some sausages, bring a frying pan and we would make a campfire. I was still in my teens and it was not so long since my student days in Germany where boys and girls slept side by side in ski huts in perfect safety! I was unaware that Mel presumed this was an invitation to take our relationship a stage further.

It turned out to be a disappointing night for him! We drove up to Box Hill; Mel collected wood and lit the campfire. I cooked the sausages on it. We cleared up, put on the gramophone and enjoyed a prolonged kissing session, at the end of which I said I thought it was about time we went to sleep as I was on duty early next morning. Telling him not to look, I took off my skirt and blouse and wrapping myself in a blanket settled myself down having assured him I wouldn't look whilst he took off his trousers. After I had thrown him the second blanket, I wished him good night and went happily to sleep.

In his autobiography, *Against The Odds*, Mel refers to that night thus: 'Moonlight, total privacy, a girl I was crazy about, and all she was bothered about was whether the fire would stay alight whilst we slept. Sausages and campfires were not quite what I had envisaged when she invited me to spend the night alone with her.'

Heinkel, now my shadow, was, if anything, uglier than he had been when I first saw him. But I loved him passionately and didn't care what he looked like. He came almost everywhere with me. If that was not possible, I could leave him anywhere even on a station platform and he would wait there patiently as long as he had some article belonging to me to guard. Even an old glove or shoe would do. When I did not have the car, one of my friends looked after him.

However, it was only a month or two before it seemed I was about to lose him.

There was no such thing in those days as an injection against distemper. It was as infectious as measles was for children, and one of the dogs on the camp passed it on to Heinkel. At the same time as I became aware he was not very well, I was posted to Ipswich on a fortnight's course. Joan, Audrey and some other girls and I were to be commissioned as, young though we were, they wanted to release the male Filter Officers for overseas service. My other close friend, Bragi, was commissioned soon after. Such early promotion did not apply to girls who joined up later so we were fortunate to get our commissions so soon. Immediately we arrived at our billet, I drove Heinkel into Ipswich to a vet in the town. By this time, Heinkel looked very sick indeed. To my horror, the vet took one look at him and said the kindest thing to do would be to put him to sleep. I was appalled, then angry.

'It's your job to save life, not destroy it!' I shouted, close to tears.

He took another look at Heinkel, told me he must have been taken away from his mother far too early; that he was obviously the runt of the litter and the pet shop had had no right to sell him to me – or anyone else. Nevertheless, he gave me some medicine but warned me it would probably not save Heinkel's life.

By now, I knew I was going to be late for the meeting we were all to attend to alert us to our next day's activities. With Heinkel wrapped in an old jersey lying quietly on the back seat, I drove off as fast as I dared. Without any warning, one of the tyres burst and we ended up in the ditch. Apart from a few bruises, I was unharmed but I was worried about the puppy whose nose and eyes were running and to whom I'd not yet been able to give any life-saving medicine.

A passing lorry driver towed the car back on to the road and changed the tyre for me. Fortunately, my absence had not been noticed at the meeting and the girls put me wise as to our programme for the next fourteen days. I remember little about them other than that Heinkel's life undoubtedly hung in the balance and I was literally keeping him alive with hourly spoonfuls of milk and glucose and the pills the vet had given me. By the end of that fortnight, he was little more than a fur-covered skeleton, but he *was* getting better. His eyes were brighter; his nose wasn't running quite so much.

I was immensely grateful to the girls who had fed and dosed him when I was under instruction. If they had not been willing to do so, I doubt Heinkel would have survived. As it was, he grew into a beautiful, healthy dog. In place of the puppy fur, his coat grew thick and shiny, a deep reddish brown. He had completely straight legs, quite long and no way did he resemble a pedigree Corgi. As a specimen of the breed, he was a disaster! But he was beautifully proportioned and more intelligent than any dog I've subsequently owned. He was part of my life for the next twelve years. My father who had never had or wanted anything but Labradors, grudgingly admitted that Heinkel was exceptionally intelligent if slightly over-protective of my belongings – and me!

Somewhat unusually, having been promoted to the rank of Assistant Section Officers, we were posted back to Rudloe – unusual because our former fellow plotters now had to take orders from us newly fledged Filter Officers as well as salute us – a strange state of affairs which in fact did not trouble anyone too much. Discipline was far stricter for non-technical Waafs. For one thing, we had men in charge of us rather than women! However, my officer status was going to cause difficulties regarding my friendship with Mel. Officers were not permitted to fraternise with other ranks. I overcame this problem by wearing civilian clothes underneath my greatcoat as I drove past the sentry when I left camp to meet Mel in Bath. We still went regularly to the Assembly Room dances and I suppose I was lucky not to be recognised by anyone who might report me for my 'inappropriate' behaviour.

I did at the time have two other admirers – one a rather shy army officer who on his embarkation leave asked me to marry him. I barely knew him although he had appeared in the mess once or twice and suggested we go to the pub in Corsham for a drink. He was almost as young as I was and reminded me of Roy since he, too, had not long left his public school. He wasn't half as much fun to be with as Mel and I turned down his proposal as kindly as I could.

The other would-be boyfriend was a Polish army officer. His name was Jerzy. One of thousands of Europeans whose countries had been overrun by the Germans, he had escaped to England and was currently stationed in Edinburgh. I had not been at all well one time that summer with what the M.O. thought was a gastric infection. In fact it was a kidney infection and as I was not seeming to get any better, I asked for sick leave as my mother was insisting I go up to Edinburgh so she could look after me. Neill had by now returned from Egypt and been posted to Scotland where my mother had joined him after their marriage in 1939.

I should not really have been travelling that day as I had a high temperature. Due to the bombing raids, trains were hopelessly unreliable and mine was stuck on a siding at Crewe for some time. When the journey finally resumed, I was barely conscious. The young Polish officer who got into my carriage attempted a conversation. I was too ill to notice it but he was tall, slim, dark-eyed and extremely handsome. When we reached Edinburgh, he took my kitbag and held my arm while we waited for a taxi. Helping me inside the cab, he asked for my address to give to the taxi driver.

According to my mother, my temperature was so high I was barely conscious for the next two days during which, she told me, this attractive young Polish officer had called every day with a bunch of flowers and fruit. He had noted my address when he put me in the taxi – his behaviour as romantic as one of the heroes of her books. He continued to call with more flowers, and hearing I had a sweet tooth, brought a whole jar of fruit drops – goodness knows where he had got them from as sweets were rationed to a mere 3ozs. a week.

After a few days under the care of the Scottish doctor, my temperature went down and I was allowed to go downstairs for an hour or two. My Polish admirer, Jerzy, called with yet more flowers and sat and talked to me whilst we had tea. He was very intense, very serious and, as it transpired when I was well enough and he took me out dancing, very passionate! He was undoubtedly good-looking, beautifully mannered and, the son of the previous Polish Minister of Finance (so he told me) had obviously belonged in the upper echelons of Polish society. My mother was delighted with him. I quite liked him and when I was up and about again, I did go out to dinner and dance with him. He was not such a good dancer as Mel and not so much fun, so there was no question of my falling in love with him which I think my mother might well have been hoping. When my sick leave came to an end, he saw me off at the station and kissed me goodbye. He stayed with me until the last moment before the train left.

I had barely found my sleeper, said hullo to the woman I was to share my compartment with, and removed my greatcoat when there was a knock on the door. Thinking it was the car attendant, I opened it. It was Jerzy. The train was now moving out of the station and supposing he had not got off in time I said we must call the attendant and ask him to try to get the train stopped at the next station. Far from wishing for this, Jerzy told me he intended travelling to London – simply in order to spend further time with me. He pulled me out into the corridor and began kissing me far more passionately than he had done before.

I was not so much flattered as frightened because he would not let me go even when a passenger passed by and I became aware that he was unbuttoning his trousers. The next moment in a state of high excitement, he exposed himself. Never having been privy to such a sight before, I was horrified and made a dash for my sleeper. The following morning when we arrived at King's Cross, I kept as close as possible to the woman who had shared my compartment. This did not stop Jerzy hurrying down the platform after me full of apologies, and I was only able to get rid of him when I gave him my address in Bath and promised to write to him.

I now lived in officers' quarters at Rudloe Manor which had been especially built for us. We had our own rooms with excellent 'ablution' facilities and unlimited hot water – a luxury we had not had at our billet in Corsham where the water supply ran out after the second bath. We also had our own batwomen to make our beds, clean the rooms as well as our shoes and tunic buttons. I dared not leave Heinkel in the room if I was absent as he would fiercely defend any item of mine and my batwoman wouldn't go in!

By now Germany had invaded Russia, so although the threat of invasion had all but vanished, Churchill warned everyone that it was going to be a long, hard struggle to liberate Europe. It was to be another six months before the Japanese attacked Pearl Harbour and the Americans finally came to our aid, so at present we and the Russians were the only countries left to fight the mighty German Reich.

Hitler had invaded Yugoslavia and Greece and was defeating our army in North Africa. It had become a question of how long we could continue to hold out.

I had seen some of the devastation in the city of London when I changed railway stations on my return from Edinburgh and of course the newspapers depicted many of these horrific sights. People were using the underground stations as bomb shelters, sleeping there night after night when the daylight raids gave way to the night-time ones, which continued until dawn. It was with enormous courage and faith that the civilian population refused to allow Hitler to frighten them into submission. My mother, who was living in London at the time, was one of them. Although she could have moved out of danger to a country cottage far from the city, she refused to be forced from her home and frequently sheltered under her Blüthner piano during the air raids.

King George VI and Queen Elizabeth remained steadfastly in Buckingham Palace although nobody would have thought the worst of them had they left the danger and gone to one of their castles. What the people had to endure, he and his wife would share, the King said, and like the people, they continued to go to their work each day. My father, too, travelled to and from London often waiting patiently whilst a troop train took precedence over his.

Back in Bath, Mel and I held hands in the cinema whilst we watched the horrors of war on the Pathe News and refused to think of the future as we danced the evenings away. On duty, we became even busier as the raids spread north and westward and there was no time now to write my stories as our work continued non-stop throughout the night.

My maternal grandfather,
Herman Klein

Wills cigarette card picture of
my mother, Denise Robins,
reproduced for 'Thirties
Nostalgia' Bookclub calendar

My maternal grandmother,
Mrs K. C. Groome, before
her elopement

1938, me aged 17, shortly
to become a journalist

A treasured photo of
my father, Arthur
Howis Robins

Below: Furnace
Pond Cottage, my
childhood home

My sister Eve, aged 6, and me, aged 4

My sister Anne, aged 16

Me, aged 8, reluctantly forced into pink satin

1936, me, left, aged 15, on a ski trip with school friends, seated
next to Ingeborg the Hitler fanatic

Das Offizier-Korps des Kampfgeschwaders 255
im Fliegerhorst Landsberg/Lech

gibt sich die Ehre *Miss Pat Robins*

zu dem am *1. 12. 1937. 16²⁰* Uhr stattfindenden

Jazznacht *wald* ... *Tanz* ergebenst aufzufordern.

Um Antwort auf beiliegender Karte
an Msf. K255 bis²⁷·¹¹· wird gebeten.

Anzug:
Wagenbestellung: 19.00 oder 22.30

Abholung mit Autobus um 15.00
vor Hotel Regina. Rückfahrt gegen
23.00.

Oberst und Kommodore
des Kampfgeschwaders 255

1937, the German Air Force invite me to a tea dance in Munich

Above: 1941. Mel in
'civvies' before his
overseas posting, with
puppy Heinkel

Heinkel, my loyal
and faithful companion
from 1941 to 1953

1943, promoted to Flight Officer –
kiss curl accidental!

1943, Ken, my Australian Lancaster Bomber
navigator, shot down in a raid over Germany in
1944, aged 26

1954, Donald and me in Benghazi with Iain and Nicky

Inauguration dinner of the Romantic Novelists' Association
– in my mother's emeralds!

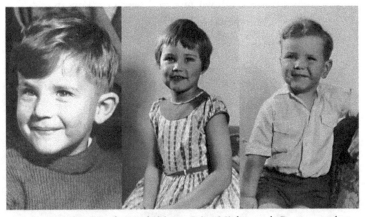

Favourite photos of my children, Iain, Nicky and Graeme, when
they were young

CHAPTER 7

At the beginning of October Mel received his posting over-seas. He was given seven days' leave and we both realised it could be years before we could go dancing again together, if indeed ever. Naturally, he wished to go home to Melton Mowbray to see his mother and siblings but at the same time, he wanted to have at least a few more hours with me. I was due some leave – a seventy-two hour pass – and I still had some petrol in the car. I suggested we could make the trip to Sussex together and I would put him on a train at Horsham.

Mel had never met either of my sisters but had heard me talk a great deal about them. He went along with my plan to stop at Newbury and see if we could get Anne out of her school, Downe House. When we reached there, I told the headmistress that one of our relatives had been posted overseas and asked if Anne could have a few days compassionate leave. To my surprise, she agreed and Anne, who had already gone to bed, was woken by Matron and told to get dressed and go downstairs.

Anne, who was only sixteen at the time, remembers that night as being one of great excitement coming as it did so unexpectedly out of the blue. Mel had a lovely singing voice and I asked him to sing some of our favourite songs whilst I drove through the night. It was a long time since Anne and I had had a chance to meet up and now she suggested that on the way home through Aldershot we stopped and saw Eve who was stationed there. Eve was equally thrilled at the unexpected visit and the presence of my two sisters kept Mel and me from thinking too much about the impending parting.

I knew I was going to miss him dreadfully, which, indeed I did, but life moved on very quickly in wartime and it was not long before the Americans arrived at Colerne with a squadron of Lightning aeroplanes. The pilots were very young and had not yet encountered the horrors of war. Looking very smart in their Air Force uniforms, with lots of everything – money, cigarettes, chocolate, silk stockings and so on – they quickly made friends with the girls in civilian clothes and in uniform. The British male service personnel somewhat resented this appropriation of their womenfolk and before long, the 'Yanks', as the Americans were called, received the designation 'over-paid, over-sexed and over here'! On the whole, they were extremely polite, good fun and only too anxious to make friends with everyone.

Jill and I were invited with others to a dance at the American base in Colerne where they were awaiting their postings overseas. Two of the pilots we met, Robert Chenoweth and David Everett, asked us if we would be their dates. When we were not on duty, they borrowed an army jeep and took us in to Bath to dine and dance. David was on the quiet, serious side and although Robert and I had started out together as a pair, after a week or two, Jill and I swapped, and David then became my escort and Robert partnered Jill. We always went out as a foursome.

It seemed reasonable at the time but looking back, 'swapping' indicates how light-hearted those relationships were. Dates usually ended with a harmless necking session. American boys were as aware as English ones that 'nice' girls didn't go further than 'petting', not that we knew even at that age, two years into the war, what 'going further' meant. I suppose there were some who did know, but neither I nor my friends did.

The boys did not stay long. They were posted off to North Africa where, so I heard later, within a few weeks Robert's plane was shot down and he was killed. David's plane never arrived and was, presumably, shot down on the journey there. I wrote to David's mother, hoping to comfort her with the news that both he and his friends had had a happy time, however brief, in England. David had a kid sister and several years later when I wrote a children's book, *Tree Fairies*, I dedicated it to her.

I began to receive airgraphs (letters photographed and reduced almost to hand size), from Mel. He couldn't say where he was of course but it sounded like the desert. He never failed to send Heinkel his love, which I took to be a euphemism for me! I wrote back whenever an airgraph arrived, telling him anything I could without mentioning boyfriends! I also had phone calls from Jerzy asking when he could come down and visit me. I always said I was too busy and my work secret so he wouldn't be allowed to come on the camp.

I spent the Christmas Eve of 1941 on duty but was given leave for New Year's Eve which I spent in Edinburgh with my mother. She was still writing and had not long finished her sixty-fourth novel, but she combined work with a busy social life. Despite the war, there were cocktail parties, dances, luncheons, bridge parties – war would hardly have seemed to exist were it not for the fact that the city was full of uniformed men from all branches of the services. The Dutch navy sent their submarines into Leith docks to be refitted and Neill and my mother knew a number of the submarine officers. On New Year's Eve there was a dance at the Castle and I was escorted by a delightful Dutch officer called Simon de Böer. He was not very good-looking being short and tubby but he was a really good dancer and as usual, I had a wonderful time. Eve, too, was on leave. She was now in the ATS – the Women's Auxiliary Territorial

Service. She danced the night away with a Dutch submarine officer called Japp with whom she fell in love. It was a significant meeting for her as it later transpired.

We were back at our respective camps when Edinburgh received an isolated bomb. It had been intended for the Forth Bridge but instead fell on The Distillers Company. Sir Harry Ross, who was Director of the company and a friend of my mother's, told her that half a million gallons of whisky went up in flames that night. Sad though it was, it seemed insignificant set against the terrible loss of life elsewhere. The news was far from good. Germany's desert army commander, Rommel, was pushing our troops further and further back towards Cairo. In Russia the advancing German armies had reached Stalingrad. The Japanese had landed in Malaya early in December and invaded the Philippines.

By January, the Japs had taken Manila and Cavite and we all now realised the seriousness of the war in the Middle East. I must say I did not give the matter too much thought as I was about to 'come of age'! On 1st February I would be twenty-one and somewhat bizarrely, old enough to 'receive the key of the door', as this yardstick was known. My father, who always gave beautiful presents, sent me a gold watch which sadly, as I dearly loved it, was stolen later on in the war. The CO gave me permission to hold a twenty-first birthday party in the Officers' Mess and I invited all the friends and colleagues I had met during the past year. My good old portable gramophone came in handy and after a buffet supper provided by the mess cook, we danced to my collection of 78's. Spirits were difficult to come by as they were strictly rationed; but as I very rarely drank alcohol, I'd managed to save and scrounge enough to provide drinks for my guests.

One of the girls I invited was – or so she claimed – one of Augustus John's illegitimate daughters. She was quite a novelty to me – very uninhibited and unconventional, but she provided a mini cabaret in the form of a dance, barefoot, unchoreographed, in a flimsy, semi-transparent dress, which went down very well – at least with the men!

I was allowed to have Heinkel with me in the mess as well as in my billet. When I was first commissioned, a Waaf Admin Officer had noticed him and reported it to the CO. He, too, had a dog, and when I was told I could not keep Heinkel in the mess, I pointed out to him that Heinkel was better trained than his dog so had a better right to stay! This was a bit cheeky to say the least but he was amused and he challenged me to prove it. To do so, I suggested we each put something belonging to us such as a glove or scarf a distance away, walked our dogs back to the Mess and at the word 'go', sent the dogs off to retrieve the objects. Heinkel, I said, would be quickest. By now he had grown into a strong, healthy animal, more like a fox than a Corgi. We had practised retrieving when I had been home on leave with my father and he was throwing a rabbit skin wrapped round a ball for his young Labrador. I knew how quick Heinkel was.

The CO admitted defeat and Heinkel was henceforth allowed anywhere I went except, of course, on duty. Joan, now one of my fellow officers, remembers an occasion when our contribution to the war was temporarily held up because I had dropped a glove when I came off duty at the entrance to the new underground Filter Room. Heinkel had automatically placed himself on guard and no one was allowed to pass him until I had been found to call him away.

It is strange thinking of the anomaly of my new status. Had I remained in civilian life, I don't doubt my activities would have been confined within the small bubble of conventional behaviour appertaining to a girl of twenty-one from my background. As it was, I had been freed from all those restrictions. As Waafs we could – and did – go anywhere, often hitch-hiking lifts in strange cars, travelling alone on trains at night, meeting, talking to strange men; picking up male hitch-hikers in my car. We never came to any harm, whereas today girls would be courting danger if they did such things. Because of the war, I was freed from parental control long before I came of age and was thought old enough to live away from home.

It was only a fortnight after my birthday that the news came saying the Japanese had virtually walked unopposed into Singapore and that over seventy thousand people had been taken prisoner. There were hundreds of civilians amongst the troops, including children. It was really only after the war was over that we all learned the true awfulness of the prison camps to which they were taken, but now several people around me had relatives out there and things looked far from hopeful.

Those of us who had friends who were pilots never knew from day to day when we would see them again. I remember meeting a young Mosquito pilot at a dance who was cheerfully making daytime, low-level sorties to strafe trains travelling across Occupied France. I promised to go out with him the following evening but received a telephone call from a member of his squadron saying he had not returned from a raid he'd been carrying out that day. It was very sad but so commonplace now that we all accepted such tragedies as par for the course.

In a way I suppose we were becoming inured to them in much the same way as civilians were learning philosophically to cope with the bombing raids – no need to be apprehensive, your number was on a bomb or it wasn't. It was very much an atmosphere of 'eat, drink and be merry', because there might well not be a tomorrow. Mostly, we managed not to think too often about the daily and nightly loss of lives and simply put as much effort as we could into whatever work we were doing to help win the war.

In May 1943, I was posted to Headquarters No 12 Group in Watnall near Nottingham and was billeted with a young mother and her two small children at 87, Main Street. Ron, the husband of my landlady, Ann Crich, was in the army overseas and I think she quite liked having someone living in the house as well as needing the allowance people were given for letting their spare rooms. She made me very comfortable and, moreover, allowed me to keep Heinkel with me – something I'd feared might be a problem when my posting came through.

Later on in the war, discipline tightened quite considerably and on a posting up north to Preston, I was told I could not have Heinkel in my billet. I was fortunate in being able to opt for a ground floor room of the building which backed on to a farm track. Opposite my window were some farm buildings and after a quick visit to the farmer, he agreed to billet Heinkel in a stable opposite me. It was easy then for me to take him to the stable, tell him to stay there until I called him, which I would do as soon as I reached my room. He would jump in through the open window and remain unobserved until I had to banish him once more to the stable before my batwoman came to clean the room. We were both quite happy with this makeshift arrangement. I have to admit I was prepared to be court martialled for disobeying orders but we were never discovered!

The work I was doing was much the same but we were kept very busy and I only had time to write an article or story if the weather was bad enough to prevent flying. One afternoon when I was on duty, the crew of a Lancaster bomber came down to the Filter Room. They wanted to see how it had been possible for them to be rescued so quickly when their plane had ditched in the Channel on the way home from a raid.

I explained how the system worked – that echoes from the coastal radar stations crossed one another; how the girls attached to the table placed their coloured counters and an arrow was put down by a Filter Officer such as myself at the point of intersection. A relative speed of the plane could be estimated by the time it took from one radar blip to the next, so even when the plane flew too low to be picked up on the radar screens, the approximate distance it then travelled could be gauged before the Mayday calls ceased. The position of a plane in trouble would be given priority as it was passed on to the ops room and a Walrus seaplane scrambled to go and pick up the crew to be found, hopefully, at the estimated point at which it had ditched.

There was a dance on at the station that night and one of the crew of the Lancaster, the navigator, asked me if I would go with him. His name was Ken Lyons and he was an Australian. I had intended to go to the dance unescorted because a particularly good-looking American pilot was going with a bunch of his friends and I'd been hoping he would ask me to dance! However, Ken was very persuasive as well as good-looking, so I said I'd meet him in the Mess when I came off duty.

Ken turned out to be far from the best dancer I'd known; but despite this disappointment, he more than made up for it with his charm. He was five years older than me and at twenty-six, struck me as being very grown-up. Instead of dancing, we sat and talked. He was stationed near Lincoln and had a very good friend, a Canadian called Arnold, who, like me, had his own dog, an Airedale. Ken suggested that if we could coincide leaves, and I could persuade a girl friend to come with us, we could all four go up to the Lake District for a walking holiday. I liked him enough that first evening to agree to the idea.

I don't know if I ever 'fell in love' with Ken – I just grew to love him. 'Nice' is such an inadequate word but that is what he was – so very nice. All the good adjectives applied to him – thoughtful, generous, kind, considerate, unselfish and so on – yet he was a really good companion, eager to meet people, explore the countryside, live life to the full. Part of his great pleasure in life was discovering England, 'the mother country' – pubs, beer, patchwork fields, small farmsteads, lakes – he was eager to see everything – and wanted me with him. I took him home to meet my father with whom he got on splendidly, and we spent several leaves in Sussex, going for long walks in the woods, on the South Downs, picking blackberries, roasting chestnuts on the log fire. They were simple peacetime pursuits which made it possible for a little while to forget the war and the danger he would be in when his leave was over.

Those days were the more precious because we both knew how likely they were to be the last. The life expectancy for bomber crews was horrifyingly short. One day I read an article about the stresses and strains pilots suffered knowing each time they were sent out on a mission, the chances were only one in five that they would come back. I decided that I should dismiss the edict that girls should not 'give themselves' to a man (i.e. have sex!) before marriage, and that it was more or less my duty to 'give myself' to Ken. The article inferred that not to do so meant one was increasing the dangers of added stress when a crew was airborne. Very sadly, my darling Ken is not here to tell my disbelieving grandchildren that such thoughts were perfectly normal for a girl brought up as I had been.

Ken and I were to spend a seventy-two-hour pass in Lincoln. We met at the railway station and I asked him to walk up the hill to Lincoln Cathedral with me where we could sit outside in the sunshine and I could tell him of the 'momentous' decision I had made! Although he tried to dissuade me on the grounds that this decision was something I felt I ought to do, not something I really wanted to do, my mind was made up. Had I known how little precious life was left to him, I would have wished I had taken this 'momentous' step before.

We rented a furnished room in Nottingham where we met whenever our leaves coincided. If I arrived there before him, I would nearly always find a letter waiting saying: 'I'll be with you very soon and I love you very much!' We were for the brief time we had left, very happy.

It was whilst I was at Watnall during the winter of 1943 that I became quite ill with pleurisy. I had had a chesty cough but it had not stopped me going down to the Filter Room on night duty, often in cold wintry weather. The Filter Room was warm but once again, it was bitterly cold outside when I had to bike back to my billet. One morning I woke in such pain that I asked Mrs. Crich to telephone the camp and ask the M.O. to come and see me.

I retain a hazy memory of the doctor saying an ambulance would call to take me to hospital; of worrying how to let one of my friends know so that they could look after Heinkel for me. My next memory is of sitting in a cold hall on a bench in the hospital clutching my medical notes, and a doctor coming up to me and asking what I was doing there. He took my notes from me and than started shouting. I found out later that he had been beside himself with anger because when my RAF transport had dumped me in Out Patients, I had been left sitting there for over an hour before anyone noticed me.

The outcome was a patch on my lung that necessitated quite a long stay. After a few days of semi-consciousness with a sky-high temperature, I began to feel a little better and to find that I had been put in a very comfortable twin-bedded room with a convalescent ATS officer. After a while, my friends came to visit me and assured me that Heinkel was all right – my biggest concern. I was allowed to sit up and then to have my portable typewriter so as I got better I decided to pass the time writing a children's book. *Tree*

Fairies was the result although it was not published until after the war was over.

Ken came to visit me. The loss of time together was made up for by the fact that I was sure to get sick leave to convalesce and there was time for him to coincide his leave. We spent it that autumn doing all the 'country' things Ken liked and finding places to make love outdoors as well as in. My mother had moved during the summer from Edinburgh to London, Neill having been posted overseas, and I took Ken to meet her. She sat at her piano and played all his favourite tunes for him and approved of our relationship which she thought very romantic.

Perhaps we were unwilling to face realitites but we needed to believe we did have a future. We even decided upon the number of children we would have and the names we would give them. I would happily have married Ken and had the first of our children but he was more realistic and told me he was unprepared to take the very real risk of leaving me a widow with child whilst not long out of childhood myself. But we cheated death for a little while, pretending our small threadbare room was our home and buying homely objects for it as, for example, our own orange teapot which we used instead of the one our landlady had provided together with an old tin kettle to heat on the single gas ring. I don't know if she ever questioned our relationship. Ken was protective of my reputation but I didn't care. It wasn't our sexual compatibility which made my time there so precious. All I needed was to be with him and to know that he was safe for a little while.

There was a glimmer of hope for us for the future, now that the Germans had been forced to surrender to Russia at the gates of Stalingrad, their forces decimated by the extremes of bitter weather. In September that year American and British troops landed in Italy and Benito Mussolini, the Italian dictator, surrendered to the Allies and hundreds of Italian prisoners were coming to England to be put in camps and to work on farms. General Montgomery with his 8th Army had finally forced the German Commander, Rommel, to retreat and now, when the German troops in Africa surrendered, Churchill was turning his thoughts to the invasion of Europe. It really did seem as if the tide had turned at last, and Ken and I might yet have a future together.

CHAPTER 8

Anne was now in the WAAF and stationed at Defford, Worcestershire in the Meteorological Office. Eve in the ATS was with an ACK-ACK Battery and in more danger than I would ever be now that the Filter Rooms were underground. We met very rarely but I kept in touch by letter with both the girls. On my way back from a leave in Edinburgh, my mother travelled down to London with me. As always, the train service was disrupted either by bombing the night before or by troop movements, and we were shunted into a siding at Crewe.

We decided to get ourselves a cup of tea from the mobile trolley. As we walked back to the carriage, my mother stopped to greet a tall, good-looking naval officer called John Sutton, who she had known when she and Neill were in Cairo. He travelled down to London with us. As always the romantic, my mother insisted we exchange addresses and made John promise to get in touch with me. This he duly did, inviting me up to London to a dinner dance on my next seventy-two-hour pass.

I would have declined the invitation but for one reason – he bore a remarkable resemblance to Japp, the Dutch submarine officer with whom Eve had fallen in love in Edinburgh. Sadly he had been lost at sea and she was quite grief stricken at the time. But at the first meeting with John, which I organised, as I expected, she found him every bit as attractive, if not more so, than Japp.

In August a year later, Eve and John were married in

Liverpool, the event dwarfed by the long-awaited Allied invasion of Europe. On June 6th one hundred and seventy-six thousand Allied troops landed on the French coast at Normandy. Because of the obvious preparations for such an enormous undertaking, the Germans had known the invasion was imminent, but not where on the French coast our armies might land. As a result, the Allies were able to move forward very quickly and on the 23rd August they liberated Paris.

One of my friends, the actor Donald Gray, had stopped by to see me on his way down from the north of England to the coast where the invasion troops were being mustered. He was among ten thousand killed or wounded that day on the Normandy beaches and was returned to England twenty-four hours later minus an arm. Although he was lucky to be among the survivors as inevitably the losses were very high, the absence of a limb did seriously curtail his career as an actor.

I suppose to some extent we had all become accustomed to the sudden, unexpectedness of death. Subconsciously, we were prepared for it. But I had begun to hope that despite the danger Ken was in every time his Lancaster flew out over Germany on one of their bombing raids, he would soon be safe on the ground. At that time, aircrews were expected to complete two tours, each consisting of thirty bombing raids. Now on his second tour, Ken had only three more raids to do. He was virtually counting the days. He had confessed to me that he was scared to death every time they took off on a raid; that any other crew member who said they were not frightened, was not telling the truth. It was not only the heavy concentrations of anti-aircraft flak that endangered them, particularly if they had not yet dropped their load of bombs, but the German night fighters which could pick them off like flies if they were caught in the beam of a searchlight. The crews all knew that at this time of the war, on average, one in four of them would not come home.

Early on this particular day in August, Ken telephoned me to tell me he would not be ringing me that evening as was his custom because the airfield would be closed down – something which always happened when a raid was to take place. I had no qualms about Ken's safety as his plane was unserviceable and he'd told me he would not be flying. However, having gone to bed at midnight following a late shift, I slept for only a few hours before I had a terrible nightmare in which I saw Ken's Lancaster falling through the sky in flames. I must have been making a noise as the other girls in my room woke up. They quickly reassured me that my fears were unfounded because, as I well knew, Ken was not flying. What I did not know was that because of his longing to complete his final tours of duty, he had volunteered to replace the navigator of another crew who was unfit to fly.

The following morning, I woke with the same horrible feeling of apprehension which increased as the hours passed. I was due on duty at twelve but knew I would never be able to concentrate as I should unless I had spoken to Ken and knew he was all right. I telephoned the airfield. Instead of being put through to the Mess as was normal, the operator put me through to the Orderly Officer. That was when I was told Ken's plane was among those which had not returned that night. One of the pilots reported they had seen a plane blown to pieces approaching the target, but could not be sure which of the missing planes it was.

It was at this point in my life that I started smoking. I had, of course, tried smoking with Tony one of his father's cigarettes at the age of ten – and hated it. Because it was very much the 'in thing' for sophisticated people to do in those years before we knew it was dangerous, as a grownup

I had tried continuously to enjoy it and failed. Now, because Ken had, among many other treasured gifts, given me an amber cigarette holder, I started smoking in earnest. It was, I suppose, a somewhat bizarre way of staying close to him. By the time I realised he was never coming back, I was addicted – and many years later, was to suffer the consequences.

I have always been too much of a realist to believe in the supernatural. The danger always threatening Ken was never far from my mind, and it was probably no more than pure coincidence that I should have dreamt that night he died when his plane was blown to pieces. Nevertheless, I still wonder sometimes if he was trying to tell me that he would not be coming back.

It was some while before the 'Missing' designation was changed to 'Killed in Action'. I did try to tell myself that it was not Ken's plane and that he had come down somewhere over German territory and was a prisoner of war. I wrote letters, started saving whatever I could to make up one of the P.O.W. parcels the Red Cross delivered once the prisoner's camp was known. But I knew I was kidding myself and that I wouldn't see him again. My letters to him which he had kept were returned to me by his friend, Arnold, but I burnt them. I did keep his letters to me, nearly all of them written when he was returning from one of his bombing sorties and talking of the future that was never to be.

Hearts, of course, do not break and time does heal. There were, however, some very difficult moments, not least each time Heinkel, who had loved Ken, raced up to an airman he happened to see wearing the Australian dark blue uniform. For a while, just for a split second, I had a flash of hope.

It was soon after this that Eve's wedding took place in Liverpool. Ken had arranged to have leave to cover the date so he could be there, so I don't remember the wedding day as being a very happy one for me, although Eve, of course, looked beautiful and her tall, naval officer very handsome. After the ceremony, a taxi bearing bride and groom was drawn with ropes by eight naval ratings through the streets to the Adelphi Hotel where they had the reception. My father had travelled up from Sussex and he and my mother were temporarily reunited for the occasion.

As the Allies advanced into Germany, and the bombing raids over England became things of the past, Hitler made one last attempt to subdue the population. That September of 1944, he launched his 'secret weapon' – pilot-less bombs fired off like rockets which soared over the English Channel and fell indiscriminately over London. Sometimes they fell in the countryside if they had run out of fuel before reaching their target.

They came to be known as Buzz Bombs because of the noise they made – a noise which abruptly ceased leaving a frightening silence in the minutes before it fell. Everyone continued to go about their business whilst the buzzing continued overhead, but stopped, holding their breath whilst they waited to see where it would fall.

Horrible as they were, no one believed they would halt the now foreseeable victory, but nevertheless, the Buzz Bombs were very draining on the nervous system and caused a massive amount of damage when they fell in a built-up area. By the end of 1944, the V2s started to arrive. Unlike the slow flying V1s, these rockets flew at supersonic speeds and the radar stations had to be fitted with special equipment to track them. Special plans were made to eliminate the launch sites, and I found myself posted down to Stanmore to play a small part in this.

By now I had been promoted to Flight Officer and I joined several others in a room at Fighter Command where we were given graphs to fill in indicating the arc of the rocket's flight. The final point of the arc was the exact position where the V2 landed. This was relayed by the Observer Corps whose job it was to pinpoint these positions. They were also tracked by Ack-Ack and Barrage Balloon sites. Over the sea, there were plots from any radar station along the coast which they were able to pick up when the V2 rose to a certain height after it had left its launch pad.

As a result, it was possible to plot an arc soon after leaving the French coast to the point where the V2 landed; but because the radar beam could not detect it at very low altitudes, the actual site position remained unknown although the rest of the arc could be drawn. By the time I started work on these graphs, the technical details of a V2's performance was well known. We could, therefore, give a fairly accurate drawing of the arc of a V2 shortly after launch, to fill in the missing start of its flight and thereby pinpoint its probable launch site.

It was concentrated work but simple enough to do and with the reward of knowing that it could result in the possible end of the V2 bombs. Our planes were sent over the Channel to decimate the sites wherever enough starting pinpoints had accumulated. As the V2s were being launched both days and nights, there was no lack of arcs to be plotted and drawn. (I may not have explained this very clearly, but at least I knew what I was doing at the time!)

The war finally came to an end on May 8th at one minute past midnight. Anne and I joined the huge crowds trying to reach Buckingham Palace where the King and Queen and the two princesses were appearing on the balcony waving to the ecstatic people filling every last inch of space in the Mall. We did not get beyond Trafalgar Square where laughing, cheering people hemmed us in.

It seemed as if the entire population of the country, including every man and woman in the armed forces, wanted to join in the jubilation of that final victory. We all knew that the war with Japan in the Far East had yet to be won, but for that night, I don't think anyone gave it a thought. At long last, the church bells were able to ring, blackout curtains were pulled down, and those who could not get to London huddled round their wireless sets toasting Churchill's promised victory after six long years of war.

An official day of celebration was announced, VE Day, Victory in Europe. All over the country there were street parties and apart from the enormous feeling of relief that at last the war was over, there was also a feeling of pride as people realised that we had for a long time stood alone against Hitler's evil regime withstanding the worst he could throw at our tiny island. It was well known that he had committed suicide in his bunker in Berlin but news was only just beginning to circulate of the indescribable horrors discovered by our troops as they came upon the concentration camps.

There were further horrors to come when the Japanese city of Hiroshima was flattened by the first ever atomic bomb dropped by the Americans, to be followed by a second on the city of Nagasaki, after which the Japanese surrendered. Any sympathy felt for the victims was tempered by pictures on the news of the skeleton-like figures of the prisoners of war now liberated from the camps. The mood of euphoria that had engulfed everyone on VE Day had all but evaporated. The privations of the aftermath of the war were universal.

I was partially inured from all the shortages that not only continued but in some cases, increased. My job on the V2s had ended and in order to find something for me to do whilst I awaited my turn for demobilisation, I was given a job as assistant to the Education Officer. Seeing my lack of any single academic qualification, it seemed a very odd choice of employment. However, it did not require any skills. My boss's task was to give lectures to officers and other ranks on the camp telling them what employment and training was available to prepare them for civilian life.

By the end of the first two weeks when I had accompanied him, I could have repeated his lecture word for word in my sleep. Came the day not long after when I received a message to say he was laid low with flu and would I give his lectures for him. I was quite happy to fall in with his wishes – until I went out on the stage and looked down on several hundred upturned, expectant faces. I had never before had any occasion to speak in public and now I was hopelessly overcome by nerves. It was not enough to know exactly the words which were supposed to come from my mouth – I could not utter one of them.

I've no doubt I looked pretty stupid standing there gaping. Fortunately, I recalled how, at the end of his lecture, the Education Officer always invited questions. Explaining rapidly that my boss was ill and that there would be no lecture, I told my audience I was familiar with the courses, openings, and the training that would be available. After answering a few such questions – I found my lost confidence and was able to give reasonably lengthy explanations when required.

When the Education Officer was not lecturing, we would go round offices, orderly rooms etc., offering information to anyone interested, sometimes together if there were a number of people in the room, sometimes separately. On one such day, I entered the room where two RAF pilots were seated. Both were former university students and it wasn't long before they realised that I knew nothing whatever about English universities. The older of the two, who introduced himself as Charles Crusoe, suggested I give up the task of trying to organise their post-war employment and sit down for a chat. His friend, he said, was a Scot called Donald Clark, an ex night-fighter pilot, then navigation officer. Don was more serious than his companion who was somewhat of a flirt, but he was very good-looking and when Charles invited me to go out for a drink with them, I suggested they both came to the flat in Gledhow Gardens which I had not long since acquired.

Discipline was far less strict now we were all about to return to Civvy Street and there had been no difficulty for me in gaining permission to live off camp. Gledhow Gardens was just off the Old Brompton Road in London and I had the car in which to drive to and from Stanmore every day. Anne, meanwhile, managed to get herself posted to Stanmore where she was involved giving talks on musical courses that might be available to ex service personnel. In her lunch hour, she gave small concerts using records provided for her by ENSA – the Entertainment National Service Association.

Anne was not yet twenty-one, i.e. an adult, and because of this, she was able to wangle permission to come and live with me as I was not only three years older but also a commissioned officer! So she and I shared the tiny flat just under the roof of the building. It was our first independent home and we were thrilled with it despite its tiny size and minute cupboard of a kitchen.

Charles and Don became regular visitors as did a number of other friends, many of whom were Waafs. We also had staying temporarily with us a former ATS friend of Eve's called Katie who had been booted out of the army when an American paratrooper, who had fallen in love with her, got her pregnant. Unable to go home because of parental disapproval, Katie needed a refuge until permission came through for her American, a really nice chap called Fred, to marry her and for her to go out with him to America with all the other hundreds of G.I. brides. Anne and I forbore to tell our parents she was there as they would have considered her 'a bad influence'. Bearing in mind that despite her size the poor girl had to stagger up five flights of stairs every time she went up to our attic flat, her pregnant state was more of a warning than an encouragement to take any risks! There was a huge celebration when Fred's permission to marry came through – only just in time, as by now poor Katie had only a few weeks to go before the birth of her baby.

There were other notable events in the year we were at Gledhow Gardens. My mother's secretary arrived there unexpectedly one evening and asked if she could have a bed for the night. It was no problem for Anne and me to double up so we allowed her to come. In the morning Anne took her in a cup of tea when we got up and came to tell me she couldn't wake her. As I could not wake her either, we called a doctor who told us she had taken an overdose of sleeping pills and sent for an ambulance to take her to hospital.

Needless to say, my mother was both shocked and very angry with the poor woman for involving us. She did survive but of course, did not continue in my mother's employ. Much later we learned she had been having an affair with a married man who had finally broken off the relationship. She was not a young woman and seeing no future happiness for herself she had decided to end her life. A few years later, she died of natural causes.

On 26th February 1946 I was finally demobbed, and Anne shortly after. I now found time to write again. Hutchinson had not only published the children's book I had written in the Nottingham hospital, but now they also published my first novel, *See No Evil*. This managed to pay the rent! Anne was now twenty-one and went to study clarinet under Albert Goosons at Trinity College of Music. At the same time, she joined the Bach choir. My mother had great hopes for her musical future; in no doubt that she had inherited our grandfather's exceptional talent.

Several friends I made before and during the war came to visit us at Gledhow Gardens. I also received a completely unexpected visitor one evening when Anne and I were cooking a meal for Charles and Don, the two RAF officers who had not yet been demobbed. I opened the door to find Mel standing there. He had broken his journey home on his way back from Italy. We had been corresponding regularly throughout the war but I'd not heard from him for several weeks, so I had no idea he had just been demobbed.

It was really nice seeing him – memories reviving of all the fun we had had an interminable five years ago. His war had been even more adventurous than mine. He had travelled from Iraq to Palestine, to the Lebanon, Syria, Egypt and finally landed with 241 Squadron in Sicily two days after the Allied invasion. From there, the Squadron had fought their way up the east coast of Italy to Treviso when the war ended.

Naturally I invited him to stay and have supper with us, but although he knew Anne from the school episode, he knew neither Charles nor Don and it was difficult for us to start reminiscing. The tango had been our favourite dance in the Bath days and I still had my old hand-wound gramophone. I put on one of our favourite dance records, 'Jealousy', and for just a few moments, we were back in the Assembly Rooms.

Neither of us was particularly at ease and not long after his arrival, Mel said he must go. I walked with him to the underground station. We promised to keep in touch but it did not seem very likely that we would do so. Mel was returning to his home in Melton Mowbray where he would have to find himself a job having nothing but his railway warrant and his demob pay of twenty-three pounds with which to start a new life. Our worlds were, as they had always been, miles apart. It was a sad as well as a nostalgic moment when we kissed goodbye. Less than a year later, we were both married to someone else.

CHAPTER 9

Anne and I soon realised that our tiny flat was too small for our needs. One of my WAAf friends, Maisie Frazier, had now also been demobbed and was looking for somewhere in London to live, so we found a large flat consisting of rooms on two floors – the ground and basement. It was in Drayton Gardens, only a stone's throw from Gledhow Gardens. The rent was four pounds a week which, at the time, was more than we could afford. Altogether there were five rooms as well as the kitchen and bathroom, so with Anne, Maisie and myself in three of them, there were two to let which we advertised in the local paper shop.

A delightful former ATS girl called Bridget took one room, a former WREN called Dorothy took the other. Accustomed as we all were to service life, we shared the bathroom, kitchen and lavatory without problems.

Anne was back at music college and I had decided to take an outside job after four years of working underground. Maisie, who was a double of the actress Loretta Young, was snapped up by Elizabeth Arden as a sales girl in their Bond Street establishment. Bridget and Dorothy both got jobs as secretaries. My job was enormous fun. I was employed at Regent's Park Zoo in the children's enclosure. In the mornings, I had to clean out the kennels, pens, cages of the domestic animals, and in the afternoon, give pony rides to the visiting children. As I was a keen animal lover as well as having always loved the company of children (and hoped to have at least a dozen of my own!) I thoroughly enjoyed my work.

Despite my inexperience with some of the animals, I only managed to make one gaffe. It happened soon after my arrival and I was told to clean out the cage containing three half-grown fox cubs. They reminded me of Heinkel when he was a puppy and I stopped scrubbing to play with them, tickling their tummies when they rolled over and scratching them behind the ears.

A passing supervisor stopped when he saw me and shouted that I was to come out at once. When I did so, he informed me that the cubs were very far from tame and that I had risked being badly bitten. Not knowing they could be vicious, I'd had no fear but now, when I went into their cage, I was nervous, as a consequence of which they growled when I went close to them. I now understand how vets get away without being bitten as often as they should.

We all had boyfriends who came to visit us or to take us out. We entertained them in the one communal room, the kitchen, the hub of all laughter, fun and socialising. Roy, brother of my Munich friend Pam, had returned from overseas and he and Maisie were now starting a romance which, ultimately, led to their marriage. Bridget had kept in touch during the war with the man she ultimately married a year after she came to Drayton Gardens. Dorothy had a whole posse of different boyfriends! I, meanwhile, had lost touch with Charles Crusoe but was seeing a lot of Donald, who was a regular visitor.

Looking back to those post-war years, it is easy to understand why the young women such as myself were anxious to get married, have a stable home and children. There had been very little permanence in our lives, many of us being posted from station to station, all of us losing boyfriends who were killed or who had disappeared somewhere overseas. We were in our twenties and after five years of insecurity we were ready to settle down. I, for one, although I was now writing again, was longing to have children. Don, I decided, would be the best of fathers. He was a hard-working, reliable, responsible person whose company I really enjoyed because he was a fount of knowledge and had an answer for nearly everything. He explained what was happening politically – momentous happenings at that time, the Conservatives having been swept out of office by Labour. I, like many others, found it hard to believe that Churchill was no longer our Prime Minister. His broadcasts had kept us all from despair when things were at their worst, and his strategies had won the war. Although he was now old and a bit doddery, it seemed so ungrateful of the country to oust him so forcefully.

I now took Don to meet my parents. He invited me, also, to meet his mother, a widow, and his sister, Isobel, who were living in Airdrie. Having lived all his life in a town and ended his education at Glasgow University, Don was not a countryman and so he and my father had little in common. Nor, indeed, did his quiet, studious background impress my mother. It was not long before she told me in no uncertain terms that she thought I would be making a big mistake if I was thinking of marrying Don. We were, she maintained, totally incompatible. If incompatible meant different, then I accepted that she was right, but it was this very difference that I found intriguing. I was hopelessly impulsive; he was thoughtful; I had had no conventional education, he had been to university and would have scored very highly on Mastermind had the game existed in those days! I think he thought me pretty frivolous so I had a job to get him to take me seriously.

I kept my job at the zoo for about nine months when my stepfather, Neill, was posted to Cairo. Immediately, my mother saw a way to break up my relationship with Donald and asked me to go out to Egypt with her. A year of separation would be proof of how durable this relationship was, she maintained. If, when I returned to England, I was of the same mind, she would give us her blessing. I was in three minds – I didn't want to leave London where I could see Don several times a week; I would love to travel; it would enable me to prove to my mother that I was far better at choosing my husband than she was. Moreover, that was exactly what I intended to do.

Don was by now thoroughly entrenched in the Ministry of Civil Aviation and working very hard. As a civil servant, he was disadvantaged by the fact that he had spent the last five years in uniform and needed now to catch up with those who had continued their education and obtained their degrees. I think he was quite pleased to have me temporarily out of the way!

Leaving Heinkel safely with Anne, I travelled with my mother down to Poole Harbour on December 23rd, in time to join Neill in Cairo for the Christmas celebrations. The flying boat named the *Silver Stag* was an adaptation of the wartime Sunderland, and would be travelling at an estimated speed of a hundred and fifty knots – not very fast by today's standards, but this was 1946. We settled into our seats which were virtually armchairs that could be tilted back to make what was tantamount to a bed. With tables, washrooms, a cocktail bar and several stewards to cater to our needs, it was the height of comfort. I recalled briefly the time I had flown in a Lancaster bomber during the war, and a further occasion when I had been flown up to a party at any American airbase in a Flying Fortress, both planes bare but for the necessities of bombing sorties.

There was to be one stop for refuelling in Augusta on the island of Sicily. We took off at half past ten on the morning of December 23rd, 1946 all of us blissfully unaware of how near we were to come to death before the day was out. Once airborne, we flew at around three thousand feet, and before long a break in the clouds enabled us to see the Normandy beaches far below where the greatest invasion in history had not long since taken place. The countryside was bathed in sunshine and we could see the shattered towns and villages and fields pockmarked by craters. Inevitably, I thought of Ken, wondering if the remnants of his plane would ever be found.

Lunch was served and passengers began to talk to one another. My mother discovered a fellow author, Francis Gerard, who was travelling with his wife and a delightful baby they had nicknamed 'Duck'. Our flight continued uneventfully until after tea had been served and then the sky suddenly darkened. Unbeknownst to us, the pilot had received a weather report from Augusta – there was a cold front ahead, which inevitably would cause the flying boat to experience some severe turbulence. He could turn back and land at Marseilles but the *Silver Stag* was scheduled to rendezvous in Cairo with another flying boat which would fly the Durban-bound passengers on the next leg of their journey. He decided to press on.

The sun went down and rain now started to cascade down the porthole windows. I had been both car and train sick as a child and as the plane bucked, I began to wonder whether I would prove to be airsick as well. The baby, Duck, had already thrown up over his mother's lap. Suddenly, without warning, the plane shot upwards, hovered for a moment and then dropped several hundred feet in an air pocket. I was far from being the only passenger to be ill as one by one, nearly everyone needed the sick bags the stewards were busy handing out. Both Duck's parents were ill and much to my surprise, my mother took the baby, she being the only passenger to remain unaffected by the continuous violent turbulence. The flying boat was in the midst of a severe thunderstorm and was being thrown about like a ping-pong ball. The pilot had not, as he'd hoped, been able to outflank the cold front and was trying to fly through it and reach Augusta as soon as possible.

However, Augusta was reporting very bad conditions in the bay, and suggested we orbit until the sea was calmer. Such was the condition of the passengers by now that the pilot felt he could not possibly delay landing much longer. Moreover, fuel was getting short. I was past caring – in fact, I thought death preferable to the continuation of this nightmare. Quite unperturbed, my mother sat nursing the baby who had now fallen into an exhausted sleep.

Five minutes later the seaplane lost height and lights appeared far below, the pilot having requested a flair path to assist the landing. The wind was buffeting the plane from side to side and it was lurching badly. Although we were unaware of it, the pilot was trying desperately to keep it steady as he brought the plane down to twenty-five feet above the water. Suddenly, the thirty-four ton *Silver Stag* travelling at ninety miles an hour hit the water with one wing down. There was a jarring crash and the port float and stays buckled as did the propeller of the outer port engine. The pilot was aware that with only one float, if a gust of wind gave a list to port, the plane would turn turtle and we would all be drowned.

We were told to put on life jackets and all the men but one steward were instructed to get out on the starboard wing despite the torrential wind and rain. Knowing that the rescue launch would not be able to reach the plane so far out in the bay, the pilot now taxied on the one remaining float towards the beach.

It took an hour before the fire floats and rescue launches were able to reach us. It was now half past nine at night. We were told to move quickly to the escape hatches and go down the ladders into the launches, leaving all our possessions behind.

Having not long since bought her first full length, very

beautiful mink coat, my mother refused to leave it behind, and still clutching the baby, put it on and struggled down the ladder. Soaked to the skin, the thunder still rumbling and an occasional flash of lightning illuminating the little Sicilian port, we were taken across the turbulent water to the jetty. Safe on land at last, we were driven in jeeps to an empty block of flats last used as billets by the Germans before they had been turfed out of Sicily.

Augusta in those days was no more than a fuelling stop and had no facilities for passengers. Someone went off to find food but I don't think anyone other than my mother and the crew was hungry. Milk was found for the baby and extra khaki blankets were found for the beds.

We were frozen with cold and exhausted. The floors were stone and the rooms bare of any comforts. At one o'clock in the morning our luggage, which had been lifted from the seaplane now beached on the shore of the bay, was brought to us. At last we were able to get out of our wet clothes and climb into cold, unaired bunk beds. I didn't think I would sleep but within minutes I was dead to the world.

The following morning I was woken by my mother's voice urging me to get up quickly and come and stand beside her. With a blanket round her shoulders she was gazing out of the window and pointing towards the beached hull of the *Silver Stag*. It was glittering in the sunlight that was dancing on the beautiful mirror-like surface of the bay. There was not a single cloud in the brilliant blue sky and we looked at one another wondering if this incredible sight could be the same scene as that of the thunder, lightning, rain and near death danger that had engulfed us the night before.

When we were dressed, we met up with Francis Gerard and his wife and baby, all of whom had recovered from our ordeal. Francis said he was going to write a book about the experience and this he did, two years later. It was a fictitious story called *Flight Into Fear* to add to his fifteen already published crime and detective novels. His description of our brush with death is far more detailed than mine and amusingly he gave my mother a pseudonym, Felise Wren, instead of Denise Robins. I still have the book published in 1948 and have used it to refresh my memory.

It was now December 24th, Christmas Eve. We were informed that a relief boat could not be sent out from England until after Christmas. The children who had been on board were devastated. How would Father Christmas know they were in Augusta and not in Cairo as they had told him in their letters? We all did our best to reassure them but realised there was no possibility we could go out and buy them presents. The little village of Augusta did not run to toyshops! We all agreed to rifle our luggage to see what we could find so that they did not wake up on Christmas morning with empty stockings!

It was surprising what people came up with – presents they had intended for family or friends they'd hoped to be with by Christmas Eve. Several of the families had been going to stay with friends with children so there were toys as well as chocolates, shortbread, a fountain pen, a Swiss penknife, bath salts and so on. So Father Christmas knew where to go after all!

My mother and I took a walk in the brilliant sunshine down to the long stone jetty where the previous night we had so gratefully put our feet on dry land. Looking out across the bay, it really was hard to believe the horror of the previous night, although the streets of the little Sicilian port, still wet from the deluge of the night before, confirmed its reality. That night together with several other passengers, we went to midnight mass in the beautifully decorated candle-lit church. It was, of course, a Catholic service, reminding both my mother and me of our convent days.

Was it God who had spared our lives last night, I wondered as the Latin words soared over my head? During the war, it had become increasingly difficult to believe in a benign Creator who seemed not to care how many lives were being lost. Why young men like my Ken, one of the sweetest-natured people anyone could know? Why Buzz, whose life had been spared when he'd been fighting that other war against the Fascists in Spain? Why good-natured, harmless Maule? Why my innocent young Lightening pilot David, or his friend Robert? Why all the hundreds and thousands of others? The horrors of the German concentration camps had now been revealed in terrible detail; prisoners of the Japanese had begun to return home, ill, emaciated, trying to forget the tortures they had endured; we had even seen the horrific picture of the devastation of Hiroshima and Nagasaki. Where had God been when these desecrations had occurred?

Yet, as we walked back to the barracks beneath a sky brilliant with stars, our breath misty in the cold air, the cobbled streets shining beneath our feet, a little of my lost faith returned. I wondered where my sisters, my father, Donald were and if they were missing me and wished suddenly that I was back home with them. Then my mother turned to look at me, her face bright with happiness. Tomorrow, she said, the relief flying boat was arriving at three o'clock and we would reach Cairo that night. Neill would be waiting with a wonderful welcome for us.

As I followed her into the barracks and up the stone staircase to our room, I realised how very lucky we both were to be alive.

CHAPTER 10

Our stay in Cairo was brief as Neill was posted almost immediately to Fayid where the British had hastily erected army quarters on the shores of the Bitter Lakes. The British were far from popular with the Egyptians at that time and there was a serious threat to the Suez Canal. This was now 1947, and the Canal, which had been conceded to an Anglo-French company for ninety-nine years, was not due to be repossessed by the Egyptians until 1968.

Although in Cairo it was a wonderful treat to be in a place where there was no rationing – I consumed platefuls of egg mayonnaise and bought all the sweets and chocolate I could eat – I was not sorry to be leaving the city. A *khamsin* had been blowing since our arrival and it was hot, dusty and overcrowded. We did have several meals at the famous Shepherds Hotel which was very luxurious and held glamorous dinner dances. But I did not enjoy the persistent attentions of an army major, a fellow officer of Neill's, who my mother had invited as my partner. I was well aware that she was hoping I would find someone she felt more suitable than the man I was hoping to marry.

In less than a week after our arrival, we were on our way to the Canal Zone, stopping at Fayid. At lunch I sat next to a very pleasant RAF Photographic Officer called Philip. When he heard my mother saying that she did not intend to live in the somewhat spartan army accommodation available for army wives but would move further on to the town of Ismailia, Philip asked if he could drive down there one evening and take me out to dinner. As my mother had had no part in arranging Philip's suggested visit, I didn't turn down the invitation, which shows what an utterly contrary daughter I was in those days. I had been entirely responsible for myself throughout the war and now resented her parental interventions in my life! Another ten years passed before the tide turned and we became the greatest friends.

Ismailia was a beautiful little town on the banks of the Canal. We were in a rented villa, which was very comfortable. Philip came on several occasions to take me out and also took me back to camp where we went sailing on the lake. I enjoyed his company but despite this, I wished I had not allowed myself to be persuaded to leave London – and Don. A few months later, resigned to the fact that I was not going to change my mind, my mother agreed to pack me off home.

Home, I discovered, was not the best place to be that winter of 1947. Temperatures of sixteen Fahrenheit were recorded. Even the sea froze. There was a stringent fuel shortage and to add to all the other attendant difficulties, which included a continuation of food rationing, there were frequent water shortages when inevitably pipes froze up and burst.

In the flat at Drayton Gardens, the kitchen became the one warm room where all of us, including many of our friends, gathered. It had a large stove with a leather-seated fireguard round it. Provided it was fed sufficient fuel it threw out a really good heat. Both coal and coke were heavily rationed but it was possible once a week for an individual to go down to the end of the Fulham Road where there was a coal yard and to buy a single sack-full of coke. We now organised a taxi to take all five of us down to the yard where our sacks were filled, and then the taxi took us back to the flat. We pooled our coke rations and managed to keep the stove and kitchen agreeably warm. I wonder now what that taxi driver must have thought – Maisie with her long, beautifully kept red fingernails and perfectly made-up face all ready to go on to Elizabeth Arden after we returned from the coke yard; Bridget and Dorothy in neat coats and skirts ready to go to their offices; Anne suitably dressed for college. I was the only one in warm trousers and boots. I had given up my job at the zoo and was now writing a novel to follow *See No Evil,* which had been published the previous year.

Anne spent hours in the freezing cold W.C. practising her clarinet – she was a truly dedicated student – the tiny room with its small window overlooking the courtyard behind the houses being the only one where the noise she made did not annoy the neighbours. She had an Alsatian at this time, Maisie had a Corgi bitch who had produced three of Heinkel's puppies, and I still had my beloved Heinkel. There was a large garden shed in the courtyard at the back of our flat and we decided that as the three of us had to walk our dogs in the park every day, we might as well walk several more and make some money. We would keep the boarders in the garden shed.

As a consequence of this not very bright idea, we advertised and immediately had two replies – one from a woman with a mongrel called Nankipoo, and another with a Scottie. Nankipoo was waiting to be shipped out to the Bahamas and we were not sure how long we were to keep him – for ever, if I had had my way, as he was the most affectionate and intelligent dog.

The Scottie, however, was a bit of a handful. As I was not tied to office hours it usually fell to me to take the five of them to Kensington Gardens for exercise. For safety's sake, I'd take them there and back in a taxi. All went well until one weekend when everyone but me had gone home for the weekend. Eve had asked me down to Potters Bar to help her with her new baby, Rosalind, and I'd thought I couldn't go because of the dogs. However, the telephone rang and a former army friend by the name of Ian Ventris asked if he could have a bed for the night. I agreed at once on the condition he fed and exercised the dogs for me.

Ian arrived and I departed to Potters Bar. The following morning Eve called me to her telephone. It was Ian – he had lost the Scottie. I suppose I should have known better than to leave Ian in charge. He was crazy! He'd been awarded the Military Cross for bravery under fire when he had charged a German gun post single-handed. When we congratulated him, he'd said he really didn't deserve the honour as he'd thought the gun post was empty! Anyway, I drove back to London as quickly as I could to find Ian on his motorbike roaring round the streets near the flat. He'd seen the dog, chased it on his very noisy bike, so scaring it that it immediately took off again as soon as it saw him coming.

I banned Ian from the scene and after ten minutes or so, was able to catch the exhausted dog and return him to safety.

One of our regular visitors was Michael Pertwee who was out of the army and now lived only a few streets away. He came to the kitchen for warmth as well as to be cheered up, having returned from abroad to find his wife had left him when he was overseas. Another frequent visitor was a young man by the name of Peter Barringer. Our meeting had been an amusing one. Anne and I were on the top deck of a bus travelling up Oxford Street, when an extremely good-looking young man went past us and sat down in the seat two rows ahead. We started to discuss him using the egg language we'd perfected in our childhood. Its format was quite simple – that of putting the sound of the word 'egg' before every sounding vowel. Thus for example, 'it is lovely' would become 'eggit eggis legguv-leggy'. Spoken very quickly, as we did, it was unintelligible to anyone not familiar with the speech. It had been a matter of great irritation to my mother when as children we made rude remarks about a visitor and she knew from our giggles they were uncomplimentary. 'Sheeg-e hegg-as egga beggig neggose'! for example, was a matter of great hilarity.

Anne and I were happily enjoying our adulation of the young man in front of us, taking it in turns to admire his brown eyes, curly hair, long legs, etc. etc., and wondering which of us would he be most likely to fancy. We had not yet reached our bus stop when the object of our admiration stood up and prepared to go back down the aisle. As he passed us, he gave us a broad grin and in perfect egg language, thanked us for a most entertaining ride.

Our blushes on the bus were as nothing compared to the blushes when a Waaf friend of mine called to see me and tell me that her artist brother lived opposite and she would introduce us. It was our victim on the No. 73 bus. As it transpired, Peter was every bit as nice as he was good-looking and we all became great friends. He was sharing a flat with a fellow artist called Peter Chadwick – the man my sister Anne would shortly marry. It was a true case of love-at-first-sight for both of them and their subsequent marriage was to last fifty-seven years until Peter's heart attack in 2002 proved fatal and Anne had to learn to live without him.

In November the year of 1947, Princess Elizabeth married Prince Philip, and we watched the wedding on the Pathé newsreels rather than joining the thousands of people who turned out in person to see the spectacle. Anne and I were married a lot less spectacularly the following year – Anne and Peter's wedding on February 11th and mine and Donald's on March 27th. We were married in Glasgow where it was convenient for Don's relations who were living in or near the city. My mother was still in Egypt but my

father, Eve, and some of my WAAf friends came up to
Scotland to support me. Clothes rationing still being in
force, my dress was second-hand – beautiful ivory silk
brocade, which I would not have changed for a new one
even had that been possible.

Unfortunately, the 27th of March was a Saturday and
Rangers were playing Celtic at home. That day football
fans from far and wide were pouring out of the station
and were making for Govan by bus or tram, and in some
cases by taxi, to see the match. The taxi my father had
ordered to take us to the Grosvenor Chapel some hundred
yards distant from the hotel, did not turn up and, so the
concierge informed us, was now unlikely to do so having
put the football supporters' interests before ours!

Time was passing and there was nothing for it but for
me, Don's sister, Isobel, my bridesmaid and my father to
walk. Needless to say, a bride in a white wedding dress,
flowing veil and carrying a bouquet of flowers was somewhat of a rarity in Grosvenor Street. I was waved at,
whistled at, grinned at and clapped at by all the football
goers; trams and buses stopped for us and by the time I
got to the Chapel I was shaking with nerves.

The service and luncheon that followed passed in a blur
and after what seemed an interminable time, Don and I
were in a taxi on our way to catch the Clyde steamer to
the island of Rothesay where Donald had booked us into
the Glenburn Hotel for our two week honeymoon. It was
quite late when we arrived in a downpour of rain. It seemed
the hotel had overlooked the booking which had been made
some considerable time before and we were informed that
dinner was off but that we could have some sandwiches in
the lounge. We were then shown to our room which was
very small, as was the bed that sported one lone pillow.
This was clearly a single room but the hotel was full and
we could not be moved. Our room, I suspected, had been

empty and hurriedly brought into service for us – empty because it adjoined the W.C. where the noise every time it was flushed was loud enough to wake me.

Don put on a brave face and told me that tomorrow, when we would be able to explore the island, I would not feel so depressed. We never left the hotel and we never explored Rothesay which I don't doubt is beautiful – but not in the rain. We were like an elderly married couple, Don sitting in the lounge doing *The Times* crossword and me playing snap and noughts and crosses with a four-year-old boy who was as bored as I was! It rained that Sunday, and Monday, and Tuesday, and every day until we decided to our mutual relief, to cut short the holiday and return to London. We had just bought a delightful little dolls house in Walton Street behind Harrods and were looking forward to starting our married life there. The house, which had cost the princely sum of two thousand pounds, consisted of one large and one small room on each of three floors – and were it to be sold today must surely fetch half a million pounds at the very least, had we kept it.

Anne and Peter now lived in a studio flat in Queens Gate. Eve and John and their little girl, Rosalind, had moved to Sussex and Eve was pregnant with her son, Murray. Maisie and Roy were married, and my Munich friend, Pam, had married Richard who was now a paediatrician living in Uckfield. My childhood friend Margaret, who before the war was a dancer with Madame Rambert's ballet, was now on the stage, her stamina no longer up to the strenuous activities of a dancer.

It was while we were still living in Walton Street that I happened to run into my former history teacher, Miss Stewart, looking a lot older but I had no doubt it was her. She got into the lift in Harrods where I was going to an upper floor. It was a cathartic moment for me. I recognised her instantly and it was as if I was back at school. Unconscious of the other people in the lift, I looked at her and said stupidly: 'Why did you hate me the way you did?' The poor woman gave me a startled glance and got hurriedly out at the next floor. I realised then that she couldn't possibly have recognised me as the twelve-year-old she had once tormented. After all I was now twenty-eight, so I suppose she thought she was being accosted by a mad woman. I am not one to harbour grudges but I couldn't prevent the thought I just had – serve her right!

That same year the Russians blockaded Berlin and prevented any food and other necessary supplies getting to the capital. British planes were once more airborne, this time to airlift supplies to the city's inhabitants. Although the costs of this operation was enormous, we were struggling not to let the Soviet Union take over the whole of Germany – which had already been divided by the Allies at the end of the war. Thirteen years later, the Russians were to enforce the division of Berlin by the erection of a huge concrete wall. It remained, separating East and West, for twenty-eight years, before it finally came down and the two halves of Germany were reunited.

We only lived at Walton Street for a year before moving to Hertfordshire where we bought a pretty little thatched cottage in a village called High Wych. We moved in one morning, confident that we would be really happy there with a nice, large garden for Heinkel – something we'd lacked in London. We did not have the cottage surveyed because the owners generously offered us their survey which, they said, was only a year old. I don't remember which one of us opened the front door on our arrival. I do remember with complete clarity how, as we did so, the back wall of the little dining room fell out! So much for the survey! It was not quite so much of a trauma as it sounds. For one thing the room was small so it was not a very big wall needing to be replaced. For another, it had been made of wattle and daub and although this had fallen out, the supporting oak beams remained in situ.

Heinkel and I were delighted to be back in the country and Don, although he had to commute each day to Liverpool Street, enjoyed his weekends. However we were beginning to get anxious because there was no sign of my becoming pregnant. Eve had two children and Anne had her first baby and I, who had wanted a round dozen ever since my childhood, seemed unable to conceive. Our local doctor told me to be patient, which was not one of my virtues. Although I was still writing – I had now published four novels and was plotting a fifth – the days seemed long and lonely after the companionship I'd enjoyed in the WAAF and in our flat in London.

Knowing my fondness for children, both my sisters used me on occasions as a child minder! Eve sent her three-year-old daughter, Rosalind, to stay with me for the weeks before and after her son, Murray, was born; and Anne did likewise when a year after the birth of David, the first of her seven children, she had her second baby. Both girls gave me detailed instructions how their offspring were to be fed and cared for, and I had no problems. However, these visits were short and the remaining days of the year were long and solitary, so I decided to get a job.

There was a vacancy for an assistant in an antique shop in Old Harlow, which I immediately applied for and was given the job. There were two other part-time girls there with whom I quickly became friendly – Betty, and Pat who was a single mother with a small boy. There was very little activity in the antique side of the business but half the shop was being used as a haberdashers, so to keep occupied I offered to help the girls who at times were kept busy. My first ever effort as a sales girl was somewhat shameful. I was asked to provide a yard of elastic. Betty had shown me the brass ruler edging the counter so I duly pulled a length of elastic off the card round which it was wound and held it from end to end of the ruler.

'Excuse me, Miss!' My purchaser looked anxious.

'You did say one yard?'

'Yes, Miss, but that there's 'alf a yard!'

So indeed it was – if you did anything stupid like stretching it.

The only other incident during my year there happened one morning when we woke to discover the alarm had not gone off. Don was frantic less he miss his train and be late for work. I, too, was due at the shop. We dressed as quickly as we could, skipped breakfast and raced the two miles into Sawbridgeworth where I saw Don off on his train. Breathing a sigh of relief that he'd made it, I drove slowly into Harlow and got to the shop just as the clock was striking the hour. It struck eight times – not nine! I was there one hour too early and realised that Don, also, would be an hour early at his office. In our belief that we had overslept, we'd not looked at the clock carefully enough. I managed a smile as I sat on a bench waiting for the shops to open an hour later, thinking of the blameless alarm clock ringing away at the right time with neither of us there to hear it.

Unfortunately, I had one other of my good ideas whilst I was working in Harlow. We were all hard up and often wished there were ways we could augment our incomes. Betty was married to a carpenter who occasionally did odd jobs for people. This prompted my idea (ahead of its time when you think of Bizzy Lizzies and other such firms hiring out domestic labour) of pooling our labour and starting a business called 'Odd Jobs'. We advertised in the local paper saying we would undertake small carpentry repairs, ironing, cooking, washing, gardening and so on. The phone rang several times, the first of these calls being a request to take in some washing.

I had anticipated this as Don and I – alone of the three households – had a brand new small twin-tub washing machine which I had thought would come in very handy when we had our first baby. In due course, a woman arrived with a bundle of dirty washing which I immediately tipped without touching it into my new machine. I was too ignorant to know that soft Chilprufe vests and knitted matinée jackets did not improve in near boiling water. Everything that possibly could shrink did so. There was nothing for it but to pay full compensation to the distraught owner, so 'Odd Jobs' looked like starting out with a large over-draft. When Don arrived home, he insisted we abandoned the new venture before anything worse happened. Another idea gone wrong!

I have to admit that my domestic skills were all but non-existent. We had a cook and maids when I was a child, and as soon as I was commissioned, I had my own batwoman during the war. At Drayton Gardens we shared the cost of a daily help and there was nearly always someone else around to do the cooking. When I married Don, my reper-toire consisted of various egg dishes, fried bacon, chips and sausages. As there was only a tiny ration of meat, sugar and fat each week, there wasn't much scope for puddings or stews. In London we did buy whale meat from a shop in the Kings Road but this, inevitably, was very fishy and no one much liked it. At the Thatched Cottage, however, the daily help I had twice a week to do the washing and clean the cottage kindly offered to give me some cooking lessons. Among other things I learned how to make a steamed bacon and onion pudding. I could have made a steak and onion pudding had we been able to get the steak! At least eggs were now plentiful as there was a farmer's wife half a mile down the road who kept me supplied.

My fellow shop assistant Pat's little boy was six years old and I always enjoyed it when they came from her home in Harlow to spend the day with me. On one summer weekend when she was with me, I had a surprise telephone call from my one-armed actor friend Donald Gray, asking if he could come down to see us. As it happened, Don was away on a three-week course so I was delighted to have the company. I knew he and Pat would get along well. In due course, Donald Gray arrived in an open-roofed car. He was wearing his artificial arm which, when I went out to greet him, he flung on to the back seat saying it was more of a hindrance than a help but that he needed it to drive!

We had barely finished lunch when the telephone rang yet again. It was Mel who, it seemed, was on his way from Leicestershire with three friends to watch Leicester football team playing in the Cup Final at Wembley Stadium. One of the three had somehow managed to either lose his ticket or leave it at home. At this juncture, they were on the main road approaching Ware in Hertfordshire. Remembering that I had not long moved to the county, Mel offered to let his chum have his ticket so long as Don and I had a television set on which he could watch the match! They stopped the car at a telephone kiosk and Mel found out my number.

Time was running short if they were to be at Wembley for the kick-off, so I agreed to meet Mel halfway between us at a village about four miles away called Eastwick. When we got back to the cottage, Donald, Pat and her son had already taken Heinkel for his daily walk, so we all settled down to watch the Cup Final. When it was over, Donald offered to take us all out for a meal. It seemed that no arrangements had been made by Mel's friends to fix a meeting place after the match, and as they would almost certainly stay on in town to celebrate afterwards Mel said he could catch a late train back to Leicester and stay now to make up a four so we could all go out together. Although we had exchanged Christmas cards and change of address cards since our respective marriages, we had not had occasion to meet since his visit to Gledhow Gardens when the war ended so we had a great deal of catching up to do.

Pat went up to the village to arrange for my daily help to come down to the cottage at six o'clock and mind her little boy. By half past six the four of us were in a pub in Sawbridgeworth. Whilst there, we discovered that there was a dance that Saturday night in the village hall so we decided to go. Donald and Pat were getting along very well (as I had thought they might), so it was inevitable that Mel and I would partner each other. It was a very basic dance hall and a very amateur band but we had great fun. In many ways it was reminiscent of the dances in the NAAFI in 1940. It was also nostalgic when, as was nearly always the case at such 'do's', they played 'The Last Waltz', at which point we were both wishing ourselves back nearly ten years in time. Just for that unexpected evening, the years had rolled away.

The three of us saw Mel off on a train to Cambridge from where he hoped to get a connection to Peterborough and then home. Donald Gray and Pat left on Sunday night and the cottage seemed very lonely again with only my faithful Heinkel to keep me company. More than ever before, I wished I was like Pat and had a child. I made up my mind not to go on waiting indefinitely. Next week, I vowed, I would go and see my doctor and find out once and for all what, if anything, was wrong.

CHAPTER 11

Our sympathetic G.P. made an appointment for us with a London consultant. There followed a number of tests and three weeks later, the consultant informed us regretfully that the chances of us ever conceiving a baby were so slight, we should think of alternatives. After the first shock, I was prepared to go along with any alternative so long as I ended up with a baby! Probably more for my sake than his own, Don chose the adoption route.

Neither of us had the slightest suspicion as to how invasive the Adoption Society's checks would be. Every last detail of our lives was investigated, our relationship, finances, hobbies, work, interests, plans for the future, and so on. Our home was investigated as well as our health records. Only then were we put on the waiting list – and it was a long one!

In retrospect, one can understand why all the questioning was desirable. The Society were, after all, acting in the babies' interests – not ours. There was no question of adopting parents walking down a row of cots and pointing a finger saying 'I'll have that one!' Their method was the opposite of emotional; it was to match as far as possible the backgrounds of prospective parent and child, the likely traits the baby could have inherited as, for example, a talent for music or art or sport; and also the physical likeness between child and parent. As they pointed out, if brown hair ran in the families of the parents, a child with red hair would face comments from school friends and visitors as to their difference from their adoptive father and mother.

This was not to say that the fact of adoption was to be kept secret. On the contrary, it was strongly advised that an adopted child should be informed of the fact; told it was A Chosen Child – which, indeed, they were. The choice was not made because of looks but from written details about the baby. A short while after we had been put on the waiting list, we were offered a baby who had half-German parentage. I would have taken it immediately but Donald – perhaps wisely – refused to do so. The war was not yet five years past and he had lost a great many friends in the RAF. Also, we had seen the horrific pictures of the German concentration camps. If the adopted child was found pulling the dog's tail, he explained, he would almost certainly think it had inherited a cruel trait. Whilst I shed tears of frustration, he pointed out that however silly I thought his reasons, it would be unfair to the baby for his father to be so biased.

He was, of course, absolutely right. Moreover, had we taken that baby, I would never have had the wonderful son who was offered to us in November the following year. Don and I drove up to London to collect him, Eve having given us Murray's carrycot – he was now two – and a variety of baby clothes, bottles and other paraphernalia as she had no intention of having any more children. Not only were we quite hard up but we were all still suffering the post-war restrictions, so we were grateful for these hand-me-downs. All the way up to town, Don kept asking me if I was sure I could look after a baby properly. As I had had both Eve's Rosalind and Anne's David when they were babies, I was totally confident.

It was a hugely emotional moment when the baby was brought in and handed to me to hold. I don't find small babies particularly beautiful and this one was no different, but he was mine! Tending always to hide my more intense feelings, I'm apt to play them down.

'He's an odd-looking little thing!' I said.

The woman stiffened and her brows drew together in a frown as she said in a cold voice: '*We* think he is beautiful!' It was a tense moment. I realised I had made a dreadful *faux pas* and was terrified she would take the baby back. Fortunately for us she did not.

With great relief, we got into the car and Don drove home. At first the baby, who we were going to have christened Iain, was sleeping peacefully, but as we neared Hertfordshire, he started to cry. Yet again, Don asked nervously if I was sure I knew how to cope.

'He's just hungry,' I said. 'I'll feed him as soon as we get home.'

The woman at the Society had given me detailed instructions as to the formula I was to use, a tin of the dried milk, and a bottle duly made up so that all I had to do was heat it. With the baby now screaming at full volume, I went into the kitchen, boiled a kettle, stuck the bottle in a jug of boiling water and took the baby back from Don who had been holding him. The moment the teat was in the baby's mouth, the screaming stopped. I looked at Don with a 'Told-you-so!' expression. It didn't last long. Out came the teat and the screaming started again.

'It must be too hot!' Don said anxiously. But I had tested it in the usual way, shaking a few drops on my wrist. I tested it again. It was perfect. I put the teat in again. A moment's peace and the screaming started once more. The infant was now scarlet in the face and unmistakably angry.

'Too cold?' Don asked without much hope. I shook my head.

'Something has to be wrong with the milk. I'm going to make up a new bottle,' I told him. I was uncomfortably aware that although the kettle had not long boiled, it would still take time for the newly made formula to cool in a jug of cold water. My former confidence was starting to wane.

Handing the baby back to Don, I went to the sink and took the teat off in order to empty the bottle.

'Oh, no, I don't believe it!' I said halfway between laughter and tears of relief. The bottle had been corked and the teat put back over it. Clearly the cork had not been put on very tightly and enough milk had seeped past it into the teat to provide those few misleading drops when I tested them on my arm.

It was the first and, I was enormously relieved to find, the last time my new baby son was going to yell at me so furiously. On the contrary, he was as good as gold, sleeping through the nights, putting on weight and generally thriving – until four months later, I nearly killed him. Accidentally, of course! My sister Anne had moved from London to a house in a village adjoining High Wych. She now had two toddlers, David and Belinda, and was pregnant with her third child. That summer of 1951, I would drive over to her house with Iain and Heinkel in the car and we would take all the children and our two dogs for long country walks. Anne lent me the pram she had used for her toddlers for Iain. Her house was on a very nasty bend so it was our habit to cross the road one at a time to get to the fields opposite.

On this particular day, Anne crossed first and waved to me when she saw there was no traffic coming round the corner. I started to follow, Iain now six months old, settled comfortably at my end of the twin pram facing the way we were going.

As I started to manoeuvre my way through the garden gate, the front springs of the pram gave way and Iain was catapulted into the centre of the road, where he now lay, the pram mattress on top of him. The broken pram blocked my exit and as I struggled frantically to get it out of the gateway, Anne shouted that a lorry was coming. It was like the very worst nightmare. I knew Iain was going to be run over; knew I could never get through the gate in time. Nor could Anne move. She was standing with one child in the pushchair, another holding her hand and the dog on its lead. She dared not run out on her own without the risk of the little ones following her.

It was little short of a miracle that the lorry swerved and avoided the bundle in the road. Perhaps, seeing Anne and the children, he thought it might be some object of theirs they did not wish flattened beneath his wheels. I finally squeezed past the front half of the pram and rushed out into the road. Hardly daring to do so, I lifted the mattress and stared down at Iain who was lying perfectly still with his eyes open. I knew at once that he was dead. I carried him back to the house and Anne joined me. She insisted that he was breathing but although I saw this was true, my relief was short lived because despite both Anne and I touching his cheeks, he did not make a sound. I was now in no doubt whatever that he was dying.

Out in the country where we were, there seemed little chance that any emergency ambulance could reach us more quickly than I could drive Iain into the doctor's surgery in Sawbridgeworth – about four miles away. Anne, meanwhile, said she would telephone to alert the doctor I was coming.

Throughout that nightmare journey when I knew every second counted, Iain made no sound. At last we reached the surgery where the doctor's wife greeted me with the news that her husband was out but that he would be back very shortly. Close to tears, I told her what had happened. She looked at Iain whose eyes were now closed and told me to try not to worry; he was probably slightly concussed. By the time the doctor did arrive five minutes later, I was nearly hysterical. I loved my baby passionately and with all my heart – and now he was dying.

'Let's have a look at him!' the doctor said quite calmly, and taking him from me, carried him over to the window.

A moment later he said with a smile: 'Calm down, my dear. There's nothing wrong with him.'

I couldn't believe it.

'But he's not crying!' I gasped. 'He was catapulted on to the hard road. He . . . he . . . he must have been badly hurt . . . *he's not crying . . .*'

'Soon see about that!' the doctor said, and lifting Iain up, slapped him on the bottom. A loud, protesting yell filled the room. Over the sound of Iain's bawling, the doctor explained that the child's pupils had narrowed and dilated exactly as they should do when the light changed which was a certain sign that there had been no internal damage. He himself had ascertained there were no broken bones.

'Babies and drunks can fall quite badly without damaging themselves,' he said. 'Not that I am suggesting you try tipping him on to a road again. Here, you can have him back! You have my word for it, he's right as rain!'

It was a salutary lesson on the less joyful aspects of motherhood, many more of which were to come. Loving one's children means fearing the worst every time they are within the slightest prospect of danger! I can recall some years later, when, controlling his exasperation, Iain said: 'Mum, I am forty-five years old. I really don't need you to tell me when I go ski-ing to take a whistle in case I get buried in an avalanche!' Ah, well . . .

I continued to write whenever I was not engaged in my maternal duties. '*Awake My Heart*', my sixth book, was published the year of the pram accident, and later that year my seventh, *Leave My Heart Alone*, came out. I started work on the next one, *Beneath the Moon*, which was published the following year. At the weekends Donald and I worked in the garden. He had made a lovely lawn where Iain could crawl. At long last we went to court and legally adopted him and had him christened. The relief of knowing that finally no one could ever take him away from me was enormous.

Living as we did not that far from London, friends visited, including Michael Pertwee who was now writing comedies for production at Ealing Studios, and was beginning to make a name for himself in television. The war in Korea which had begun the previous year was mercifully over and life at the Thatched Cottage was relatively peaceful. However, Don was finding the train service to Liverpool Street Station was both tedious and unreliable so the following year, we decided to move to a larger house, preferably in a location with a better train service for him.

We had no difficulty selling the Thatched Cottage and we found a five-bedroomed house in Buckinghamshire tucked under the hills in the lovely little village of Whiteleaf. It had a large garden and on the other side of the lane leading to the house, another half acre of orchard. My mother, meanwhile, had moved to Monks Risborough, adjoining Princes Risborough, and was only a few miles away, so Iain, Heinkel and I often walked down the hill and spent afternoons with her.

We had barely moved into our new home, Under Rood, when my beloved Heinkel died. Needless to say, I was heartbroken but there was no way his death could have been prevented because his heart had simply stopped beating. He was twelve years old and he had come through the war beside me. He was a remarkable dog and for at least seven years after the war was over, if I passed someone who had been at Rudloe or any of the other stations where I had been posted they would come up to me and say: 'Aren't you the Waaf who had the dog called Heinkel?' They remembered his name, but not mine!

A few days after we buried Heinkel in the garden, the King died. Despite his difficult stutter, he had been forced to take up the crown when Edward, now called the Duke of Windsor, had abdicated. He and the Queen had remained in London throughout the horrors of the Blitz and he was much loved by everyone. At that time, Don and I were the only people in the lane with one of the newly produced television sets. We invited all our neighbours to come and watch the funeral which was being televised. I felt that the sombre notes of the funeral march were appropriate also for Heinkel. The King's eldest daughter, Elizabeth, now succeeded King George and her Coronation followed the next year in June 1953.

We had wanted a larger house because we had put our names down on the Adoption Society waiting list for another baby – a daughter, and had supposed we would have another long wait. We'd only been in Under Rood, the new house, a few months when the telephone rang and it was the Adoption Society asking me if we would like to consider adopting a six-week-old baby girl who they thought would fit in wonderfully well with our family. They realised that it was a bit soon – we had specified two years between the children's ages – but as the baby seemed to be exactly what we wanted, they thought we might waive the time span.

Although it meant I would have two very young children with only twenty months between them, we went up to London to see the tiny girl and fell in love with her. She had weighed only five pounds at birth so was still on a special formula – this time I made sure I uncorked the bottle before giving it to her – and she quickly put on weight. She was without question a beautiful baby who we called Nicola. She was so good that one summer evening I put her out in her pram in the garden after her six o'clock evening feed – and forgot I had left her there as she so very rarely cried. Soon after ten, I prepared her food, went upstairs to fetch her and the cot was empty.

I tore downstairs in a blind panic telling Don she was missing – that someone must have kidnapped her. We never locked doors in those days and anyone could have got in whilst we had been watching television, and taken her away.

Don, ever calm and practical, told me not to be silly and went upstairs to find her. When he came down, he was not quite so confident.

'For Heaven's sake, where did you put her after the six o'clock feed?'

It was only then I remembered she must still be outside in her pram. When I rushed out, she was still sleeping peacefully but the pram was covered in dew and except for the starlight, it was pitch black! I went back indoors shame-faced but also worried lest the Children's Officer got to hear of it. Until the actual Court decision to legalise an adoption, a Children's Officer called on a regular basis to see if the baby was being properly cared for. Don thought it would serve me right if she did find out!

I now saw a great deal of my mother. She was as busy as ever writing her novels and her publishers Hutchinson's were planning a big party for 1952 when her hundredth book was due to be published. We were fast becoming really good friends. After my somewhat stormy childhood relationship with her, we discovered we had a great deal in common – as well as our shared birthday. She was not very child-minded but was always sweet with the children, finding little presents for them and making sure they had their favourite things for tea.

She became particularly fond of Iain who was not only an entrancing little boy with a crop of tight golden curls and huge blue eyes, but because some years later an incident occurred which she never forgot. She was about to cross a busy road and said they must wait because there was a lot of dangerous traffic which could hit them.

'Hold my hand!' Iain said offering his. 'You'll be quite safe with me.' He was about three years old!

Neill was more complimentary about Nicky with her beautiful almond-shaped brown eyes and pretty heart-shaped face. She attracted compliments wherever we were.

Donald spent hours feeding and nursing her, particularly when she was teething.

We spent our fortnight summer holidays on the north coast of Cornwall with Eve and John and their two children, renting a house overlooking Watergate Bay. The holiday was a success and we repeated it several years running. On one occasion, Don and I ran out of money so I drove into Newquay to Barclays Bank. The cashier refused to give me a blank cheque because, as he pointed out, I had no proof of identity with me. I demanded to see the manager and in due course, was shown into his imposing office. The conversation went as follows:

'Good morning! How may I help you?'

'I need some money – ten pounds to be exact – and the cashier won't let me have any because I haven't got my cheque book or any form of identity.'

The manager had the hint of a smile as he said in a very friendly voice:

'But of course you may cash one of our cheques. How much would you like?'

Whilst he telephoned for a minion to bring both cheque and money to the office, I asked for an explanation as to why he trusted me and his underling had not.

'Well, Madam,' he said, smiling openly now, 'we don't often get criminals coming to see us with quite your decorations!'

I followed his gaze and saw that I had a row of five very large blue and pink safety pins dangling in a chain down my chest. In those days disposable nappies had not been invented and we used terry towelling washable nappies, which were folded into a triangle and fastened at the sides with these large pins. Wanting to get down to the beach as soon as I could, I had rushed off to the bank after dressing the children without stopping to look at my attire. Seeing the look on Don's face when I told him about the bank clerk's refusal to serve me, I argued that the nappy pins had served me very well in the end.

Sadly, Anne and Peter were too busy – and too hard up – to join us having just produced twin girls not long after moving to a larger house near Epping. Peter, the artist, was employed at Hutchinson's producing book jackets – a job he didn't much enjoy as he had decided that what he would really like to do was become a sculptor rather than paint pictures.

Life was now fractionally easier for us all on the catering side, tea having finally come off ration. We now all had identity cards which were a nuisance if you mislaid them but would have come in very useful had I had mine at Barclays Bank! By the end of the year, sweets and sugar rationing had ended but we could not yet dispense with our wartime ration books. It was not until the summer of 1954 that all rationing ended.

December also brought a posting for Donald. He was offered the position of Director of Civil Aviation for Libya. We would be living in Tripoli on the north coast of Africa, and would be there for about a year. Did I want to go, he asked me? It sounded exciting compared with the drab, daily struggles in post-war Britain. It would be an important posting for Donald and I was sure the children would enjoy it, too.

'Of course we'll go!' I said, having no idea of the difficulties to come.

CHAPTER 12

We tidied the house, packed the things we thought we might need and let the house to some newly weds who had not yet bought a house of their own. Our flight out to Tripoli was for the most part uneventful. Nicky, always such a good baby, slept most of the way. Iain I kept amused reading his nursery rhyme book to him. However there was not much in the way of child-friendly equipment on board and towards the end of the flight Iain somehow managed to bite a chip out of the glass of orangeade he was drinking. Fortunately I didn't discover this until the stewardess pointed it out to me when she collected the tea tray.

Needless to say, I panicked – not audibly, I'm glad to say, but in whispers to Don. Suppose Iain had swallowed the piece of glass? Suppose it was lodged in his throat like a fishbone? Suppose . . . Don pointed out there was no sign of any blood, nor did Iain seem in the least discomfited. Nevertheless, after consultation with the stewardess, it was thought advisable to take him to the hospital in Tripoli to be checked as soon as we arrived.

There were no taxis at the airport and after an interminable wait; we took one of the horse-drawn gharries to drive us there. The children loved it! I was too anxious to enjoy the ride, the view or the sunshine. Half an hour later, Iain having been given a clean bill of health, we were in the same gharry the driver having thought fit to wait for us, and were driven to the hotel that had been booked for us. Not only was it in an unacceptable part of the town but also we were accommodated in one room. There was only a ceiling light around which I had to tie a scarf when we put the children to bed. Not unnaturally, they were confused by the fact that there was no 'light's out!' after their story was finished. They were thoroughly unsettled by the changes and unfamiliar routine. Iain announced very firmly that he wanted to go back to his house – a plaintive wail that was to be repeated all too often in the ensuing weeks when things went wrong.

The following morning, Don went off to make alternative arrangements for us which ended in our being given rooms in the house of an Italian woman and her husband in a residential area. The children were far happier there where they had a room of their own and were more or less back to the daily routine. I discovered that there was a beautiful sandy beach a short taxi ride from our house and I took the children there every day where they could play to their heart's content. My one problem was the language. The Signora did not speak a word of English and my knowledge of Italian was limited to one term of lessons at my Swiss school. It is surprising how quickly one picks up the words you need when, if you don't, you go without!

Within a few weeks, Don learned that the Government was intending to move forthwith to Benghazi – a large harbour town on the northwest side of the Gulf of Sidra, and he was to go with them. Benghazi had been much fought over during the war, changing hands between the Germans and the British five times before our 8th Army finally took possession in 1942. Don decided to leave me in Tripoli with the children whilst he went ahead to find appropriate accommodation. The Libyans were responsible for housing us but when he reached Benghazi, Don was taken to a one-bedroomed house furnished with little more than one large bed for the four of us, and opening on to a dirty Arab back street. The Libyan accompanying him could not understand why Don was complaining, among other things, at being offered only one bed for the four of us. 'But you have only two children!' was the reply. He could see no reason why Don refused to move his family into such quarters. Finally it was only by threatening to go straight back to England that Don was allocated by the British Embassy an army officer's spacious flat on the sea front opposite the yacht club.

As was customary, we employed a houseboy, Ali. Ali was a tower of strength to me. First of all, he knew how to cook on the paraffin stove whose workings flummoxed me completely. He cleaned the flat, took me to the local market and bargained furiously with the stallholders to get me what he called a good deal. He loved the children and was as happy to be working for us as I was to have him. Once we had all settled down, he asked me to teach him to read which I attempted to do using some of Iain's nursery rhyme books for the purpose. He proved himself utterly trustworthy and I eventually allowed him to take the children across the road to the yacht club where there was a swing and a sandpit for them to enjoy. Iain particularly missed his large garden where he could ride his tricycle and run free.

With the children off my hands for an hour or two, I was able to send home quite a number of stories about my life which I banged out on my ever faithful portable typewriter. My mother gave them to her secretary to type out neatly and send off to my old magazine. These were all published and my editor suggested that if I could find the time, I should write a book in instalments which he would print each week as one of the two serials that regularly appeared.

So I wrote *Love Cannot Die* – a novel about a girl who goes out to Benghazi to look after her sister's child and comes face to face with a past love. It was serialised before being published in 1955, my fourteenth novel.

Before we left Whiteleaf, I had made three very good friends, all of whom had children the same ages as mine. Inevitably, we walked together and spent time in each other's houses. One of my new friends, called Rosemary White, lived only two doors away. The other two, Betty Henry and Lilias Atkinson, lived in Whiteleaf village. Lilias' husband, Bob, was a pilot for BOAC, British Overseas Air Corporation and from time to time, he flew to Benghazi whilst we were out there. This was always a great pleasure and he acted as postman, bringing presents from my family and taking things back. Unfortunately, it was always a 'turn-round' trip so he could never stay for very long. I missed my friends and family and looked forward to going home in June the following year.

Apart from annotating the articles and stories I sent home to my mother, she was proving invaluable to us, keeping tabs on our tenants, the sundry workmen who had had to be called in to do some repair work; sorting out money, clothes, books, papers and writing numerous letters back to us with news of the family and home. She had been wonderfully supportive when we were adopting the children, and when she wrote to say she and Neill might come out to visit us, I was thrilled. The visit did not take place, but every time we saw Bob he brought presents for the children, comics, toys, photographs, all carefully chosen by my mother to please me and the children.

We did not remain friendless in Benghazi for long. In fact, Don made so many contacts through his work that we actually gave a drinks party for forty people – some from his government department, others from the army, BOAC, Shell, the Legation and so on. Several of these new friends had children, which was good for Iain and Nicky. There was also a couple who were anxious for Bridge partners and roped us in despite the fact that I was a beginner and pretty hopeless at the game. Nevertheless, we went to their flat about once a week leaving one of the army wives to baby-mind.

In March we went on a four-day holiday to Cyrene, a tiny little village two thousand feet above sea level and about a four-and-a-half hour's drive from Benghazi. The road ran through scrubby desert as far as Tocra Pass before climbing up into hills covered with cypress trees, mimosa bushes and shrubs with feathery pink blossom, and pink, white and yellow flowers. We drove past deep gorges where high up on the rocky sides, there were caves where people once lived.

The hotel, an army leave centre, stood in a fir forest the floor of which was a carpet of white anemones. Unbelievably, the little village of Cyrene was once one of the greatest cities in Africa! Nearby was Appolonia and we visited the ruins of the Sanctuary of Apollo.

The children loved Cyrene, particularly Iain who felt he was halfway home with the trees and flowers and freedom to run about in the garden where there were see-saws, swings, a sand pit and plenty of shade beneath the fir trees. There were other couples there with children for mine to play with. We were given a very nice suite of rooms which we really enjoyed but for one night when a Major General turned up and we were obliged to doss down in a dorm-itory whilst he occupied our accommodation! There was even a special high tea laid on for the children and cinema shows at night for the adults.

We could all have settled there quite happily but Don had to be back at work in Benghazi. He did, however, take a day away from us driving down from Cyrene to Tobruk. The Allied garrison had been besieged in the town of Tobruk for nine long months during the war in North Africa and preparations were now being made for the Queen's visit there during her tour of the Commonwealth. Don was back at the hotel in time to celebrate our sixth wedding anniversary. Sitting in that glorious sunshine in such beautiful surroundings, it was difficult to imagine the rainy, windswept vista from our honeymoon hotel in Rothesay six years previously, and I was thankful we were not there!

Despite the time lapse since we had left Under Rood, and all that had gone on since, Iain never stopped talking about home and asking if we could go back there. He even dreamt of it! It was for all of us – but for him most of all, I think – a wonderful day when we actually boarded the aeroplane to take us back to England. When we did finally arrive at Under Rood, he tore round the house and garden like a puppy let out of boarding kennels as he rediscovered all his special places. My mother had moved again from Monks Risborough to London but she was at Under Rood to welcome us back. Nicky was too young to remember her but when Iain rushed up to hug her calling: 'There's my Gam!' as she was known, Nicky toddled up and with a furious glance at her brother said: 'My Gam, too!'

There was an equally joyous welcome for our dog, a yellow Labrador called Morne; and Chloe, the tortoise-shell cat. I had not intended to replace Heinkel after he died but, unexpectedly, a request had appeared in the local paper asking if someone would give a good home to a two-year-old Labrador. The owner was not selling her as he had grown fond of the dog but couldn't keep her because when he took her shooting with his other dogs she had started to eat the game. My father had always had Labradors for shooting and I knew how exceptionally good they were with children. I had therefore answered the advertisement and Morne became part of the household before we knew we were going abroad. Fortunately, the couple who leased the house were perfectly happy to take care of the dog as well as the cat with an allowance made for their food and care, so the animals were there waiting for us on our return.

Don returned to his job at the Ministry of Transport and Civil Aviation. Two more of my novels, *Hearts Desire* and *Heaven in Our Hearts*, had been published and now I was offered a regular contract for three books after which a further contract for another three would be offered to me. Obviously, my publishers Hurst & Blackett hoped I was going to be as prolific as my mother who was now on her one-hundred-and-fourth book! Following my articles on Benghazi, I was still in touch with my former editor and he now invited me to take on the magazine's children's page. This was something I knew I would really enjoy doing as apart from the material for the page itself, lots of the children wrote in and I loved answering their letters.

I found a reliable daily woman who was also prepared to cook an evening meal for me to give Don when he got home. We wouldn't normally have been able to afford a regular help but, as I pointed out to Don, it made economic sense to employ her as I could earn more than her wages if I did not have to spend time on domestic chores.

Iain and Nicky started to go every morning to a delightful little nursery school called Ladymede, recommended by my three friends whose children also went there. We only had one car which Don took every morning to the station but Rosemary's husband worked in Aylesbury and he would drop the children off on the way to his office. I therefore had my mornings free for my writing. In the afternoons, my three local friends and I took care of each other's children and it was a really happy summer for all of us.

Despite Eve's decision not to have any more children after Murray was born, she was now pregnant with a third child which was due in September. Anne had four children and I desperately wanted a third – I didn't mind if it was a boy or a girl. The Adoption Society would only agree to allocate two babies per couple so I asked my doctor if he knew where else I might find a baby needing parents. By chance, he knew of a nursing home in Aylesbury who sometimes took in pregnant unmarried girls, and he gave me a letter to give to the Matron.

Matron was a charming, sympathetic woman who told me that the mother of an eighteen-year-old girl had booked in her daughter who was due to have her baby that August and the baby would have to be adopted. The girl had younger sisters and the mother refused to have her eldest daughter and baby home as she felt it would be a bad influence for her siblings. Sad as it seemed for the baby's mother who had wanted to keep it, I couldn't help but be elated by the news. Knowing I already had two adopted children, Matron promised that as soon as this baby was born, she would let me know.

Somewhat to my surprise, Don agreed to go along with my wishes although stipulating that once the baby was born, it must have the same stringent medical checks that were enforced by the Adoption Society. I could not have been more excited had I been the girl awaiting the birth. At last the day came when Matron rang to tell me her patient had had a little girl. A sister for Nicky, I told Don, and made the appointment with the paediatrician in Harley Street as I had promised. Two days later, I collected Matron and the baby who I now considered to be mine and drove up to London. The doctor had already received a letter from my doctor telling him of the circumstances and he showed us into a waiting room whilst he took the baby away for her examination.

Matron and I were still discussing how soon I could take the baby home when the consultant returned. He was not smiling as he handed the baby back to Matron and asked me to follow him into his consulting room.

Then he told me the news. When X-raying the baby's chest, quite by chance the picture had included her spinal column. He was very sorry to tell me that there was an abnormality which was going to require a great deal of physiotherapy and exercises for a good many years to come. I told him at once that I would do whatever was necessary; that I had been waiting for the birth for months and looked on this baby as mine, and so the news would not deter me.

'Your doctor will report matters more fully,' he told me, 'and then you and your husband can decide if you wish to go ahead! It will be quite a big responsibility, you must understand.'

Of course I was going ahead, I told Matron, but at the same time, I was very far from sure how Don would feel about it. I took Matron and the baby to the nursing home and waited anxiously for Don to return from work. His answer was brief.

'I'm sorry, but my answer is no – under no circumstances!'

I begged, I pleaded, I argued, I wept. He would not be moved.

'You are forgetting that you already have two small children,' he said. 'You made yourself responsible for them. How are you going to give them the time and attention they need if you have a handicapped child to take to hospital? A child who is going to need special exercises; who may have to have operations; who may need a wheelchair? It's not even as if you were qualified to look after the child properly. I'm really sorry, but no!'

Miserable though I was, a tiny part of me had to admit that maybe Don was right. I was never very good in a sick room – it was always Don who had to cope with the children when they threw up! I tended to panic if their temperatures went up even a few degrees and couldn't sleep at night if they were ill. Matron, too, thought it was for the best and told me not to worry – she was sure the baby would find other parents before too long.

I rang her several times a week to see how what I still thought of as MY baby was progressing. Every time I put the phone down, I was in tears. The slightest thing upset me and to add to my depression, I woke up every morning feeling sick.

'I didn't know misery could make you feel so awful!' I said to my friend Lilias as we sat in the sun on a beautiful August day. Her two children and mine were playing happily in the garden and she was trying to cheer me up.

'It's probably morning sickness!' she said.

'If only!' I replied. 'It is odd though, as I do feel queasy in the mornings!'

Lilias looked at me quizzically.

'When did you have your last period?' she asked me.

At first I wouldn't even bother to think, but when she persisted, I started trying to remember.

'This is a waste of time,' I told her. 'I can't possibly be pregnant. That doctor was adamant that the chances of my ever having a child were all but non-existent.'

Lilias nodded, saying pointedly:

'So he said it was highly unlikely – not that you couldn't.'

'All the same, much as I'd like to think you were right, I don't think there's a chance in hell. I probably picked up a gastric bug somewhere,' I argued.

Lilias wouldn't drop the subject until I promised to go and see my doctor next day. When he had listened to me he did some tests and said he'd like to do the frog test to make sure.

'Make sure what?' I asked him.

'That you are pregnant,' he said smiling.

I didn't bother to go back for the result until after the weekend, so certain was I that this simply couldn't happen.

When he confirmed the fact that it *had* happened, I still said I didn't believe it . . . that the test must be wrong.

'It's always right if it's positive,' he told me. 'There's some doubt if it is negative – but yours is not.'

He went on to assure me that it was by no means uncommon for women who had adopted or were fostering a child to finally get pregnant themselves. No one was quite sure why, but it could be because of the tension of would-be parents whilst they waited each month to see if this time it had worked, the deep depression when they found out that yet again it had not – all those factors disappeared once the would-be mother had children to nurture. Something to do with the hormones, he supposed.

I still found it hard to believe him; after all, I had just been through a very stressful and depressing time when I'd failed to adopt my third baby.

'It's an act of God that you didn't!' Lilias said when she heard I was indeed nearly three months pregnant. 'You'd have had a six month-old handicapped baby to look after as well as your new born and the two you've got. Congratulations.'

It really did seem an act of God because the following day I received a phone call from Matron – a couple who had been over the age limit to adopt a baby from the Adoption Society were going to adopt 'my' baby. As the wife was a retired nurse, the couple felt that God had meant this handicapped infant to be theirs. They had only wanted one child anyway so could give her all the care she would ever need.

It was wonderful news and as I had no doubt that the former nurse would make a far better mother than I could have been, I could now rejoice both for her and her husband and the baby.

When I told my mother I was pregnant, she was delighted. When she heard that I favoured a natural birth at home as I didn't want to be parted from Iain and Nicky, she at once offered with her usual generosity to pay for a maternity nurse to look after me for the first three weeks. I was thirty-five – no longer a youngster and women of my age usually went to hospital for their first babies. I knew Anne had produced all her children at home with the greatest of ease and I saw no reason why I should not do the same.

I hired a girl to come and live in the flat over our garage and act as a mother's help. She assured me she was more than competent to look after Iain and Nicky for the few days I would be in bed. I stopped feeling sick and, in fact, felt better than I had in a long time – physically better, but mentally I was worried. Would the children think I'd love this one more than I loved them? My mother, Eve, several friends were all saying that I would now discover the 'special bond' there was between a mother and baby at the moment of birth. I personally didn't think any mother could love her children more than I loved mine and I didn't want my two to think otherwise.

As it happened, I need not have worried. Some years after the birth of my second son, having left him and Nicky playing in the bath, I heard piercing screams coming from the bathroom. I rushed in and was confronted by a scarlet face and a furious voice shouting:

'SHE . . .' pointing at Nicky, '. . . SHE says you *chose* her and you didn't choose me.' Gulp! Gulp! Sob! 'SHE says I was in your tummy and you had to have me whether you wanted me or not!' A few more gulps and then the furious voice said: 'And I HATED it in there and I couldn't wait to get out!'

Although the new arrival, who we called Graeme, couldn't know it, he was absolutely right about his birth. Due on the first of March, he decided to arrive early – so early that I had not yet done as I had been told and got the maternity pack needed for the confinement; nor had I bought any nappies. Moreover, we were in the middle of a spell of bitter arctic weather. All but one pipe had frozen and the house was freezing cold. It was the unlucky 13th February.

We had acquired a flock of geese to keep the grass down in the orchard and, hopefully, to provide a nice Christmas dinner and some extra cash. Unfortunately, the gander decided soon after his arrival that the grass in the neighbouring farmer's fields was a lot tastier than ours. He was an extremely fierce bird with everyone but me, the provider of food, and despite my pregnant state, I had frequently in answer to a phone call, to walk across the fields and fetch him. If I had him under my arm, all his wives would meekly follow.

On 13th February, he decided to take his flock to the farm and I had had to struggle back with him, no easy task with my large extended tummy. I was not unduly disturbed as the baby was not due for another two weeks. I was not even particularly tired when I went to bed. Soon after, however, I found I was lying in a pool of water. My waters had broken. I telephoned the doctor who said it would be a little while before he could get to me as he would have to get up and dress and hoped he could get his car out of the drive. Everywhere was frozen, including the steep hill leading up to Whiteleaf village. By the time he did arrive, I was in labour – and in considerable pain. The baby meanwhile had decided not to wait for the doctor and had tried unsuccessfully to push his head out.

The doctor removed his tweed jacket and instructed Don to phone the nurse who lived over the hill in High Wycombe as he realised he was almost certainly going to have to operate to get the baby out and I would need an anaesthetic. The gas and air was certainly not proving adequate relief. Clean sheets were put on the bed which was raised on eight of my twenty-six volumes of the Encyclopedia Britannica so that the doctor could reach me. Both bedside lamps were focused on the makeshift operating table. By this time, all I was really conscious of other than the pain was the doctor saying:

'Push! Push! Listen to what I'm saying – PUSH!'

But I couldn't. I didn't even want to obey him. I wanted only to shut my eyes and be done with the whole pain-ridden affair.

Needless to say, the road over the hill behind the house was as iced up as it was on our side. The nurse rang to say she couldn't come – her car was stuck in a ditch. Pretty frantic by now, the doctor recalled that there was an elderly retired nurse at the end of the lane. Don was sent to get her. Fortunately I was not sufficiently conscious to hear the doctor say that he thought they would lose the baby. Then when they had extricated him with forceps and the help of thirty-six stitches in my lower regions, he managed to stop me bleeding to death. The walls, bedclothes, lampshades were all blood spattered when I awoke next morning, but I was alive.

My mother, having been telephoned by Don, had collected the maternity nurse she'd engaged and driven her down from London by morning. I awoke to the sound of her voice as she came into the room holding a bundle.

'Look, darling!' she said. 'Your very own baby son!'

It was not the most tactful remark for her to have made, however heartfelt the sentiment. This baby didn't feel in the least like mine – in fact far less so than Iain and Nicky.

'Isn't he beautiful?' my mother said, holding him for me to see.

He wasn't. His face was scarlet; he had two nasty marks on his forehead where the forceps had gripped him, a tuft of dark brown hair and an expression not unlike that of Winston Churchill.

'Please,' I begged, 'can you take him away and bring me a cup of tea? And most of all, I'd like a cigarette!'

Well, how was I to know in those unenlightened days that nicotine was harmful, especially to mothers with breastfed babies?

I don't know which hurt the most, my mother's feelings or my rear end. Then Sister Dickenson, my maternity nurse, came into the room, and all hell broke loose!

1975, our near fatal car crash in Chalons, France

Publisher's request: 'More sex please!'

On the receiving end of John Osborne's wisdom
in his garden in Shropshire

Yorkshire Post Literary Luncheon. Me on left with Sue McFarlane,
Jan Leeming, Leslie Thomas and Sandy Gall

Worzel Gummidge (Jon Pertwee) with Emily and me on the promotional boat trip for *House of Tomorrow*

Working on my wordprocessor in my study

Graeme and Sarah (with Arthur) in Cornwall

Iain and Nicky on holiday in Majorca

Chiswell Barn, photographed from the garden

Heather, on holiday in France, the year before she died

All my grandchildren together in Portugal; from left to right: Jemma, Thomas, Tilly, Emily, Max, Polly, Arthur and Charlotte

Mel, taken on his
80th Birthday

above: Anne with her
puppy in the garden at
Chiswell Barn

Eve on her golden wedding
anniversary

My 80th birthday weekend in Crans, Switzerland with all the family

CHAPTER 13

Sister Dickenson was accustomed to nursing the aristocracy and that included royalty! She was expecting a nursery suite installed with every last piece of equipment, a nursery maid exclusively for her use, and every possible comfort for herself – and warmth. Her arrival that Valentine's Day was to say the least a very nasty shock for her. The house was freezing; my bed and bedroom were a disaster area and the cat was asleep in the hot cupboard on the only nappies she could find for the baby! The doctor had attended to me in his everyday clothes and, as she later told me, she was in no doubt whatever that I would get blood poisoning.

I was moved into a small spare room which she had instructed the girl who I'd employed as a mother's help to clean and disinfect from floor to ceiling. I was all but bathed in Dettol. Phyll, my mother's secretary, was sent hurrying into our nearest town, Princes Risborough, to fetch what she deemed to be necessary nursery and baby equipment. Fortunately my mother was there to pay for all this, bills we had definitely not budgeted for. We had become used to 'making-do' during the war, whereas Sister Dickenson had been accustomed to the very best of everything.

We were all frightened to death of her. She took over our double bedroom and packed Don off to a corner room adjoining mine which was even colder than ours as it had big picture windows on two sides. I only saw the baby at feeding times because, she said, I needed sleep. Sleep was hard to come by because I was in such discomfort with all the stitches. I was doused in Dettol what seemed like every five minutes. Why, oh why, I wondered tearfully, couldn't I have adopted this baby instead of giving birth to him? Downstairs I could hear frequent yells from Iain and Nicky, and Sister Dickenson reported that the girl looking after them was not only totally inefficient but was physically hitting the children when they disobeyed her.

'You must get rid of her at once!" she informed me.

'But who will do the housework? Do the cooking? Take the children to school?' I wailed.

To my utter astonishment, my maternity nurse announced that she would. Moreover, she said, she would train the baby to sleep through the night so that after she left, I would get plenty of sleep as, clearly, I was going to need it.

The Gorgon was transformed into an angel. She looked after us all beautifully and I think it is more than possible I owe my trouble free (if painful) recovery to her. Still weak from lack of the blood transfusion I would have been given in hospital, I remained bedridden for nearly ten days. Then my stitches came out and Sister Dickenson helped me into the most marvellous bath I ever had before or since.

With her help, I slowly recovered some strength, and was able to spend time with the two children. I have to be honest here and say that they were my prime concern. I felt the baby was Sister Dickenson's concern and all I had to do was feed him. This took precious time as he wasn't inclined to hurry, which I wished he would, so that I could get back downstairs to the children. Where, I asked myself, was the special bond mothers were supposed to feel when they had given birth? Today I watch these programmes on television where after the birth, a crumpled, red-faced bundle is put into the mother's arms and she gazes down at it in adoration. I stared down at the infant Graeme as I fed him. Although the forceps marks had all but disappeared, although he was not so crumpled and red as when I had first seen him and although he was a ten pound baby and did not, therefore, resemble a skinned rabbit, he was nowhere near as responsive or reactive as my six-week-old adopted babies. I confessed as much to Sister Dickenson who had now become my friend.

'It's because you're not yourself yet,' she said. 'You'll feel quite different in a week or two.'

She was right, of course. Once he started smiling at me and – or, indeed – yelling at me, I knew there was a good chance I was going to love him as much as the other two. I shed several tears when I saw Sister Dickenson off on the train to London at the end of her three-week stay. She told me that after the somewhat disastrous start to her visit, she had been really happy with us and had decided to buy the vacant plot of land adjoining our orchard and build a bungalow there for her retirement. By the time she did retire, we had moved back to my home county, Sussex, to our new home, Little Surries, in Ashurstwood.

For the time being, life continued much as before at Under Rood. I had managed to build with the help of my next door neighbour, a little house from the big wooden crates which had contained the furniture we'd brought back from Benghazi. The children loved this and the small paddling pool I dug in the garden. As we had employed a new and far more efficient mother's help, I was also able to continue with my writing – when I could find time. That year saw the publication of two more novels – they usually took me three months to produce – *The Foolish Heart* and *Give All to Love*. Graeme was such a good, contented baby, I could work every morning when the children were at nursery school and he was outdoors in his pram with the daily to keep an eye on him.

Iain, now six years old, and our neighbour Rosemary's eldest son, David, were always up to mischief. Iain was a

very athletic little boy and would obviously enjoy a more
sporting environment than his nursery school could provide.
It would not be long, I thought, before he would be ready
to start prep school. Don had had an excellent education
in Scotland and saw no necessity for Iain to go to an English
public school, but I considered that our state schools were
on the whole inferior to the Scottish ones, and as my
father had been to Marlborough, I was anxious for Iain to
have the same advantages. In the end, Don allowed me to
have my way as it would almost certainly have to be my
literary earnings which would be paying the school fees!

Meanwhile, Eve's son, Murray, two years older than Iain,
was happily attending a prep school in Cobham called
Feltonfleet, and we decided that as we intended to move
back to Sussex, it would be a convenient school for Iain.
It also meant that we could save a bit of money by having
Murray's outgrown uniform. So Iain's name was put on
the waiting list.

Don and I now started house hunting. This was far from
an easy undertaking as we had such different opinions as to
what type of house we should have. Both the Thatched
Cottage and Under Rood had been temporary residences
until we could afford to move to a permanent home. Don
opted for modern buildings, I preferred old houses. One
thing we agreed on was that it must have a large garden for
the children and must be in the Home Counties with a nearby
railway station for Don to get to London within the hour.
We put our names down with estate agents in Sussex, Surrey
and Kent, and from the dozens of particulars arriving by
every post in the week, sorted out the 'possibles' and went
house hunting at the weekends. The children quite enjoyed
these outings which were frustrating as nowhere seemed to
fit our requirements. It was fun, however, when we were
looking in Sussex as Eve and John had now moved to Cowfold
and we could stay over Saturday night with them.

It was always a rush to get away on a Saturday morning, and on one occasion, I was so behind when Don was ready to leave, I just pushed everything into the back of our Morris estate car saying I would sort it all out when we got to Eve's. We had reached a large six exit roundabout in the middle of Slough when disaster struck – the engine packed up. With cars hooting furiously as the traffic began to foul up, Don lifted the bonnet and announced we would have to call the AA as the trouble was too serious for his limited emergency surgery.

The recovery vehicle arrived in record time but by then, we were surrounded by angry motorists wanting to know what was going on. We opened the back doors and there was a slow exodus of dog, children, the pink bucket full of last night's dirty nappies; a basket full of washing ready to put on Eve's washing line; the dog bowl full of food for Morne's lunch; carrycot, bedding, bottles, children's toys and so on. I stood there holding the baby and wishing with all my heart that I had packed everything properly. The whole lot was somehow squeezed into the AA man's car whilst some of the motorists and Don pushed our vehicle on to the side of a road ready for it to be carted off on a transporter.

From that day on, I packed whatever we needed the night before in case we ever broke down again.

We finally found the house that we both knew instantly we wanted. It had the solidity and good workmanship Don desired, and having once been two Tudor cottages the central rooms were oak-beamed which I liked. All the downstairs rooms had parquet floors and there was a lovely big kitchen, wide staircase, a regency-style drawing room and a huge billiard room which would make a magnificent nursery for the children. The house was painted white and all the windows had pale yellow shutters. The style was distinctly Dutch and we found out later it had been enlarged from the Tudor cottages by a Dutchman.

Outside were two acres of very pretty garden with stone ornaments and a barn covered in clematis *Montana*. There were two garages, sheds, a three-acre field and two large ponds. It also had a small two-roomed self-contained staff flat at the back of the house.

The trouble was, not surprisingly, the price. We had a maximum of £4,000 to put down, £3,000 of which we expected to get from the sale of Under Rood. The asking price for Little Surries was £8,000 – this was the 1950s. On the way home I suggested I telephone the estate agent next morning and see if the owners would accept an offer of £6,000. Not unreasonably, Don told me not to be silly. But I did it all the same and was shattered when a few hours after, the phone rang and I was told we could have the house at our price. I telephoned Don at his office who said there must be something very wrong indeed with the property! So we had it surveyed and there was. There was Death Watch beetle for a start; then the house would have to be rewired before we could be reconnected to the electricity supply; there had been a fire in one chimney which would have to be dismantled and rebuilt as it was unsafe, to name only three of the major problems.

To my huge relief, Don was as much enamoured of the house as I was and he decided to take out an even larger mortgage than we had envisaged and have the work done bit by bit. We moved in that summer. All the pretty stone ornaments had disappeared. So too, had the oak garden furniture and a dozen or so huge oak trees that I had particularly noted on our inspection day. There was not even a light bulb left inside the house. It wasn't long before we realised why. I tried to order some goods from the village but as soon as I gave the name of the house, the order was refused. We made enquiries. The previous owner had left 'in a hurry' owing thousands of pounds to all the surrounding tradesmen. He had sold the trees twice – once

when he instructed a timber merchant he could cut them
down next spring, and again when he told another timber
merchant he could cut them down then and there. Rumour
was he had been so much in debt that he had started the
fire in the roof hoping to claim the insurance, but a neighbour had seen the smoke, called the fire brigade and it had
been put out with only the chimney damaged!

Gradually, all the indoor work was done. We now had
a beautiful home but no money left for carpets, curtains
and additional furniture. It was a question of 'making do'
with what we had brought with us from a far smaller house.
We also had a very large garden to keep up because it was
far too pretty to neglect. Iain was now at prep school,
Nicky at a local day school and Graeme in a nursery school
in the village. I therefore had a little more time on my
hands for my writing – a necessity as we needed the extra
funds for the children's education.

Apart from the garden, I also had a retinue of pets to
look after. Not the least time consuming of these was our
billy goat. Before we moved to Little Surries, the milkman
had presented the children with a tiny white goat kid. I
knew nothing about this particular species of animal but
it was not long before one of my neighbours warned me
that it was only a matter of time before the little goat grew
into a big one and the entire lane would be poisoned by
the smell peculiar to the male sex of the breed! Anyone
who has been near to an adult billy goat will know what
I am talking about.

In due course, Goat, as he was always known, was the
size of a Great Dane and sported some singularly large
horns. The vet now removed these, warning me they would
grow again, and castrated the animal. The children had lost
interest in him but I had become quite fond of him and
despite Donald's misgivings, insisted we took him with us
when we moved.

Goat now had a large three-acre field and stable to himself. He much preferred the garden which was full of tasty rose bushes and similar vegetation. We tethered him but it took less than a morning for him to pull up the stake and appear at the back door. I went down to the ironmonger who suggested an iron stake and chain such as he sold to owners of bulls. We had no doubt this extremely heavy – and costly – piece of ironmongery would keep Goat securely confined. But . . . we did not take into consideration Goat's intelligence. Within twenty-four hours, he had realised that if he pulled the chain and stake from east to west for a few minutes and then from north to south, by repeating these movements often enough, the stake would become loosened and he could once again make his way up to the back door his stake and chain clanking behind him. Nor did he stop there. I had in the past got a biscuit from the tin in the kitchen to tempt him back to his field and now, if the kitchen door was open, he would knock over the tin and butt it around until the lid came off then help himself – not to one but to the entire contents.

Curbing his desire to have Goat permanently removed from our lives, Don was persuaded to buy sufficient quantity of pig wire to encircle the entire field. We spent two exhausting weekends staking and fixing it. At last Goat was secure. He missed our company so, to compensate, I always took him with me when I walked the dogs in the surrounding woods and lanes. We made a somewhat unusual column – Iain, Nicky, Graeme, Morne, Gigi, the Griffon, a new arrival, Sirikit, the Siamese cat and Goat. As he thought he was a dog, Goat went, as the dogs did, without a lead.

Goat's belief in his canine species became even more apparent a few years later following a memorable telephone call I received one morning. The conversation went as follows:

Caller: 'I understand you have a pet goat.'

Me: 'Yes, that's right!'

Caller: 'Oh, I do hope you can help me. You see, my husband has just been posted abroad and we have a pet nanny goat and we are all so fond of her, we simply must find her a happy home. Do you think you could possibly have her? I wouldn't want anything for her.'

I gave it a few moments thought and decided that as Goat might enjoy some female company in his latter years and as he had been neutered, I need not fear lots of little goats needing my T.L.C. I told the caller I would have her pet.

Caller: 'There's just one thing I should warn you about her,' she said hesitantly. 'Hattie has false teeth!'

I was speechless until I recalled a neighbouring animal lover who told me about a lamb she had raised who remained with her into old age when the sheep had lost nearly all her teeth. Being a wealthy woman as well as a devoted one, she had persuaded a vet to fix into the animal's jaw some false ones. I was now worried about the age of the caller's nanny goat as I didn't want to undertake the expense of an ageing animal.

Me: 'How old is your pet?'

Caller: 'She's three!'

Once again I was silenced. False teeth at three?

Me: 'How old was she when she had false teeth?' I asked, beginning to think this conversation was somewhat unreal.

Caller: 'She was born with them!'

Now I knew something was very wrong. Either I had a lunatic on the other end of the telephone or I was dreaming.

Me: 'Could we please start this conversation again? You just told me your nanny goat was BORN WITH FALSE TEETH?'

It was several minutes before the caller stopped laughing. The animal did not have false teeth. She had FOUR TEATS

– which made milking the goat difficult, she added, if such was my intent.

The next day, my caller arrived with Hattie – a dear little black and white nanny only half the size of Goat who was watching as her owner led her into the field. Catching sight of Goat, she let out a loud series of high-pitched 'Bahahas'! Goat was terrified. He ran to the furthermost corner of the field glancing apprehensively at the newcomer. I suppose I should have realised that he would never have seen a goat before, let alone heard a bleat. He was used to dogs. He LIKED dogs. He went for walks with dogs. When he could, he ate their dinners. Dogs barked. They never bothered him as this new animal was now doing as she chased after him with blatant female enthusiasm.

The caller and I left them to it and went indoors to have a cup of coffee and a laugh about the false teeth. I was glad to be able to write to her a few weeks later telling her that the goats had settled down and were now best friends.

I now added an aviary of canaries to our menagerie of pets, which included Nicky's rabbit, the cat and a litter of kittens, Morne the Labrador, and Sirikit the Siamese cat, and of course, Goat. We had taken on Gigi, a little smooth-haired Bearded Griffon who my mother had bought as a puppy but found too much to handle with her other dog. She had moved yet again, this time back to our old home, Furnace Pond Cottage, and I took the children there in the summer to enjoy themselves in her swimming pool. Don was working as hard as ever but was able to relax at the weekends building bonfires, mowing the lawns and tidying up the large garden.

In December 1957 my father had died. He had never been in really good health because of his unhealed First World War leg wound, but he was an immensely courageous man and I loved and respected him. Living as we had been in Buckinghamshire, I'd not seen much of him since my marriage. Travelling with two under sixes and a baby was not easy. Nevertheless, there was always a big welcome when I went home. This was not very often and I was, therefore, unaware that he was suffering from cancer.

After the horrible experiences he'd had in hospitals during and after the First World War, he would not see a doctor who he knew would recommend an operation. By the time the pain became too much for him and he was rushed into the Middlesex Hospital, he was beyond medical help, and he died two days later.

When I went to see him the day before he died, my mother was at his bedside holding his hand. In the twenty years since their divorce, my father had never stopped loving her and knowing this, she put her life on hold and stayed with him until he died.

His much loved black Labrador, Nimbus, outlived him but anticipating this, my father left Jenners, his pretty cottage in Slaugham village to Nimbus and a sum of money to a woman to go and live in the house and take care of the dog until he died. The *Daily Mirror* got hold of the story and pictures of Nimbus and the cottage were all over the centre page.

At the time we were worried that the reporter might get hold of the story about my father haunting the graveyard! Anne and I thought it was very funny but my father's eccentricities were not always looked on with humour by other people. It happened shortly after the war when a newly elected Labour council refused to allocate funds to keep Slaugham Church graveyard in good condition. Of Norman vintage, the church had several vast old yew trees and some fascinating and historic gravestones. As the grass, brambles and debris accumulated, my father tried on several occasions to get something done about it. He, himself, had opted to mow the village green which, incidentally, he did with a small new petrol mower wearing an L-plate round his neck!

When still no tidying up was done, he told the council that the dead would rise out of their graves and haunt them all. Needless to say, this threat, too, was ignored so when night came, he pulled a large sheet over his head, crossed the road to the church and wandered round the graves calling out 'Whooooooo' in a loud voice.

Unfortunately, the village children who he had not intended to frighten, were nevertheless terrified. Their parents had a good idea who the 'ghost' was but could not be certain so they got a posse together to go ghost hunting.

Fortunately for my father, he was extremely well acquainted with the church as well as the grounds, and when he heard them coming, he was able to escape back to his house without detection. After that, he felt it politic to stop the haunting and eventually a local gardener was called in to restore the graveyard to its proper state. The church is well worth a visit and it is often chosen for picturesque weddings.

As far as my father's dog was concerned, Nimbus lived on for several years after which the house, which was left in trust for me and my two sisters, was taken over by Eve, who bought Anne and my third shares. The article was reprinted recently when my sister Eve died and her children decided to put Jenners on the market.

Although Don and I now had Iain's prep school fees to contend with as well as Nicky's day school, I decided to use some of the money my father had left me to have a hard tennis court built. Iain was keen to play and Eve and I had always been above average players having had a grass court at home as children. It was one of my better ideas as Iain became very keen and was a very good player. Nicky was not quite so keen but could hold her own with her peers.

Time seemed to race by with every day filled to capacity with one activity or another. By 1960 I somehow managed to produce three more books, which generated enough income for me to pay for a regular daily help we called Nan, who took all the domestic chores off my shoulders. I also had a three-day-a-week secretary called Joy Tait who typed finished copies for me and dealt with any correspondence. She left work when I was fetching the children from school and always left cryptic little notes in my typewriter telling me what she had accomplished. These were so amusing, I finally told her she should be the author rather than me. She rejected the idea saying she couldn't possibly write a book. Two years later, she showed me the opening chapters of a novel which I insisted she finish. That novel won the Best Unpublished Novel of the Year award from the Romantic Novelists' Association and she went on to write four more books.

The Association had been formed in 1960 by the author Alex Stuart, and my mother was President. Barbara Cartland later became President when my mother retired. Barbara and my mother were good friends and she and Neill often went to stay with her and her husband, Hugh, at their house in Great Barford, Bedfordshire. In those days, my mother's fame far outshone Barbara's although she was rapidly making a name for herself.

Iain loved his prep school where he had made many friends and was doing very well, most particularly on the football field! He had decided that he did not want to go to Marlborough as it was a rugger school and Don and I agreed he could go to Bradfield when he was of an age to move, where football was the preferred game. Nicky was not so happy at her convent school. She was an exceptionally pretty child with slightly slanting brown eyes and a heart-shaped face that caused people to stare at her, particularly the male sex. Even small boys were attracted to her, including Iain's school friends as well as porters, bus conductors, waiters, shopkeepers and so on.

Unbeknownst to me, there was a man up at the farm who used to waylay her. It was my habit to send one of the children up to the farm that adjoined our garden to collect a big jug of milk from the dairy. Nicky always made what I considered a ridiculous fuss when it was her turn to go. When I demanded an explanation, she said there wasn't one, and I would get quite angry with her. Things went from bad to worse. Unhappily, it was not until many years later that I learned what this man had been doing to both her and Graeme.

In the fifties, molestation of children undoubtedly went on but was never talked about as it is today. I had never heard of such a thing. Although I did not much like the man and generally avoided getting into conversation with him, it never once crossed my mind that he was capable of such dreadful behaviour. In fact, had anyone but Nicky herself told me about it at the time, I doubt I would have believed them even had I believed her. The children were sworn to secrecy by him and threats were made that both I and his wife, my daily help, would be sent to prison for not looking after the children properly, and then they would be put in a children's home because there would be no one to look after them.

Had Don or I known the truth, I think we would have taken a gun and shot him. As it was, the man died many years before Nicky told us what had transpired. That was not until 1987 when I was writing a book about Jeanette Roberts, a woman who had been sexually abused by her father. It is easy to decry some of the absurdities of our so-called 'nanny-state', and personally I don't think that youngsters should be taught about sex at all until they reach puberty. But having said that, I agree utterly with the outspokenness regarding paedophiles and telling parents and schoolteachers how to spot telltale signs that a child is being abused.

As it was, my beautiful young daughter who should have had the world at her feet, lacked self-confidence and confidence in any grownups. Moreover, she hated being pretty, stared at, having her head stroked, her photo taken, her hand held – and worst of all, she could no longer trust me and her father to keep her from harm. Blissfully, horribly, I was unaware of why she was no longer the happy, laughing little girl she'd once been and was now difficult to manage. Her teachers all reported she could do so much better at her work if she tried.

Mistakenly, I supposed at the time she was jealous of her brothers, of Graeme who, being four years younger, tended to demand and get more attention; and of Iain because he was doing so well at school and was both popular and happy. I decided she would be happier away from them and arranged for her to go to a girls' boarding school near Horsham which one of my godchildren attended.

With Graeme now at nursery school and the two older ones boarding, as I had ceased writing for *Woman's Illustrated* when Graeme was born, I took on the task of writing the children's page for another magazine called *Woman's Realm*. I was a bit bored with writing novels and knew this would make a pleasant change.

I wanted to make my children's page a little different and better than the ones in other women's magazines. After some thought I came up with a suggestion – somewhat unfortunately as it turned out. The readers' children could join the 'Star Club', as I called it. They were issued with a little booklet with outlines where they could paste a silver star when they had collected the requisite number of silver foil milk bottle tops. Five silver stars warranted a gold star. The aim was for the children of the magazine to be instrumental in buying a guide dog for the blind. When we had collected sufficient weight, the foil was to be dispatched by carrier to a recycling centre who would pay a sum of money for it. I visited the training establishment for guide dogs, took photographs and told the children briefly about the charity in their star collection books – and we were away.

What I had not anticipated was how enthusiastically my club members would embrace the idea. Not only did they write enthusiastic letters often including photos of their pets, all of which had to be answered, but milk bottle tops started arriving at our house in boxes, packages, envelopes, even tins. More often than not, the cost of posting was far higher than the amount of money which could be raised from the foil itself. Many of these bottle tops had not been washed, the milk on them had turned sour and the smell was dreadful when I tipped them into the Hessian sacks which were the only containers the carriers would accept.

'For heaven's sake, put them in the garage,' Don said firmly when he came upon one of these evil smelling contributions in the kitchen or hall. 'We'll move the car outside.'

The postman, too, started complaining. A mention on my children's page – 'Dear Children, PLEASE wipe the bottle tops before you post them' – was of limited avail. All I can say about that idea was that we did manage to pay for one guide dog to be trained before, at my request, the club folded.

I approached my editor with a better idea – we could put a photo of one of Battersea Dogs' Home's unwanted dogs in the magazine each week and ask if anyone would give it a home. SAVE A PET would be the name of the scheme as we could include unwanted rabbits, goats, guinea pigs, cats etc. My editor sent me off to the headquarters of the RSPCA to enquire as to their approval and cooperation. I was given an appointment with the head man who agreed the RSPCA would approve the idea provided each

would-be-owner's house was vetted before a dog was sent
to them.

He gave me a book – henceforth known as The Bible
– with the names and telephone numbers of all the RSPCA
inspectors throughout the country. I organised a form
consisting of a single piece of paper divided into three
sections; the first for the proposed owner's name, address
and telephone number and the parent's signature approving
the child's application; the second for the description and
details of the animal to be rescued; the third, the RSPCA
inspector's name and signature of approval. I would be
responsible for sending off the approved form to the nearest
RSPCA inspector.

A photographer was sent to the kennels to take pictures
of a delightful, very appealing mongrel. The response, when
the magazine appeared a few weeks later, was enormous.
It seemed as if half the children in the country wanted to
give it a home. Once again, sackfuls – this time of letters
– arrived at the house. With the editor's approval, I employed
a girl to come and help me deal with the forms. I had
supposed that after the first few weeks, the demand for
animals would lessen as those who had requested them
were duly supplied. However, this 'good idea' turned into
a very bad one – but for once, through no fault of mine.
I sent off the hundreds of completed forms to the appropriate local inspectors, matching the applicant's locality to
the local inspector's address which I obtained from The
Bible. A week or so later, applications were still coming in
in their hundreds but so, too, were letters from parents and
children who had already applied. It was now two, three,
sometimes as much as four weeks since their application,
they pointed out. Why had nothing happened? Their child
was upset, worried, unhappy. Please could they have an
explanation by return of post.

The reason for the delay was quite simple, as I soon

found out. The inspectors had had no time to go round the various homes to check the occupants' suitability to have the dog/cat/goat/rabbit etc. It was a matter of the top of the tree not knowing what the grass roots were doing. When I was given the go-ahead, the top brass in the RSPCA was unaware their inspectors were already more than fully occupied with their regular duties – attending market days, following up cruelty complaints and so on.

To say my editor was displeased is an understatement. Far from the publicity improving the magazine's ratings, readers were growing more and more frustrated as the weeks went by. I was able to approach the Canine Defence League who managed to send off a few dogs needing homes, but for weeks after the scheme was brought to an abrupt conclusion, the editor was still receiving angry letters from the parents of disappointed children. I was glad I lived down in Sussex.

CHAPTER 14

After the disaster of my 'Save-a-Pet' scheme, it seemed a good idea to stop having any more good ideas so I resigned myself to writing my usual brand of light romantic novel. In any event, I had still to finish my twentieth novel, *The Lonely Quest*. I was at work on this one morning when the phone rang. It was my mother to say she had been asked to write a sequel to *Lady Chatterley's Lover* but felt she must refuse the request because she was too well known for romance, and her readers might not like the obvious association with sex. The book had been banned until the recent court case allowing publication. The *Sunday Pictorial* had now come up with the idea of a story about Lady Chatterley's daughter. They were offering a very large sum of money. Would I like to do it instead of her, my mother asked?

I had been used to writing sequels to other authors' books because Graeme, whenever we came to the end of one of his favourite books, had always demanded more, so I would type out a few more chapters. But this proposal, to put it mildly, was in a very different category. Although I, too, wrote light romantic novels, I was not anywhere near as famous as my mother, but I presumed my publishers would not want my good name linked with a book of such renown for its sexual content!

I now told my mother that as I had three children at school and a husband in the civil service, it was unlikely they would appreciate the inevitable attendant publicity. Moreover, women's weekly magazines in those days such as the ones who published my short stories and serialised my books, insisted sex be implied rather than described. Moreover I was not at all sure if I could write a sexy book if this was what they desired.

However, I was reluctant to turn down the offer of two extremely large payments for serial and book rights. There were now two lots of school fees, uniforms and extras to be found, and in a few years' time, when Iain went to public school and Graeme to prep school, the fees would go up even further.

Finally, we thought of a compromise – instead of writing a sex-related story, I would make Lady Chatterley's daughter rebel against her mother's liberal ideas and behaviour. This aversion to sex could have caused a psychological hang-up thus making a will-she, won't-she plot. My mother promised to edit my manuscript when it was written and now we had only to persuade the Sunday paper that they could get as much publicity as they wanted by saying I was Denise Robins' daughter.

The publicity they came up with was brilliant – an exact replica of a birth certificate for the daughter of Lady Chatterley and her gamekeeper husband, Oliver Mellors. This was accompanied by a nation-wide publicity campaign – forty-five mentions on TV; huge advertising columns in the press; thousands of posters and house-to-house leaflets. I should have realised that despite my insistence that I was not to be involved in any of it, inevitably I was. For one thing, it increased the *Sunday Pictorial*'s sales by one hundred thousand copies – and this before Consul Books produced a paperback edition in July the following year.

So successful was the *Sunday Pictorial* publicity that there were pre-orders for over 200,000 copies for the book prior to its publication two months' later and the book had an initial printing of 500,000 copies. It quickly went into the bestseller lists at number four.

I was persuaded by this new publisher, John Watson, to at least attend the launch at which Adam Faith would also be present as his autobiography *Poor Me* had reached number thirteen in the bestseller lists. Despite being a fan of the pop singer I was reluctant to go and pleaded that I had no suitable clothes to wear at a smart London function such as this. My mother then arranged for a friend of hers living in London to equip and dress me as befitted the occasion. This delightful lady, Miriam, was the mother of two girls – the actress Patricia Roc and Eve's school friend Bunny, who married the tennis champion Fred Perry. Seeing how nervous I was, Miriam insisted I drink a glass of brandy to calm me. I have never liked spirits but I managed somehow to get it down me. I began to feel a little more confident once I was wearing the beautiful designer clothes my hostess found for me from her vast wardrobe.

The strong dose of brandy went to my head, unused as I was to drinking spirits – or any alcohol come to that. Even a small glass of sherry tended to make me dizzy and I liked to be in full control of my senses if I was at a cocktail or dinner party. I do remember arriving at the venue where the book launch was taking place. I remember being introduced to Adam Faith and thinking I must get his autograph for the children; but after that, everything was a blank. I learned afterwards from my publisher that I had been in excellent spirits, amusing and very talkative. Later, I was to agree that this was more than likely but for the time being, I could remember nothing. Totally unaware that I was unfit to be behind the wheel of a car, I started to drive myself back to Sussex. Of this journey home, I recall a level crossing. As I approached, the barrier started to come down.

What a very stupid man, I thought. If he isn't careful, he is going to hit me. I still don't know how I got over safely.

My next memory is of Don saying he thought I should go straight to bed. Next morning, he told me I had arrived home talking completely unintelligibly. Obviously, I had had far too much champagne on top of Miriam's double brandy. This became even more obvious several days later. The phone rang and when I answered, a completely strange man said:

'Hello, Patricia, when shall I come down to help you with the chickens?'

At that time, Don and I had tried to augment our income by keeping young hens in one of the vast milking parlours that were abandoned when the farmer retired. We had bought the farm buildings and the ten-acre field adjoining our garden so as usual we were even more impecunious. At the same time, we had moved a couple highly recommended to us into the flat attached to the house, the idea being that the man would feed and water the chickens and collect and clean the eggs and pack them up ready for the twice-weekly collection.

Unfortunately, the man's previous employer had recommended him for one purpose only – to get rid of him. He flatly refused to do a single day's work at the farm and we had, ultimately, to have him formally evicted. Now, with Don as busy as ever at his job in London and not arriving home until eight o'clock at night, it had temporarily fallen to me to cope with the chickens. Cleaning and sorting the eggs was the most boring and time-consuming job which I really hated doing. But it had to be done.

After the sixth man telephoned to tell me I had invited him down to help with the eggs, I realised that I must have been drunk enough at the launch party to see a way out of my hated chore. Doubtless none of them believed for one minute that I truly wanted them for farm duties, rather that it was a euphemism for: 'Come up and see my etchings'!

After that, it was several weeks before I would answer the phone and I made the daily or my secretary, Joy, ask if the caller would like to speak to my husband as I was up in Scotland visiting friends! Inevitably, there were lots of reviews of the book, including the one I had been expecting asking who did I think I was daring to tamper with D. H. Lawrence's work. On the whole, I think, people took it for what it was – a gimmick, and the publicity furore soon died down.

It was whilst we were trying to evict our non-working chicken manager that I was also without the domestic assistance of his wife. I had put frantic calls in to the local domestic agency knowing that without the self-contained flat as an inducement, it would not be easy to find a willing cook-general. To my surprise, a foreign lady telephoned to ask for an interview, informing me that she could start at once. She arrived on our doorstep that very afternoon complete with suitcase.

I have to say that my first impression was that she was far, far too . . . an appropriate word escapes me. Beautifully dressed, coiffed and by all accounts one hundred per cent accomplished, the middle-aged applicant informed me in a pronounced Russian accent that she would be happy to work for me in any capacity and for the minimum wage that was all I could afford to pay.

I'm not sure if I would have employed her had I not been so desperate – and without references, too. However, she took her suitcase up to the spare room, unpacked and reported in a multi-coloured, lace-edged apron that she was ready to start work. Thereupon she took over the kitchen in the most efficient manner.

The following morning, she had cooked the breakfast even before the children were up and dressed. What would I like her to cook for dinner that night? she enquired as she had found nothing in the larder. Whilst searching my mind for a possible shepherd's pie or toad-in-the-hole, she took over the decision-making. She would cook a Boeuf Bourguignonne. My 'buts' that we had no suitable ingredients were swept visibly to one side. She would go up to London that morning where she would be able to do any shopping she required.

I did not discover until that evening when she returned laden with Harrods' green carrier bags, that this was her normal grocer. She had purchased the best beef fillet, cream, bottles of Burgundy and brandy, bacon, sundry herbs and a magnificent Pavlova and a carton of cream for pudding. Aghast, I pointed out that she had spent an entire week's housekeeping money on one meal; that we were really hard up and could not afford such luxuries, however delectable, on a daily basis.

Her reply was quite simple – I had no need to reimburse her; *she* was not hard up; she would be happy to pay.

It was not long before the mystery of her sudden appearance became clear. I was told that if the telephone went and the call was for her, I was to decline all knowledge of her existence: nor had I ever spoken to her. The mystery deepened. Was she in hiding from the police? From some foreign assassin? Was she an undercover agent? No, she was in hiding from her son, a well known British actor who, she informed me, was preventing her from seeing her grandchild. If he discovered where she was hiding, I was to inform him that she had threatened to kill herself and that I was in no doubt she would do so.

She was wonderfully dramatic and I could see from whom her son had inherited his acting talent. Needless to say, within twenty-four hours, following some highly charged telephone calls, the erring son came to collect his mother and they were (not for the first time, I believe) reconciled. I was once more without domestic help and I have to say, I missed her!

Some years after the publication of *Lady Chatterley's*

Daughter, my mother had a particularly nasty bout of 'flu. She was nearing seventy and its effects were very weakening and quite long lasting. She was, she told me, worried about her next book which it seemed unlikely she would be able to produce on time. I suppose she was hoping for one of my so-called Good Ideas to solve the problem. I came up with the suggestion that I give her one of my books. The one I had in mind had had an extremely short life in hardback shortly after the end of the war, and had been out of print for all of twenty years. If she were to change the names of the main characters, I said, and their occupations, and domiciles, appearances, etc., and add her very personal flavour to it, we could be practically certain that no one would recognise my story.

After a great deal of debate about the moral ethics of this way out of my mother's predicament, I was able to persuade her to do as I had suggested. There had been so many times in the past when I had benefited by her advice, criticisms and encouragement, I so much wanted to help her that I put all other considerations aside.

Like so many of my ideas, this turned out to be a bad one. Although the book, much altered by my mother, ultimately became one of her best-selling novels, our deception was discovered by one of her fans. Unbelievably, the good lady wrote from Australia warning my mother that there was another author who had plagiarised her story – and proceeded to quote long passages which she had extricated verbatim from my book. My mother, she said, must get in touch at once with her publisher, have the author traced and take her to court.

Fortunately, after a letter to her fan thanking her for her astuteness, nothing more came of our misdeed, and we never, ever repeated it!

Lady Chatterley's Daughter was of considerable financial benefit to me not least because the publisher commissioned three more books which were supposed to be a bit more risque than my romantic novels but were actually pretty tame!

I had a little money saved from the Lady Chatterley saga and when I saw in the paper that there was a package deal for a ski holiday in Zermatt on offer the coming Easter holiday at very reasonable rates, I knew the children would love it if I could possibly arrange it. I had not been skiing since before the war and it seemed a wonderful idea. The trouble was the economy package deal was for quite a large number of people to go as a group. I set about trying to find them.

To start with, I contacted the parents of each child's preferred friend, a boy each for Iain and Graeme and a girlfriend for Nicky, explaining to them that I thought it would be a good idea if all the children earned some of the money to pay their expenses. I also invited a local friend of mine called Patricia Foster and her two children. They were all accomplished skiers and were keen to join us. She asked if she could bring a friend of hers called Joy, but even then I still needed more people to make up the required numbers. All the other children's friends already had other arrangements made for them.

I tried some more of my own friends but most were married and had other commitments. We now had a very nice tenant in the farm cottage which had fallen vacant. He was an architect called Ian Horsborough and had spent a great deal of his youth climbing in the Alps, so was very keen to join the party. I was still three people short. I looked once again through my address book and came across Mel's name. He and his wife, Kay, had two daughters about the same ages as my children. Elaine and Susan were keen to come but Kay was no more interested in skiing than was Don. But with Mel, Elaine and Susan and a friend of hers, we had the necessary numbers. As far as I know they all took holiday jobs and contributed to the ski holiday as I had suggested.

It turned out to be the greatest fun. We were housed in a hotel annexe which was fairly primitive, not surprisingly so bearing in mind the low price we were paying. At that time, English people were not allowed to take more than fifty pounds out of the country, so we were all in the same boat where spending money was concerned. Mel bought soft drinks from the local supermarket and set up a bar in the salon of the annexe so that the children could buy cheaper drinks there than in the hotel bar.

A wonderful old ski guide by the name of Ambrose was brought out of retirement to teach the children to ski. He was a grocer in the summer months but as there was a shortage of ski guides, he had volunteered to help out. He took a fancy to the children and promised he would have them all passing their bronze medals before the end of the fortnight – and he did.

Retrospectively, it was probably not the best of ideas to invite Mel to join the party. Inevitably, we slipped back into the easy companionship of our Bath days. All five of us adults got on extremely well as, indeed, did the children. We allowed them to go out in the evenings to the local disco provided they were back by midnight, and went out ourselves with the same curfew! Having dined and danced at a very nice restaurant on our 'night off', walking back to the annexe holding hands beneath a brilliant star-lit sky, Mel and I were both wishing ourselves back on Box Hill again, and I realised it was a long time since I had had such fun. When it came time to say goodbye, everyone wanted to repeat the holiday again the following Easter holidays. It is generally agreed that it's a mistake to try to repeat something that went so perfectly, but although we never went back to Zermatt, we continued to go skiing as a group on a regular yearly basis.

On one of these occasions eight of us drove out in two cars to a ski resort in France instead of going by train. This worked well until the return journey when four of us, Mel and his daughter Sue, Graeme and I, were involved in such a horrific car accident that we were lucky only to write off the car and not lose our lives.

Whilst passing a long vehicle on a long straight stretch of road, a car suddenly emerged a short distance ahead of us from a dip we'd failed to see. I knew there was insufficient time to fall back behind the long vehicle but the car coming towards us was moving too fast for either of us to avoid a head on collision.

God must have been on our side. There was a grassy bank to my left dipping down into a field. As I turned our car to go over the bank the oncoming car caught our back wheel turning the car sideways. Thus, instead of going over head first we went sideways, turned over and landed upside down in the field. Because the winter snow had only recently melted, the ground was soft and although the roof was pushed in as far as the steering wheel, we had been thrown sideways as had our two passengers, so we were more or less unhurt.

Fortunately we were fully covered by insurance and after an emergency stop in Paris, we flew home to Lydd airport next day only a little the worse for wear. I did develop a belated minor concussion which caused me to put words and numbers in the wrong order. It was not particularly painful and quite funny when I heard myself saying such things as: 'Can you give some cat to the milk!'

There was one very small blot on our first holiday in Zermatt. He was Graeme's school friend and his name was Jonathan. I shall recount the details thus:

The party scheduled to leave that day for Austria assembled in a group at Victoria Station. I counted fourteen – one was missing. I looked anxiously up and down the platform

as the train was due to leave before long. Had Jonathan
and his mother gone to the wrong place? But no, they came
hurrying towards us. Jonathan's mother was a tall, imposing
woman who I had not met before.

'It's frightfully good of you taking Jonathan with you!'
she greeted me. 'I do hope he won't be too much trouble.'

I had gathered that the boy's brother and sister were
already grown up and Jonathan's arrival had somewhat
upset the family routine. His mother was, therefore, only
too pleased to have him satisfactorily organised for the
Easter holiday. I assured her that between us five adults,
we would take great care of him.

We were scheduled to catch the boat train to Paris where
we would then board an all night sleeper to Vest. Arriving
next morning, we would catch the train up the mountain
to Zermatt. Seeing the large heap of luggage now accumulated on the platform beside us, it was clear some
organisation was needed.

'I'll be responsible for the luggage,' Mel offered. 'I'll
need the two older boys, Iain and his friend Matt Rogerson,
to help with the loading and unloading when we change
trains.'

This seemed a good idea and I volunteered to be responsible for everyone's passport and tickets. Mel counted the
luggage – thirty-three pieces which were now put in one
large heap. Suddenly, our train came gliding in and we
waited till the passengers had disgorged. As soon as I had
located a couple of empty carriages and put the big windows
down, Mel instructed the boys to start loading.

Leaning out of the first of the carriages I had earmarked,
I saw Mel looking anxious.

'We're one piece of luggage missing,' he told me. 'I counted
each one as it went in. There are only thirty-two.'

There was now a frantic search to find the missing piece
as the minutes before departure ticked by.

'There it is!' announced Graeme, pointing a little way up the platform. Beside a small suitcase stood Jonathan. There was a banging of doors as they were shut by the guard and grabbing Jonathan and his suitcase, Mel jumped quickly on board. Once we were on our way, I called Jonathan into my carriage. Why, I asked him, when he had been told that Mr. Hack was in charge of all the luggage, had he removed his from the heap and taken it elsewhere?

He looked apologetic.

'My mother told me I was to look after my own things and not be a nuisance to you,' he said.

That was a warning I should have heeded. We managed the rest of the long journey with all its train changes without further mishap. That evening, after we had unpacked and sorted ourselves out, I called a meeting in the big *salon* into which all our rooms opened.

'We are at a high altitude here and as it is April, the sun will be especially strong as will the ultra violet,' I cautioned. 'It is therefore absolutely essential that you all put on high-altitude sun cream before you go out on the ski slopes tomorrow. It's dangerous not to do so. I have brought plenty with me so if anyone has forgotten to bring their own, let me know and I'll let you have some.'

There were, of course, other instructions – from Mel about the use of the bar; from my friend Patricia Foster about the dangers of going off piste for whatever reason; from me about the need to keep rooms tidy, be dressed neatly for the evening meal in the hotel, and to take note of the rules about going into town which I had pinned up on the *salon* door. There was also a reminder from Ian Horsborough to take care of the ski lift passes with which they would be issued in the morning as they would have to pay to get them replaced if they were lost.

The following morning, the sun blazing down on spark-ling new snow, we handed over the children to Ambrose

and took to the slopes. It was an exhilarating day as any
skier will know but we were all tired at the end of it and
went early to bed. I was none too happy to be woken by
Graeme in the early hours of the morning asking me if I
would go into their room and look at Jonathan.

'What's wrong with him?' I asked.

'I don't know – he just looks funny.'

Indeed he did. His face had swollen to one big blister
and he was trying not to cry. After an early morning visit
to the clinic, I put Jonathan back to bed as the others all
set off for their day's skiing. Trying not to sound cross, I
asked him why he had not put on his sun cream. He had
not forgotten to put on some cream, he told me forlornly,
but it was ordinary Nivea cold cream which, he said: 'My
mother told me I was to use!'

Fortunately, he recovered quickly and two days later, he
was back on the slopes.

I thought I had at last got it into Jonathan's head that
from now on he was to do what I – and not what his
mother – had told him. There was one other occasion when
he took all the hot water because, he explained, his mother
had said he was to wash his feet every night; but apart
from this it was plain sailing until the final day. I was in
the *salon* where everyone had been instructed to bring their
luggage. I was also trying to make sure all the drawers in
the rooms were empty and nothing had been left under the
beds. In an hour's time, the hotel porter was coming with
a trolley to follow us on foot down to the station to catch
our train home.

I cannot recall how many times Jonathan came to the
door asking if he could speak to me. Finally I lost patience.

'NOT NOW JONATHAN!' I told him. 'How many more
times do I have to tell you – I'M BUSY. We're leaving in
a minute and I have a lot to do. For goodness' sake GO
AWAY AND LEAVE ME IN PEACE!'

There was a brief moment of silence, and then a small voice said:

'I just wanted to give you this. My mother said I had to give it to you before we set off home.' And I was presented with a box of chocolates he had somehow managed not only to hide but also not to eat all the time we were there. It was my turn to say sorry.

There were only too more minor incidents concerning Jonathan. On the sleeper going home, the third-class paper bed sheet had been folded in an unusual way. Graeme and Jonathan were trying for some time to discover how they worked. Finally there was a shout from one of the upper bunk beds.

'I've done mine!' Graeme said. 'It's really quite easy!'

'Let's see!' said Jonathan and with one tug proceeded to undo whatever arrangement Graeme had discovered would work.

I waited for the angry outburst I knew could be expected from Graeme who had been landed with Jonathan's company most of the holiday, the pair being six years younger than the bigger boys. No sound was forthcoming, and then a cold accusing voice said bitterly:

'You bloody fool!'

For once I did not reprimand my young son for using bad language.

Poor Jonathan. He was actually a very nice little boy and grew up to have an extremely prestigious job in the City. But for the moment, we had yet to get him home. When finally we arrived back and emerged from our train at Victoria station, a tall stately figure came hurrying down towards us. Kissing Jonathan somewhat absent-mindedly, she shook my hand and said:

'I DO hope he hasn't been too much trouble.'

'No trouble at all!' I told her, and kissed Jonathan goodbye.

CHAPTER FIFTEEN

All this time, far more important things had been taking place. For one, the Russian Yuri Gagarin survived the first exploration into space. For another, the Beatles were emerging with their revolutionary influence on the younger generation who not only embraced their new type of music but their long hair and their 'All You Need Is Love!' policies. It was not an easy time for parents. The great train robbery, too, took place in 1963 with mail bags containing two and a half million pounds stolen from the Glasgow-to-London mail train, some of which was never found. Far more shocking was the assassination of the American President Kennedy on the 22nd November on a visit to Dallas. Even the youthful Graeme was affected, writing from the prep school he now attended: '*Poor President Kennedy was shot yesterday. It was a Winchester rifle what did it!*'

Graeme's letters, unlike Iain's which were short and to the point, or Nicky's which were observant and discerning, were personal and very vocal. They were peppered with capital letters, the size of the writing indicating the force of his feelings, e.g. '*I HATE the food here*'. And such-and-such a master '*is DISGUSTING*', in even larger letters. One of his best efforts arrived following his first French lesson. It read as follows:

> *Chère Mère et Père,*
> *Je hope tu est well. Je suis.*

Lots of love from Graeme.
P.S. I bet you've never
had a French letter from
a boy as young as me before.

His enlightened headmaster said he would love to have printed it in the school magazine but feared it might shock some of the more straight-laced parents.

Iain loved school and was in all the sports teams. According to his school reports, he was often up to mischief but was doing well at his lessons. Graeme hated school when he started. He was a very strong-willed child, liking to do things his way and was not therefore much interested in team games. His compulsory I.Q. test, given to all the pupils, showed him as extremely high academically and low emotionally. This imbalance was a problem for him, particularly as he always wanted a logical reason for being made to do something and, understandably, his teachers were not going to stop to explain! Fortunately, he settled down and won a bursary to Brighton College.

Nicky was not very happy at her boarding school but she never indicated this in any of her letters. Although she was at last free from the traumas she had suffered at the farm, the experience coloured her thinking. As is now well documented, children who have been abused feel that somehow they were responsible. They feel unworthy and live with the fear that the same thing could happen again. Nearly all her reports said that she could do so much better if she tried. She was, and still is, a talented artist but has never used her talent professionally.

Although I was now seeing a great deal of Eve and my mother, Anne moved down to Wales where she and Peter had bought a small farm. Whilst it was ideal for her seven children who could run free, keep ponies as well as dogs, cats, chickens, a milk cow and a pig, and attend the local

Welsh school in Pwllheli, they were desperately hard up and my mother worried continually about them and baled them out when something drastic happened such as the roof caving in. Sometimes I would drive her down to Wales to visit Anne during the term time when I was not preoccupied with my own children. I was still writing novels but was really getting very bored with it and was glad to be doing yet another children's page once again, for a different magazine, *Princess*.

Despite my promise to myself not to come up with any more 'good ideas', I had just bought a Great Dane puppy when our Labrador, Morne, finally reached the end of her days. We called him Humphrey and without doubt, he was the stupidest dog I'd ever owned. He followed Gigi, the miniature Griffon, everywhere and if she dived through a rabbit hole in a hedge, he presumed he could do the same. When he gave up the attempt to get more than his big head through the hole, he would turn and look up at me as if to ask, 'Why not the rest of me?' It was the same in the evenings when Gigi liked to sit on my lap. Inevitably, Humphrey tried to do the same, managed his front legs then his body, at which point his front legs would fall off on to the ground. Moving his back legs up, his body came off and there he'd sit, once again looking at me as if I could solve the problem for him.

The idea of writing a series of articles for the magazine about Humphrey occurred to me one day when I was out walking. There were many small incidents on these walks which I related in my letters to my children and which, I realised, might amuse other children, too. I think the very first one was a little story about the day Gigi, on one side of a hedge, chased a rabbit through to where Humphrey stood on the other side. The rabbit quite literally ran into his mouth. He just looked very surprised and dropped it.

The series went well with no horrible repercussions. Once

a week a local photographer came to take photos of Humphrey meeting other animals known in the magazine as his friends. The pictures were very good and I made the articles into a scrapbook for my children, which I put away in a drawer after they had lost interest in it. If it had continued to lie there, the next half of my life might have been different in very many ways. Such is Fate! As it was, I found it one day and thought that with some serious editing, it could be made into a children's book.

Early in 1966, a publisher by the name of A. Wheaton and Co. had produced the children's book I had really written for Graeme who was only eight at the time. It was called *The Hundred Pound Reward*, and sold quite well. However, the publisher was not interested in the Humphrey story. My agent, Miss Blackborough of Hughes Massie, suggested I went to see a new young, up-and-coming publisher called Desmond Elliott who had recently published a children's book about pandas.

I made one of my rare trips to London and called to see Desmond Elliott in his small, upstairs office in Duke Street. I was surprised to find someone younger than myself although I was aware that he had only expanded from literary agent to publisher a short while ago. With his fair hair, blue eyes and small stature, he looked even younger than he was. I showed him my Humphrey book and he told me that regretfully he could not envisage doing another children's book so soon after his panda publication. He then began to question me about my writing career and, of course, my relationship with my mother. Had I thought of writing historical novels, he asked me, because he thought there was a gap in the market in the United States.

I told him regretfully that my knowledge of history was simply non-existent, and moreover, I had now thirty-three published light romantic novels under my maiden name and such readers as I had would be expecting more of the same. Lastly I was under contract to Hurst and Blackett for two more of a three-book contract,

Desmond was nothing if not persistent. We could invent a pseudonym, he said. He had good contacts in the States and thought he could sell an historical novel there as well as in England. He could, he promised, make a great deal of money for me.

I could do nothing but reiterate that I would very much like to write something different and the money would come in very useful but – and it was an insurmountable but – King Arthur and the burnt cakes, King Canute and the sea and 1066 were about the limit of my historical knowledge.

I supposed that would be the end of our brief association, but far from it. Periodically, the telephone would ring and Desmond would enquire if I had changed my mind. Sometimes my good friend and part-time secretary Joy Tait took the calls,

'You really ought to have a go!' she said, knowing I could do with the money. 'Why not compromise and write a contemporary story with something historical in it?'

I rang Desmond who was enthusiastic. He would, he said, be delighted to consider it. How quickly could I do it? A few months I suggested, provided it doesn't have to be too long. That night I lay awake wondering what on earth I could write about; and suddenly remembered a story Granny had told me when I was a teenager about a young woman travelling home on a liner who had fallen in love with the ship's blind pianist. I'd always liked the idea and decided now to weave a plot about a blind man for whom music was his greatest consolation.

The result was a book which I called *A Voice in the Dark*. The heroine was a modern girl who finds herself drawn into the lives of an old aristocratic Italian family – hence the historical element – as I knew I could get the details from the library of a palatial old Italian villa from an illustrated guide book. I really enjoyed writing that story which was basically a romance but with a theme of danger as the family's past caught up with the present. Desmond was delighted with it and acting as my agent, sold it to Avon Books publishers in America.

By this time, he had invented a pseudonym for me; I was to be Claire Lorrimer so that I was virtually leading a double life – Patricia Robins who wrote romantic novels for Hurst and Blackett, and my new persona, Claire. I did not want to risk giving up my novel contract until I knew I could earn the same income as I had been getting, so I wrote two more romances, *Sapphire in the Sand* and *Return to Love*.

Avon was pleased with *A Voice in the Dark* and asked for three more of the same! I was happy to produce these as they were not very long and I enjoyed the new challenge. Desmond now found an English publisher, Souvenir Press, who bought hardback rights for *A Voice in the Dark*. English paperback rights, foreign rights, large-print rights, followed. In all, the book has appeared over the years in sixteen different editions, has never been out of the libraries and now, in 2006, forty years later, is about to be reprinted yet again by Chivers in a large-print edition. It remains one of my favourite stories and I live in hope that one day, someone will see what a hugely pictorial television play it would make!

It was now 1974, Iain had got his degree at Exeter University, and was sharing a flat in London with Eve's son, Murray. He had a job he enjoyed with Schroeder's merchant bank in the city. Nicky had left my old school in Switzerland where she had had a year learning French and was now working on the fashion page of a weekly magazine. She, too, was living in London, in Putney. Graeme had failed to get into medical school despite two A grades and a B grade for his A level exams. It was a big disappointment and he now decided to go to Bath University, where he had been offered a place to read engineering.

Despite their adult status, all three children were still anxious to join the Easter skiing party which I was busy organising when a far more pressing concern occupied my mind. Don had had a persistent cough but as usual would not go to the doctor. Suddenly, spots of blood had appeared in the sputum and at last he agreed to go. Our G.P. said he wanted Don to be scanned; that he'd make an appointment for him which hopefully would be in about a fortnight's time. I was very far from happy, knowing how important early diagnosis could be if this turned out to be anything horrible like lung cancer. I telephoned my mother who was always a fount of knowledge where specialists were concerned and had many friends amongst the medical profession. She would make contact with an appropriate consultant, she told me. I was not to worry.

Miraculously, within twenty-four hours Don and I were on our way to the King Edward VII Hospital where a Mr. Brain operated. Don was to be admitted when we arrived and was to have an immediate bronchoscopy. I stayed that night at my mother's pied-à-terre in London and went straight to the hospital next day. Don greeted me with the news that there was a suspected abscess on his right lung and that Mr. Brain had suggested he operate to remove it the following day.

I learned later that the policy at the time was not to tell a patient they had cancer unless the patient particularly stated they wished to know. It was an extremely worrying time. Although Mr. Brain told me the next day that the operation had gone very well, Don looked dreadful when I went to see him in the intensive care unit. However, thanks to the remarkable surgery Mr. Brain had performed, despite being without a part of his lung, Don slowly recovered. He had some wonderful nurses in the King Edward VII Hospital and finally returned home weak but slowly getting better.

It is always easy to be wise after an event but at this time, I did not fully realise how weak Don still was. He had not wanted to come out to the ski resort where we were scheduled to go at Easter although I was sure the beautiful mountain air and sunshine would have done him good. Instead, he decided to go to one of the holiday hotels we'd been to in the summer in Cornwall, and convalesce there. As it was, the trip was too much for him and he returned home to an empty house. Fortunately, we had a gardener, George Stevenson, and his wife living in the flat and his wife, Ivy, did the cooking and housework, so Don was not totally abandoned, but it set his recovery back quite a bit.

As is usual after such operations for cancer, Don needed regular check-ups for which he had to produce the X-rays taken at the time he was in the King Edward VII Hospital. The surgery had been so innovative and well executed that doctors and surgeons at the local hospitals kept asking to see the X-rays and on one occasion managed to lose them!

It is now over thirty years since that operation and Mr. Brain would be delighted to hear that at the age of eighty-six, Don is in excellent health.

In December that year, I managed to write *The Shadow Falls*. It followed *Relentless Storm* and *The Secret of Quarry House* and was the last of the four contemporary mystery romances I produced for Avon in America. I would soon be writing for another publisher instead.

CHAPTER 16

Desmond now started once again to beg me to write a long historical saga. He had been lunching with the President of Bantam's in New York who had expressed an interest. I told him my lack of historical knowledge made it impossible for me to do as he wished. It was then Joy intervened once more. She suggested that perhaps we could collaborate. History, she told me, was her favourite subject and if she provided the historical background, could I write the story to go with it?

We mulled over the idea. I was nervous. Joy was insistent that we COULD do it – and Desmond had offered a thousand pound advance even before I had written a word. That was a great deal of money in those days. I signed the contract, explaining that I still had one more book to do under my last three-book contract with Hurst & Blackett. We agreed that I would start writing the historical saga for which Desmond had already chosen a title, *Mavreen*, at the end of April when the children went back to school after the Easter holidays.

The cheque arrived and went straight into the bank to pay the most recent school fees. Joy and I now jointly decided to carry out her suggestion to set the story in the Napoleonic period, her favourite. Two weeks before we were due to start on the first chapter, there was a phone call from Joy's husband, Ian. Joy had gone to hospital for a minor check up but been informed that she must stay for further tests; it looked like an immediate operation

would be necessary and, Ian concluded, Joy thought it best
to warn me that she might not be back to work for a long
time.

I was appalled. The contract was signed and I had already
spent my advance. I would have to find someone to replace
Joy as my historical collaborator. I opened my address book
and telephoned every friend I had as well as some who
were more acquaintances than friends – all to no avail.

'Stop panicking,' Don said, 'and do the research yourself.
The library will have plenty of books. Start with a biography of the Duke of Wellington.'

I calmed down and went into East Grinstead to the
library.

'Please . . .' I said to the middle-aged librarian, '. . . could
you tell me where I can find a book about the Duke of
Wellington; and also if you have it, a book about Sir Arthur
Wellesley?'

I won't try to describe the perplexed look on her face
as she asked me to repeat my request. Blissfully ignorant
of the fact that they were one and the same person, I asked
once more for books on either of the two men. When I
opened the books at home I was deeply ashamed. Quite
probably my three children would have known better than
to make such an embarrassing mistake. I lay awake that
night wishing and wishing that I had stuck to my guns and
never agreed to write the beastly book.

Prepared to eat as much humble pie as was needed, I
returned to the library next day, called the librarian aside
and confessed my ignorance. I then told her the reason why
I needed her help. Alas I have forgotten her name but I
was then and still am eternally grateful to her. She found
for me books not only on historical events and characters
but on clothes of the period, poets, social mores, nearly all
potted versions in simple editions printed for children, which
I could easily and quickly absorb.

Had anyone told me prior to that event that I would end up totally fascinated by history, I would have gone to the gallows before agreeing with them. Yet there I was, sitting on my study floor surrounded by books and so deep into them that not only would I forget the time but also I was doing no writing. I had to ration myself, dividing my time between research and typing the next chapter.

My plot began fairly simply – poor, illegitimate daughter of an aristocrat – Mavreen – grows up to be so beautiful and clever, an elderly, rich titled man wants to marry her and launch her back in Society, whilst she has fallen in love with a young French viscount who has to make a suitable marriage. The characters came easily to mind, for example, the usual upstairs/downstairs household full of faithful servants. Amongst these was an elderly butler. As my saga was to cover a great many years, I was well into the story when I realised my butler was still around serving his master's brandy, but would now be approaching his hundred and twelfth birthday. Moreover, a pregnant housemaid was still pregnant two and a half years later. My heroine had miraculously aged four years in twelve months and not least, I had described a beautiful coming-out ball on the day of the King's funeral.

I can laugh about it now but at the time, it meant a huge amount of work, all but starting the whole story again. I realised I could not just put a piece of paper in my typewriter, head it Chapter One and continue to the required eighty thousand words as had been my habit with all my light romances. This complicated historical saga must be PLANNED. I had no choice but to start all over again.

Apart from the time spent that first month doing research, the story took over and I had no trouble writing it. Fortunately for both Joy and me, she was not convalescent as long as her husband had feared and she relieved me of the task of finding suitable books, reading them and high-lighting passages she knew from the plot would be of interest to me. This saved an enormous amount of time. Moreover, she made valuable comments and criticisms whenever I made an historical gaffe; in fact she was so helpful I insisted she should have a share, albeit very small, of the financial benefits – if there were any! Now, thirty years later and eight years since, very sadly, Joy died, I am still able to send one of her grandchildren little cheques from time to time for royalties for *Mavreen*.

Desmond was pressing me to get the book finished before he went off to New York. He seemed more interested in placing it with an American publisher rather than an English one but I didn't realise why until much later.

Grateful when at last I had completed the six hundred-page saga, I managed to get the manuscript to Desmond shortly before he was due to catch his plane to the States. Then, knowing how long publishers took to read and decide upon acceptance or otherwise of a book, I more or less forgot it as I was busy helping my mother move from Furnace Pond Cottage to a smaller house in Haywards Heath. Despite the work involved in a move she continued writing her novels, although she was by then in her eighties. As Granny, her mother, was still writing books when she died at the age of eighty-six, my mother said she saw no reason why she should not do the same!

The following week, I had a frantic telephone call from my sister, Eve. There had been a terrible accident on the Moorgate underground station. It was not only the route Murray took to work, but also the accident had occurred at about the time he travelled. It transpired that forty-two people had been killed. Murray was on the train but by an incredible stroke of luck, he was late that morning and instead of getting in one of the front carriages as was his habit and where all the terrible damage had occurred, he'd been obliged to get in the last undamaged one. As soon as he could, he telephoned Eve and she was able to relay her relief to my mother and to me.

Down in their Welsh smallholding, Anne and Peter had come to the conclusion that they should move back to England where their seven Welsh-speaking children could go to English instead of Welsh schools. Furthermore, as Peter was now producing sculptures for Heredities, he needed to visit the firm from time to time. They found a cottage in the beautiful Cotswold village adjoining the famous Hook Norton Brewery.

I was not expecting the telephone call from my new agent, Desmond Elliott, when it came one lunchtime. He had read *Mavreen* on the plane and within a week, had 'sold' the American paperback rights for two hundred thousand dollars. Was I prepared to accept the offer, he asked? Not knowing how many dollars went to the pound, it sounded a lot so I said 'yes'. I telephoned Iain who, as he worked in a merchant bank, I knew could give me the exchange rate. He said I must have written the amount wrongly – miscounted the noughts. I had written the figure down very carefully so I now read it out to him. When he told me I had been offered the equivalent of about one hundred thousand pounds, I could not believe it. Nor, indeed, could Don when he came home that evening.

There was one snag which Desmond now related to me. The publishers, Bantam Books, wanted me to put in more sex. This was equally hard to believe! How did one interject sex sequences into a story that was already written? And could I write about sex? My training writing for women's weekly magazines always insisted sex was left at the door of the bedroom never inside it! But for the unbelievable sum of a hundred thousand pounds, I was prepared to try anything.

The consequences turned out to be quite far reaching.

For one of my sex episodes, I created a highwayman who robbed Mavreen, fell in love with her, found out where she lived and because he was very attractive, she more or less allows him to seduce her. In fact, he turned out to be such fun as well as attractive that he more or less took over as the man I wanted Mavreen to end up with rather than her somewhat effete French aristocrat. I therefore devised a really neat twist at the end of the book. Mavreen had finally found in Russia the Frenchman she thought she loved. Realising she doesn't love him after all, she departs on her *troika* with her faithful servant when from out of the forest gallops the highwayman who 'claims her for his own'. Very satisfactory, BUT the publisher didn't want it – the French Viscount was to remain the hero, and that was that.

I was quite upset. I was half in love with my highwayman myself! However, I was in no financial position to argue with a hundred thousand pounds. Besides, Desmond had now decided to publish a hardback British edition and was talking happily about an English paperback edition and foreign royalties. He went ahead and published the hardback that year. The following year, Bantam's produced their paperback version and it went straight into the *New York Times* bestseller list. Much to Iain's delight, I also managed to make the *Financial Times* top ten bestseller Romance League table with the Corgi paperback edition where it remained for several weeks. Ultimately the book sold over three million copies and was reprinted thirteen times.

Early the following year, in 1977, Desmond told me Bantam's wished me to go over to New York to meet their sales staff and he arranged for me and Iain, who agreed to accompany me, to stay at the St Regis Hotel in New York for a week. Also invited was a young author, Richard Doyle, whose fictional book on flying boats had just been published.

The three of us were newcomers to New York and after the talks, publicity lunches and parties were over, we were able to sightsee. It was heat-wave weather and as the weekend before our departure approached, we decided to spend it with Desmond's approval by the sea. Richard had written his book without ever having been in a flying boat and hearing that there was an air service from New York to a resort called Fire Island, he suggested we should go there. Desmond told us he thought we would not care for it but he gave no reason why, so as Richard was so keen to go we booked seats on the four-seater plane for the following day.

The flying boat trip, short though it was, did remind me uncomfortably of my ill-fated journey to Cairo after the war. However, we landed safely in the little harbour and armed with a picnic basket and our swimming gear, we started to climb up the dunes. I'm not sure which of the three of us was the more startled to see two men, arm in arm and totally naked, walking towards us. We continued to the top of the sand dunes and stared down at the beach on the other side. It was a beautiful day – not too hot, a lovely calm sea, blue skies and a wide, sandy beach . . . covered for the most part with nude bodies; nude male bodies sunbathing, some with straw hats or towels protecting their more vulnerable parts!

I thought it was very funny although I was, like the boys, embarrassed. There was no going back as the plane was not returning to collect us until the end of the day. I was the only female to be seen and no way was I going to appear in my swimsuit and walk down to the water's edge with all those hundreds of pairs of eyes wondering who on earth I was. Not long out of their public schools, the two boys were even more embarrassed than I was at the thought of stripping off in front of me; nor did they wish to look stupid putting on their swimming trunks when every other male was nude. In the end, the extreme heat overcame their reluctance and they all but flew across the sand into the sea and stayed there!

Next day, we thought it best not to tell Desmond where we had been and muttered vague reference to a beach whose name we couldn't remember. Fire Island, however, is etched forever on my memory, vaguely associated with *Mavreen*!

The year prior to our New York adventure, I had had to face the fact that with Iain and Nicky living in London with their own jobs and friends, and Graeme at University, I was frequently very lonely. Don was a workaholic and tired as he was when he commuted home at the end of a long day, he was loathe to get involved socialising. We rarely went out and our friends were limited to those I had made with parents of the children's associates. I was not then required to entertain my publisher or the sales force as happened after the success of *Mavreen*.

I did go to London quite often to lunch with Desmond who was always invigorating, full of enthusiasm and new ideas. He was a very remarkable man. Having grown up in a Masonic orphanage, he started work as a paper and string boy at Hutchinson's the publishers. There as a clerk he had met the Chairman and Managing Director of the firm, Walter Hutchinson, a remote cousin of my mother's, although this was unknown to Desmond at the time. Desmond related to me how one day Walter came into the little room where the three junior clerks sat squashed together at their respective desks. Looking around him Walter remarked that they seemed to be over-crowded. At once, they all vehemently agreed.

'That's easily settled,' Walter is supposed to have said, pointing at Desmond's two colleagues. 'You and you – you're fired!'

Amusing as these lunches with Desmond were whilst he was urging me to write a sequel to *Mavreen*, they were but a tiny part of my empty days. I thought back to the wonderfully happy, fun times I'd had on our skiing holidays and finally faced the fact that really, Don and I were about as incompatible as any couple could be. I think we had only agreed on two major issues – to adopt our children and to buy Little Surries! I finally admitted that my mother had been right all those years ago, we were not well suited. But one thing was certain, I could not have wished for a more hard-working, responsible, reliable husband and father. Now, when I had stopped being a mother whose great pleasure was organising birthday parties, holidays, picnics and tennis parties, I knew I needed a different kind of life to the one I was leading. I think Don, too, wanted a different kind of life to the haphazard one I so often presented him with when all he wanted was a bit of peace. He did not need companionship in the same way I had always done. I often thought he would have done much better to have married Eve who also liked a peaceful life and was often fed up in our childhood with my persuasions to 'come and do this or that'.

It was not until the publication of *Mavreen* widened all my financial horizons that it became possible for Donald and me to go our own ways. I could now be independent – set up a new home for myself and fill it with as many of my own and the children's friends as I wished. All three children were old enough now, I hoped, not to find the proposed separation of their parents too disturbing. What I had not envisaged was that my life was about to change far more radically than I could ever have imagined. When Mel heard about my plans, he immediately announced he wanted to join me.

Looking back now to the post-war years, I realise how easy it was for so many of us who had been in the services to have rushed into marriages with the wrong partners – perfectly nice, admirable, worthy people but not necessarily the people we would have chosen to marry in pre-war years. Nothing was permanent in the services for many girls like myself who had joined in their teens and early twenties. There were postings to new environments; there were new colleagues, new boyfriends, lovers who never came back from their particular bit of the war. We were ready to settle down, have our own homes, choose what to do with our lives. And with our biological clocks ticking away, most of us wanted husbands and children to complete the picture.

Mel, too, had married believing it would be forever, but although he had made a big success of his life and owned his own flourishing motor distributorship which enabled him to have more or less anything he wanted, you couldn't, he told me, buy the fun and companionship we had shared in the Bath days; nor, indeed, on our skiing trips.

Neither of us was sure if we could make such a relationship work now, at our ages. We were no longer young – Mel was sixty and I was fifty-five. Moreover, he was far from sure whether he would like living south of the Thames. He had a very large circle of friends in the Midlands with whom he played golf, tennis, fished, shot and partied. He even had his own shoot which he would have to leave behind him. Nevertheless he had no hesitation in moving down to Kent where we bought a lovely old converted Tudor barn with an exceptionally pretty garden.

Chiswell Barn needed a huge amount of improvements – windows put in, walls removed, re-wiring, painting and so on. At one time, we had sixteen workmen on the premises, but it was 1976 and throughout the summer there was a continual heat wave, so we all but lived in the garden. We decided upon a swimming pool and in his summer holiday from Bath University, Graeme and a friend built a lovely sunroom overlooking it, where we were to have some great parties once all the work was done.

Don had a bad dose of flu shortly after I had moved out. This was, of course, some time before our divorce and his subsequent marriage to a charming German divorcée called

Charlotte. So I went back for two weeks to look after him – Mel understanding completely my wish to do so. I also accepted the need for his frequent trips back to Melton Mowbray to see to his business affairs and make sure his wife and daughters were coping without him. Nicky came to live with us for six months following the breakdown of a relationship she had with a fellow student at Eastbourne College where she was doing an art course. Mel let her use the workshop he had organised at the top of the garden to start a small business painting children's furniture and kitchen utilities. Eve and John were frequent visitors and as Mel had taught me to play golf – he had a shelf full of golf trophies – we made up a regular foursome both on the golf course and at Bridge which I was only just learning. My mother and Neill also exchanged visits and got along famously with Mel, which was lovely for us both.

From time to time Don and 'Lotte would come over to lunch with us or we would visit them in the charming house they bought near Battle. We ourselves were always popular in the summer because of our lovely garden and the swimming pool! Many of Mel's friends came to stay and we exchanged summer and Christmas parties with our new neighbours.

Unfortunately Joy, who was quite a bit older than I was, found the distance from her home in Lamberhurst too far to travel as she had done when I was at Little Surries, and said she must retire. We still visited each other and we played foursomes golf with her and her husband; but I did have to find a new secretary as I was busy writing *Tamarisk*, a sequel to *Mavreen*. I can still smile remembering how anxious I was to start the new book as I fully intended to kill off the French Viscount as soon as possible and let Mavreen marry her highwayman. This time, nobody complained!

My new secretary was ultra efficient, but was having

marital problems and I was probably not easy to please
as I was missing Joy with whom I could always have
chats and giggles. Fate was, however, once more very
much in my favour. After the new girl had left, I was
bemoaning the absence of a secretary to my next-door
neighbour, a young mother with two little girls and a
baby boy in a carrycot. Her name was Penrose Scott. A
former secretary, she was married to a patent expert called
John. A day later, at Mel's suggestion, she came round
to our house and asked if she could work for me on a
part-time basis.

I won't take up too much space describing how very
lucky I was to have chosen a house with the perfect replace-
ment for Joy literally on my doorstep. Pennie, as she has
always been known, was – and still is – quite invaluable
to me, not just as a secretary but as a P.A., a researcher, a
bookkeeper and not least a friend as well as a kindly neighbour. Like Joy, I can bounce ideas off her and get back
intelligent comments, criticisms if I need them, suggestions
if I'm flagging. That baby son in his carrycot is now thirty;
her little girls are both married and her husband has retired,
but Pennie is still with me, partly because I won't agree to
let her go, but also because I think she has actually enjoyed
a lot of the ups and downs of my literary life.

Our houses are in a dead-end, mile-long lane with a
farm and a further fifteen houses spread at intervals along
it. I used this environment for my first ever Whodunit,
Over my Dead Body. The Scotts are on our left and to
the right our neighbours were the playwright John Osborne
and his future wife, Helen. Our first meeting with the
Osbornes was in 1976 whilst we were in the middle of
the house improvements, and they stopped to see what
was going on. Without any idea who they were, we invited
them in to look round as they were obviously curious.
Eventually we sat out in the garden and Mel offered them

a drink, it being a scorching hot day. One drink turned into a prolonged drinking session during which John's language became quite outrageous seeing we were total strangers. He was, like a naughty schoolboy, doing his best to shock me.

When finally they left, walking unsteadily back to their house up the road, I said to Mel that if they were typical of our neighbours, I didn't much want to get to know them better. The following morning, our bearded neighbour arrived at the back door bearing a bottle of champagne. It was John, coming to apologise for yesterday's behaviour! The four of us became really good friends. I have subsequently heard people levelling criticism of one sort or another at John but apart from our first meeting, I never again found him anything but kind, polite, amusing, generous and enormously hospitable. Most of all I remember how particularly sweet he was to my mother in the early stages of her Alzheimer's. He sat beside her in the garden when she was offering him some incomprehensible advice about how he was to manage his teenage daughter, listened to and agreed with her as if her opinion was of the utmost importance to him.

John always gave wonderful summer parties to which the whole village were invited along with such well-known people as Ralph Richardson, Lawrence Olivier and Joan Plowright, Edna O'Brian, Edward Fox, Adam Faith, Jack Nicholson, John Mortimer to name but a few. We had a rather tiresome Canadian visitor on one occasion who was very full of his own importance. John, of course, told us to bring him along to the party. When we arrived, our visitor sailed up to John, held out his hand and said: I'm Maurice Gaye! To which John replied: Don't apologise!

We were all sorry when he and Helen decided to move up to Shropshire. We stayed with them there on two occasions but on our last visit, John was not very well and in

1994 he died. Helen survived into the new century outliving him by ten years.

Mel and I continued to give our own summer parties in the garden to which mutual friends and neighbours came. Jon Pertwee, alias Worzel Gummidge, and one of the many Dr Who's, came with his wife, Inge. I'd known Jon for as long as I could remember and never let him forget that he had once pushed me off the side of a punt in a boathouse when I was four! Sadly, only a few years after his last visit Jon had a heart attack and never recovered.

His brother, Michael, my favourite of the three Pertwee brothers, contracted the big C and his death particularly affected me. He was a very modest man with a wonderful sense of humour. He'd had an extremely successful career writing farces in which Brian Rix, Peter Sellers, Terry Thomas and Dennis Price all starred. He also wrote regularly for television and was a co-author of the musical *A Funny Thing Happened on the Way to the Forum* in 1966. Michael was one of our most frequent visitors in the heady post-war days in our flat in Drayton Gardens.

Apart from enjoying our garden, golf and entertaining, Mel and I went on some exotic holidays, perhaps the most memorable was to the Seychelles where Nicky came with us. We were there before the 1977 *coup d'état* when the dictator France Albert René took control of the country so the tourist scene was pretty much still in its infancy. It was the most romantic place. We drove across to the opposite side of the island where there was, as yet, no development. The whole island was beautiful, and I was able to use it for background in my saga, *Chantal*, the third in the *Mavreen* trilogy.

The guests in our hotel, the Beau Vallon, were of all nationalities, including German. One evening, a large party of them sat down at the table near ours. As this was before their hotel management became sophisticated, the waitresses consisted of young untrained Seychellois girls who did not speak a word of any language other than their own. Their service was somewhat haphazard to say the least but they were always smiling and hugely anxious to please. The German host demanded for the third time in a loud voice for a mustard pot missing from their table. It was not forthcoming because the girl had failed to understand what it was he wanted. He started to berate her and she ran out of the room in tears.

Mel stood up, lifted the mustard pot off our table, walked slowly over to the German's and without a word, banged it down in front of him. Other diners had been equally conscious of the scene and now one and then another took their mustard pots to the table until there were little short of a dozen in front of the complainant. From then on, there was an uneasy silence from the man and his guests, and they did not appear in the dining room again.

At night, we danced under the stars to the music of an extremely pleasant group of local musicians. They were of mixed race like most of the population – Indian, Chinese, French, African, Portuguese. When it was too hot, we dived into the swimming pool before returning to the dance floor. One memorable night, one of the female guests quite literally fell down dead. She had had a heart attack. Miraculously for her there was a British doctor sitting with his family watching the dancing. The woman was laid on the floor where he carried out coronary resuscitation and brought her back to life. It was both a shock and a relief to see her sit up and start talking.

Another long distance holiday we had was in The Gambia, West Africa. We had only been there a few days when I heard a voice calling across the hotel foyer: 'Hi there, General'. It was a nickname I'd been given by Matt Rogerson after the Zermatt skiing holiday because the organisation had gone so smoothly. Unbelievably, it was Matt himself.

He was now married and he had his lovely wife, Sue, with him. I think he was as much surprised to find us as we were to see them in such a remote part of the world.

We had one unusual adventure there. Once again, I was researching suitable background material for a future book, and we learned that it was possible to make a two-day boat trip up the river Gambia to the undeveloped interior. The boat was small, we were warned, with limited facilities and it would be advisable for us to book one of the very few cabins. The boat carried supplies to and from the villages along the riverside, and the local population travelling on it slept and cooked on the lower deck. Mel made a noise about my being a famous novelist who was only used to 'the best', as a result of which we were allocated the President's cabin.

The day we boarded we were informed that unfortunately the President's cabin was need by the gentleman himself and we would have to sleep elsewhere. After a great deal of fuss, we were led down below where a door was opened into a tiny, evil-smelling cabin, the floor awash with filthy water and dirty covers on the bed. Aware that there was no way I would consider even going into the room, let alone sleep there, there was another noisy interval at the conclusion of which we were shown to yet another cabin – this time with four bunk beds, two of which appeared to be spoken for. However, there was a toilet and minute washbasin in a tiny cupboard leading off the small room, and as the boat was already under way and we could not disembark, we settled for the shared cabin.

I was unpacking our overnight bag when the other two occupants came into the room. They were two young German students who seemed not a little put out to be sharing their accommodation with an elderly couple like ourselves! Because of the restricted space between the bunks dressing and undressing was extremely difficult, let alone making use of the toilet facilities; but we made the best of it. We spent all day on deck watching the passing scenery, the wild animals on the river banks, and most interestingly, the primitive villages, mainly small riverside gatherings of huts where the harvested peanuts were loaded on to boats and stores offloaded.

At one of these makeshift docks a new, somewhat rickety wooden jetty had been built, alongside which our boat was scheduled to draw up. The village chieftain in white robes with a retinue of followers, one holding an umbrella over his head, came out on to the jetty to perform the opening ceremony. Alas, the weight of so many people was too much for the flimsy structure which gave way and in slow motion, sank beneath the muddy water. We had cameras with us with which to catch this hilarious if unfortunate moment. However, the Gambians also saw the funny side and a very noisy burst of hilarity heralded the exodus of the wet bodies as they scrambled back on to the riverbank. With no jetty, supplies had to be ferried to and from our boat in small rowing boats and on rafts.

We were able to disembark at the point of turn-around, and wander round the village with its few stalls selling fly-ridden meat and fish and locally made baskets and ornaments. There was a small school with smiling African children sitting on the earth floor of the clearing listening to their teacher with serious attention until they were told they could say hello to us. The poverty was extreme yet everywhere we went we were met with smiles.

For the return journey we were finally allotted the President's suite as presumably he had been on a one-way trip! How to describe our prestigious accommodation? One very small cabin with a double bed which filled it and toilet facilities no different from the other cabin. There was a slightly grubby curtain at one window which looked out on to the deck – an improvement on our last below-deck cabin. But this, too, was constantly filled with the smell of paraffin and food being cooked by the below-deck passengers, seemingly at all times of the day and night. But despite the deprivation we both thoroughly enjoyed the two-day adventure although we were pleased to get back to our bathroom and have a lovely long bath when we finally reached our hotel.

On another occasion we joined my mother and Neill on a holiday to Madeira where we soaked up sun, danced in the evenings, played golf and toured the island. We also went skiing in Crans-sur-Sierre – a regular haunt of theirs – our trip coinciding with my mother's and my joint birthday. My mother, of course, did not ski but enjoyed the sun and shops whilst she waited for us to come down off the slopes. We went there three years running, once when Nicky came with us. We also went to Jamaica as guests of Land Rover, one of the motor companies for which Mel's firm was a distributor. In the daytime we swam, played golf, visited the local market, rafted down the Rio Grande and climbed the Dunn's River falls.

There was a welcome party the night we arrived. As this was at the equivalent time of four a.m. in England, we were pretty exhausted and ready for bed, but felt we should make the effort and attend the cocktail party. We'd been advised to take suitable clothes for such a function so despite our fatigue, we duly changed and went downstairs. To my dismay, everyone else was in the clothes in which they had travelled. One thing was for sure, I said to Mel, we would not make the same mistake again. When the last day came and we were invited to attend the farewell party, we arrived in our daytime holiday clothes to find everyone else in formal attire! They, of course, had been informed of the correct dress during the daily seminars and no one had thought to tell us. After this, we were not sorry to be going home!

CHAPTER 17

With *Mavreen*, *Tamarisk* and *Chantal* still selling in the States, and with a Transworld paperback version in Britain as well as hard and paperback and foreign rights in Europe, my bank balance was in a very healthy state . . . in fact as some of the proceeds of the three books was overseas, it seemed an excellent idea to spend some of it. Mel and I had decided to visit Spain to play on some of the golf courses where he had played for the Massey Ferguson team in the past. We chose a package deal to the Costa del Sol and were given accommodation in a hotel in Mijas – a resort in the hills above Fuengirola very popular with tourists like ourselves.

Unfortunately our visit coincided with that of a film crew as a result of which the hotel management thought fit to limit some of the facilities such as the swimming pool and dining room to guests. We rang our travel agent to complain. They agreed to us moving the following day further along the coast towards Marbella to a really lovely hotel called the Los Monteros, (I used the name 'Monteros' much later for a family in *Frost in the Sun*, a book set in Spain about the Spanish Civil War).

We knew there was a golf course nearby so deciding not to waste our first day, we found our way there. To reach it, it was necessary to drive along a rutted lane across the side of the mountain for a mile or two before it joined a slightly better road at a T-junction leading to the golf course. Four kilometres down the hill was the town of Fuengirola;

up the hill the road again became rutted and potholed and had a signpost pointing to Coin and Mijitas. It also said that there were apartments for sale in Mijitas for as little as eight thousand pounds. After we had played golf, we lunched in the clubhouse and decided to drive up the hill to look at Mijitas and see what these apartments were like. We might between us consider buying one so that we had a holiday home to come to.

The road twisted its way upwards with very occasionally a villa on one side or another. At the top, however, we found an Andalucian village in the process of being built. The few houses which were already completed, some occupied, were enchanting and we could not believe it was possible to buy one of these so cheaply. A drive down into Fuengirola to the offices of the vendors ensued and the agent, a Mr. Tugwell, showed us the plans for the future development of the village. If we purchased a place now, he pointed out, we would have a fifty per cent reduction on green fees.

That spur-of-the-moment visit ended eventually in our buying a one-bedroom apartment known as B41, already built with an option to buy the restaurant which was only half complete, and two other plots near the entrance suitable for a bookshop and a launderette. With only half Phase 1 and all of Phase 2 and 3 yet to be built, we could see the potential of the complex.

We returned home full of plans. The terrace of the restaurant overlooked the smooth green fairways of the golf course and far beyond was the beautiful blue of the Mediterranean. If we had been younger, we agreed, we'd have gone out there to run the restaurant ourselves. This thought prompted me to suggest that maybe Nicky might like to go out there. She was currently working in an antique shop owned by the boyfriend of one of her girlfriends. On the floor above the shop, there was a picture-frame restorer

– a young man by the name of Arnold with whom she had become very friendly. When she came down to see us at the weekend, I asked her if the idea of going to live for a year or two in Spain appealed to her? We arranged to fly out with her on a brief visit so that she could see what we had in mind.

Not yet entirely sure of her feelings for Arnold, Nicky decided that if he wanted to go to Spain with her, it would enable them both to discover more about one another. Arnold, understandably, asked for some sort of agreement which would compensate him for the loss of his current business were the restaurant not to prove the success we all hoped for. We drew up this agreement which we all signed, Mel agreeing to finance the expenses the project incurred; and until the business was making profits, to finance the running costs. The agreement wasn't legally viable, our local solicitor told us, but with the four of us and, in addition, Iain signing all five copies, we felt this was adequate.

It was a rash venture, not least because we had no idea what the Spanish laws were like about non-nationals working out there. The Spanish lawyer we employed in Fuengirola soon alerted us to the fact that Nicky must be a resident in order to obtain a work permit. Arranging this was the least of our worries. The Spanish businessman who owned most of the mountainside on which the proposed village was being built, was nothing less than a rogue. Items such as air conditioning units never appeared; electricity came from an extremely noisy generator, which was supplanted when he had the main cable tapped into so that we were all using electricity illegally whilst still having to pay the bills. But by the time we found out all the many defects, the restaurant was built and Nicky and Arnold were installed in B 41.

Mel and I took frequent trips out there staying in another

apartment on the complex. Mel had bought the couple a small car without which they could not have made the necessary trips to Fuengirola to get groceries, sign documents and so on. We sacked our Spanish lawyer who we found to be in cahoots with the owner and found an English speaking, reputable lawyer in San Pedro. He did his best to help us with the sundry difficulties but it seemed he already had a thick folder of pending court cases against our villain! Nothing in Spain happened quickly as we had, by then, found out.

It was a disastrous undertaking as we were gradually to discover. Although Arnold presented account books for Mel's inspection whenever we went out there, they never balanced and Mel had to find more and more money to meet the so-called costs. As most of the houses in Phase 1 were yet to be built, there were not many customers eating at the restaurant which, after innumerable delays, was finally up and running. Arnold was a good enough chef but was not particularly hardworking and chose only to open in the evenings. It was not, therefore, available to golfers at the end of their game to call in for a drink or a meal; nor for the few residents who might have enjoyed a good English breakfast there.

It was not an easy situation for any of us. Arnold managed to quarrel not only with the agent who could otherwise have been helpful to him, but with some of the residents as well. Nicky was in the far from happy situation of having divided loyalties. Whilst the launderette had been built and equipped and the bookshop used as offices, neither proved profitable and we decided to sell them. As for the restaurant, Mel thought it best to put in Spanish tenants who, when he did so, began to make a go of it. Nicky and Arnold, meanwhile, moved to Bordeaux where they started up an antique business with the proceeds of the family agreement pay-off – a sum of money Mel believed should have been coming from Arnold to him! It was not a happy time as I, too, had divided loyalties.

A few weeks after one of these trips to Spain – but not connected to it – Mel was rushed into hospital with a pulmonary embolism. It had started with a swelling behind his knee to which he did not pay much attention. However, as he was due in hospital next day for a routine heart test, he agreed with me he would let a doctor there look at the swelling. Strangely, by morning it had reached his shoulder. Luck for once was not with him as there was no doctor at the hospital and the technician using the test machine suggested we should return home to see our own doctor at the surgery.

It was a Saturday morning, and by the time we reached Edenbridge, the surgery was closed for the weekend. There was football on the television that afternoon with a match Mel did not want to miss so he now argued strongly that we should stop bothering and wait for further developments on Monday. I was strangely uneasy and rang our local cottage hospital to see if there was a doctor there. One was due to call in at the hospital that afternoon.

I drove a reluctant Mel down there, he arguing that he felt perfectly well and I was fussing over nothing. Half an hour later, I was driving him to the large hospital in Pembury. The doctor had diagnosed a pulmonary embolism which had already moved up his body on the way to his heart, and he thought I could get Mel there faster than if we called for an ambulance which would have had to travel twice the distance.

When finally Mel was put to bed in the ward, there were more wires attached to him, machinery around him and medical staff in attendance than when he'd had a triple bypass at the London Hospital. That night I had to telephone his family to warn them how ill their father was. It was a question of whether the doctors could disperse the clot before it reached his heart. Mel was now in extreme pain and I could not help but wonder what on earth would have happened had he stayed at home to watch his football match.

His recovery took some weeks but he hated being ill and did all the necessary things to hasten his convalescence. When I had a pulmonary embolism years later, I knew better – thanks to Mel – than to delay going to see my doctor at the very first recognisable symptom.

We decided that summer to holiday in the mountains where the air would be good for us. Never having been there in summertime, we chose to go back to Crans, one of our favourite ski resorts. It had a championship golf course as well as the beautiful mountain walks.

On our first ascent, unaccustomed as we were to long walks, let alone climbing, by the time we were halfway up the mountain we were exhausted and decided to return to the hotel. Looking around, I thought I could see a short cut down to the village. I pointed out this seemingly good idea to Mel who somewhat reluctantly agreed to try it. It was a disaster. Half an hour later, emerging from a dense pine forest, we stood facing a deep unnavigable gorge. We had but one option – to retrace the half hour walk through the forest and descend the way we had come up!

Tired though we were after those long treks, we still spent every evening dancing in one or other of the night-clubs which, being European, played our sort of music rather than the rock and roll our children enjoyed.

We had another lovely holiday on the north coast of Italy near Genoa when – and golfers will not believe this – we played in a Pro-Am tournament – professional player with amateur. As Mel was a five-handicap golfer, it was perhaps not quite so incredible, but I was a complete beginner and did not even have a handicap.

We had chosen a package deal holiday where golf was included in a very reasonable all-in price, the more so as a chauffeur driven car was included to take us to the course every day and collect us when we wished to return. When we arrived, we discovered a vast Edwardian-like hotel with huge crystal hanging chandeliers in the massive dining room, an immense foyer, a bedroom that could have been made into a flat, ballroom-size reception rooms but very few guests to be waited on by the innumerable members of staff. We learned later that before the war the hotel was filled with wealthy clients but those affluent days were gone and the owner had finally been obliged to consider offering package deals for the masses. We were among the first such arrivals.

The golf course was beautiful and for the first two days we were driven there and back and had leisurely rounds of golf. But on the third day, we were informed there was a Pro-Am in progress. Our driver had already returned to the hotel and when Mel explained our disappointment to the secretary, he told us with a delightful smile that we were not to concern ourselves; we could enjoy our game as arranged by the hotel; we could be fitted into the Pro-Am as soon as we were ready to play.

Had I had my own transport, I would have turned round and gone straight home! Mel, however, said we might as well do as had been suggested. It was of no consequence that I was a beginner. He would drive off first so it would be thought when I played that I had just had a bad first drive.

I was even more nervous when the official showed Mel on to the men's tee. The whole area was a teeming mass of golf fans who had come to watch their favourite players. Undaunted, Mel put down his ball and gave it a hefty thwack. This would normally have travelled around two hundred and forty yards, but on this occasion, it hit the metal sand box on the ladies' tee ten yards in front of us, ricocheted off and landed behind where he was standing.

In total panic, I hit my ball which, unbelievably, travelled a reasonable distance and then, thanking the Gods, we were off. It was a remarkable day. All the Pro-Am participants were incredibly kind and if we caught up with a foursome, they chatted to us whilst they waited to play off.

Towards the end I was almost beginning to enjoy myself until we came to the last hole – a short one – where two rows of people standing four deep lined the fairway and curved round the green. They were holding their programmes and, it seemed, every one was staring at me. I knew what they were thinking: who was this *signora* – the only female on the course? Was it a *signora* or perhaps a longhaired *signor*? Who on the list of professionals was less than five feet five?

'Use your five iron and for pity's sale, keep your head down!' Mel hissed as he went to drive off his tee. Mercifully, his ball hit the green and there was a loud burst of applause from our audience.

'Just keep your eye on the ball and HEAD DOWN!' Mel repeated as I put a ball on my tee peg.

It landed even nearer the flag than Mel's. I was in such a state of nerves, I don't now remember what I was feeling as we were clapped all the way to the green. I can only say that I have never forgotten that day, or indeed could it ever have been repeated. We both laugh when we look back on it, but I certainly wasn't laughing at the time!

My sister Eve's children were by now all married and her eldest daughter, Rosalind, and her artist husband, Milan, had produced Tim, Eve's first grandchild. The second was to come five years later when Susannah arrived. She was to grow up to be a talented musician like her Aunt Anne and her great grandfather. Anne was now playing regularly as first clarinettist in the Banbury Symphony Orchestra and, twenty-nine years later, Susannah has been travelling round Europe playing the flute in first her school and then in her university orchestras.

My own children were also married – Iain in February to a lovely girl called Heather, and Nicky to Arnold later that summer. She and Arnold had given up the antique shop in Bordeaux which they'd had to leave with a number of debts, and were now back in London working in an antique emporium in north London.

Graeme had had a somewhat chequered few years. After his failure to get into medical school, he was awarded a degree in engineering by Bath University – a second best choice. His main interest there had been in starting up a hot- air balloon club, spending valuable time sending hundreds of handwritten letters to businesses in order to find a sponsor. Having achieved his aim, he qualified as a pilot and later, came third in the National Hot Air Balloon Championships. He was eventually made safety Officer for the British Hot Air Balloon and Airship Club. Unlike Iain who had religiously worked his way up to a position of importance in his merchant bank, Graeme decided he did not want to be an engineer but preferred to join the recently modernised Metropolitan Police and help to put the world to rights.

After less than two years, during which time he and his girlfriend, Sarah, were married, he decided that the promised improvements in the police force were not taking place after all and that he was unable to improve anything, including some very obvious shortcomings, so he started up a printing franchise in Clapham not far from where Iain and Heather were now living.

In 1983, Heather and Iain presented me with my first grandchild, a little girl called Emily. I don't think I have ever been more thrilled – not even when Desmond had telephoned me about *Mavreen*! I now hoped that I would prove to be a really good grandmother as I knew when Heather married Iain that I would probably be about the worst mother-in-law a wife could have. I had not been called 'The General' by our young skiers for nothing! I warned Heather – and ultimately my second daughter-in-law, Sarah. The way to cope with me, I suggested, was to listen patiently to all my suggestions as to how to run their lives, tell me what really good ideas they were, and then as soon as I'd gone home, do whatever they meant to do in the first place. I promised that even were I to notice my ideas had been ignored I would never object.

Back in 1981 I somehow found time to write the first of my second trilogies, *The Chatelaine*. This was followed by *The Wilderling*. These two have turned out to be my personal favourites of all my books. They were duly published in America but Desmond switched my publisher from Bantam's to Ballantine's and I did not get on too well with the editor who had taken over from my wonderful Bantam's editor, Linda Price. Certainly neither of these books nor the subsequent third in the trilogy, *Fool's Curtain*, made the same headlines as *Mavreen*, *Tamarisk* and *Chantal*.

Desmond, who was both my agent and publisher, had now built Arlington Books into a significant publishing company. Jilly Cooper and Leslie Thomas were but two of his best-known authors.

By March 1983, Desmond was so busy with his growing number of authors and his frequent trips to the States that I felt he no longer had the time to nurture my career. My paperback English publisher, Transworld, suddenly refused to buy the rights of one of my books. I was devastated by this sudden announcement, not least because I had a wonderful editor, Diane Pearson, who, an author herself, I found completely compatible, and I had no desire for a change. When I asked Transworld why they were no longer interested I was told that my agent had bumped up the figure for the advance to one that was impossible to achieve in sales. It was pointed out to me that the costs of productions were steadily rising and there was a limit to the number of sales big books such as mine could achieve.

I understood his point but Desmond disagreed. It was by putting a high price on something that it became a valuable and 'wanted' object, was his reasoning. I felt it would be better if I had a separate agent who was not also my publisher. Naturally I had no wish to lose Desmond as my hardback publisher. I wrote asking him if he would agree to my going back to Curtis Brown who had originally been my literary agents, whilst remaining one of his authors.

I suppose I should have known better. Desmond was very sensitive and he took this request to be an act of extreme disloyalty on my part. It was, he pointed out, he who had created 'Claire Lorrimer' and 'made her the popular novelist she now was'. He now no longer wished to publish me and I could remove myself elsewhere.

We had been together for almost ten years and had Desmond proclaimed that he was still as enthusiastic about my career as ever he had been, I don't think it would have taken much for me to be talked into leaving things as they were. But Jilly Cooper was really hitting the headlines and in his smart new premises in Mayfair and with many more successes since *Mavreen* had hit the big time, I felt he really was too involved to have more than a cursory interest. So we came to the parting of the ways. I don't think he ever forgave me although we did meet subsequently at a book launch where we exchanged polite remarks. Otherwise I did not hear from him and he ignored my Christmas cards. I was invited to his funeral twenty years later when I wrote a tribute to him. But for him, I would never in a thousand years have written an historical romance, so he was as much responsible for the ultimate fifteen of them as he had been for *Mavreen*, and I will always owe him a big debt of gratitude.

I don't think Desmond would disagree that *Mavreen*

played a very large part in putting his fledgling publishing company, Arlington Books, on the American map. After all, on the strength of the success of *Mavreen*, he had been able to launch Richard Doyle and obtain half a million dollar advance for a two-book contract for him. So Desmond and I were mutually beneficial and I was saddened to hear of his death.

My new agent from thenceforth was Anthea Morton Saner of Curtis Brown and it was she who secured a contract for me from Rosie Cheetham of Century Publishing for my sixth historical saga. Rosie published *Last Year's Nightingale* in 1984 and arranged for me to speak at one of the *Yorkshire Post* Literary Luncheons in company with Sandy Gall, Jan Leeming and Leslie Thomas.

Despite the publicity tours of the country I had carried out under my publicist Tony Mulliken's umbrella, talking on radio stations and to newspaper reviewers, I was still nervous when I was obliged to appear in public. At the *Yorkshire Post* lunch, I was supposed to be the third speaker but was unexpectedly announced second. As I rose to my feet, the elderly gentleman on my left moved to pull back my chair for me and upset his glass of red wine all over me and the table in front of me. He was so upset that I felt obliged to comfort him while a waiter mopped up, and by then I had forgotten to be nervous and, hopefully, was able to give my speech without too many ums and ers.

The book signing session which concluded the lunch was less of an ordeal than I had feared, imagining no one would ask me to sign a book. Desmond had once told me a story about an author's book signing session in a shop when no one at all had turned up. The manager of the shop then surreptitiously alerted his staff to go out of the back door, in by the front and keep going up to the author as they went round for a second time or third. If the author had happened to look up and recognise one of them, they were to say they had forgotten to get a copy of the book for their aunt.

I had thought that story very funny until I sat at that table waiting for the first would-be fan to approach me. To my relief, some did!

During the year Nicky and Arnold were selling antiques in an emporium in north London, their relationship was deteriorating and Nicky discovered Arnold was having an affair with one of their clients. Nicky had been seriously thinking of leaving him and this discovery was the catalyst – she told him the marriage was over. Arnold now showed himself in his true colours. Whilst she was away on a walking holiday with a girlfriend, he removed their entire stock.

Within a few days, Nicky discovered he had stored them in a barn in Nottinghamshire whose address she was given by one of their friends. The only problem in retrieving them lay in the fact that Arnold had cleverly listed the goods as HIS personal property. Would she be permitted to repossess them? Many had been given to Nicky either as wedding presents or by her grandmother when she'd moved to a smaller house, and were of quite some value. She telephoned to tell us what had happened.

Mel now decided the time had come for him to intervene. He had suspected Arnold of falsifying the accounts in Spain, and later, pointed out to me that Arnold, rather than using his own name, had cleverly put the Bordeaux antique shop in Nicky's maiden name. When that had got into financial difficulties, it had been Nicky's responsibility to clear the debts. Mel was now in no doubt that Arnold had been using the few profits they made in Bordeaux to buy and sell goods behind Nicky's back. Aware that Nicky, his meal ticket, was about to leave him, he was now trying to take possession of her few remaining assets.

Nottinghamshire adjoined Leicestershire and after so

many years in business in the area, there was hardly a farmer Mel did not know. He also had a great many friends and business acquaintances through his sporting activities and other social contacts. This proved of enormous benefit as he knew the owner of the barn where Arnold had stored Nicky's belongings.

It was only a short time before Mel made contact with him and managed to persuade his friend (who at first insisted that he could not release the goods to anyone but Arnold), that they rightfully belonged to Nicky. Mel now arranged for one of his firm's big lorries to collect them immediately before Arnold could sell or move them elsewhere. There was one snag, however, and it proved to be a big one – it was snowing heavily. Nevertheless, the lorry was dispatched with two stalwart men, who arrived safely enough but had a nightmare journey back as the snow was falling even more heavily and even the main road traffic was down to a crawl.

The furniture – what there was of it, for some had already been sold by Arnold as we now discovered – was stored for a short while at Mel's business premises. It was then put into an auction in Nottingham where we were able to recoup quite a lot of money for Nicky. Undoubtedly Arnold would have sold it all and kept the proceeds but for Mel's very timely intervention.

Arnold now tried to reclaim the antiques we had sold so I put the matter into the hands of London lawyers. Retrospectively it was a question of throwing good money after bad. Although Arnold was ultimately taken to court, there was no financial recompense for Nicky, and the lawyers' bills ran into thousands of pounds. There was one small moment of satisfaction – the lawyers did manage to get Arnold put in prison for 'non-compliance with Court Orders'.

Subsequently the divorce came through by which time

Arnold had moved to Foye where he was living with the girl with whom he had been having the affair. She was of similar background to Nicky and had been an air hostess. Using her savings, Arnold bought a restaurant which he put in her name. Learning of this from an old friend of Arnold's, Nicky did try to warn the girl that all the debts Arnold would undoubtedly accrue would be her responsibility. But she was as gullible as Nicky had been. The restaurant inevitably ran into heavy debt and Arnold disappeared leaving his girlfriend and their two-year-old child with the creditors on her back. Some while later, Arnold repeated his fraudulent behaviour with yet another woman, and may probably still be doing so. Needless to say, we all agreed to take more notice of Mel's opinion if he thought some new contact was untrustworthy even when he could not justify it.

Our frequent trips to Spain gave me the idea for my next big book which was to be published by Century. I chose the Spanish Civil War as the historical period not only because of its obvious plot possibilities and the details I'd learned from my cousin, Buzz, who had been a participant, but because as children, my sisters and I had been to Andalucia five years before that bitter conflict had taken place. My mother had found a beautiful Spanish hacienda called Santa Clara on a rocky promontory below which was a tiny sardine fishing village. The hacienda was owned by a Spanish girl who had married a Rhodes scholar and between them they had converted the stables surrounding the outer courtyard into accommodation for visitors. On the edge of the Mediterranean, there was a path down from the hacienda to a deserted beach. To the north were orchards of orange and lemon trees and great expanses of olive trees. Near the garden were fields of sugar cane. The place was called Torremolinos.

It is impossible for people arriving today in the huge

skyscraper, burger-bar, English-pub environment of
Torremolinos to imagine the peaceful isolation of that tiny
part of the coast when my mother took us with our governess
to holiday there three Easters in a row in the early 1930s.
To get there, we had a horrible four-day boat trip to Gibraltar
there being no aeroplane service in those days. Nor did the
boats have stabilisers and I was invariably seasick when
we sailed through the Bay of Biscay. From Gibraltar we
were driven by taxi along the coast road to Malaga. The
sides of the road were cobbled as the main form of transport consisted of donkeys. These were laden with heavy
panniers hanging from their sides and as often as not, a
man sat astride the heavily laden animal as well.

We loved the donkey rides and picnics up in the hills
almost as much as we loved playing on the sandy beach
which we had all to ourselves with the exception of our
audience – an ever present group of small, brown-faced,
dark-eyed Spanish children who came to stare mainly at
my two sisters who were a curiosity to them being very
blonde and blue eyed. We also loved watching the sardine
boats coming in at the end of the day and seeing the men
offload their catch of fish. The village air always smelt of
fish frying in olive oil. Another pleasure was to watch the
owner of a herd of goats, their bells ringing when he came
to our hacienda in the mornings. He milked them in the
yard according to our needs. There were cows in the farms
but they were infected with tuberculosis and foreigners
were not supposed to drink cows' milk. As it was, I loved
goats' milk, still warm and frothy straight from the jug.

That was in the 1930s and the poverty for most of the
Andalucian people was rife although we children were
unaware of it. Whilst crops were harvested and sold in
spring and summer, the farmers and their families were
often starving in the winter when they had little or nothing
to sell. The fishermen, too, were totally dependent upon

their catch. Ten years after the Spanish Civil War, that isolated coast became the Costa del Sol, a popular tourist region, and sadly its former beauty disappeared beneath the concrete. The orchards and olive groves along the road from Malaga to Gibraltar gave way to a wide coast road and then a motorway, and the golden sands were buried beneath beach cafés, sun umbrellas and lounge chairs. Torremolinos became all but a city of skyscrapers and Santa Clara, our hacienda, no longer exists. However, the population must have welcomed these many new vast openings for employment and the huge influx of wealth from the tourists that has ensued.

Mel and I decided to research the parts of Spain which had been the scenes of such terrible fighting during the Civil War, a war which was so much the worse for the fact that families were often divided, the Republicans against the fascist Franco's invading army. We drove the car to Paris and then took the night train to Madrid. From there we drove slowly south over the mountains through beautiful old towns such as Toledo where I could talk to the inhabitants, see castles and dungeons and battlefields.

I learned then that more soldiers died from frost and cold in those mountains than died in battles during the whole of the war. That was when I decided to call my book *Frost in the Sun*. There was so much to write about that the book ended up over seven hundred pages long. Although it was published twenty years ago, some copies still remain in the libraries and continue to be a popular read for anyone going to the Costa del Sol who will find places, names and even people who are familiar!

CHAPTER 18

On May 1st, 1985, my mother died. The news was reported on the radio and on television throughout the day and there was hardly a newspaper which did not carry an obituary. It was a comfort to me and my sisters that she would have been so pleased with the publicity. She had written one hundred and eighty-nine books which were published all over the world, and I have copies of every English-language novel in all its formats in my study. It is quite remarkable that although it is now twenty-one years since her death, her library returns show that she is still being very widely read. Her books continue to be reprinted in large print and recorded on audio cassette and I sometimes get letters from faithful fans who want to know where they can find past novels.

A memorial service was held at St. Bride's church in Fleet Street at which my son, Iain, read the Lesson and my sister Anne, now a professional musician, played Rachmaninov's 'Vocalise', a clarinet solo which was one of my mother's favourite pieces. It was very moving. As she had lived to her late eighties, many of her contemporaries had died, but despite this, the church was full and there were many celebrities there.

For the previous three years, my mother was in a nursing home following the onset of Alzheimer's. It seemed such a very sad and inappropriate end to her long, creative life. For a short while, she continued to know us but she also knew something was very wrong with her brain and as her thought processes deteriorated, she became more and more distressed. It was therefore a relief to us all when finally she was unaware of her surroundings, and it was then rather than when she died that I knew she had left us and I mourned her loss. We had become very close in the latter part of her life when we were able to look back on my stormy childhood with mutual understanding. Her autobiography *Stranger Than Fiction* was reprinted when she died and I wrote a new foreword for it in which I expressed the comfort it gave me to remember how often she expressed her continual pleasure in following the progress of my career. She was the most generous person, not only with her wealth but also with her love. Her greatest pleasure where her own work was concerned was in knowing how many thousands of hours of happiness she had given to her readers – so often a longed-for escape from their often humdrum lives.

In my foreword to her autobiography, I wrote:

For a woman who wrote so many billions of words about love, it is perhaps not surprising that it was more important to her than anything else in the world. She believed in it utterly and I have little doubt that she would wish not only to be remembered with love but as its purveyor. Perhaps it was part of her own particular brand of genius that she could inspire it not only in her family but in all those who knew her personally and through her books.

Glad though I was that she was at long last at peace, I missed her in many ways. Quite often in the past, I took a manuscript over to her for her comments, or I asked her advice about a new plot. Sometimes she discussed her work with me. In a way, we both strove for different goals. Her stories were mainly about love as women wanted it to be – a wonderful form of escapism. I have always tried to be more realistic! With any book I have written, I asked myself at the start: 'Could this really happen in real life?' If it couldn't, I scrapped that idea and found a more realistic scenario. My mother and I often debated the subject. She acknowledged that in real life some men were selfish, dogmatic, unfaithful, unkind, unromantic and so on but, she maintained, women didn't want their heroes to have any faults. The villains were villains and the heroes must be perfect in every way. However, I thought that my highwayman in *Mavreen* was far more attractive as a bit of a rogue than if he had led an exemplary life!

I have no doubt that but for my mother's influence I might never have become an author. When I am invited to give talks about my work, I always invite questions at the end. Sooner or later, someone remarks that I must have inherited this ability from my mother. Having given the matter a great deal of thought, I don't think this is true. I think it was the environmental influence – seeing my mother busy at her typewriter and deciding with a great deal of encouragement from her to do the same.

I was an imaginative child and my mother actively encouraged it once she saw that writing my 'good ideas' as stories avoided the frequent disasters that occurred when they were unchannelled. With very few exceptions, I believe all children are born with vivid imaginations, but remarks such as: 'There's a horrible big bear in the garden' or: 'My (non-existent) friend wants a lollipop, too,' are nearly always greeted with: 'Don't be silly', or: 'Don't tell fibs!' and make-believe soon gets lost. I was lucky in another way, too, when my little sister believed everything I told her and asked for more!

Very often at the end of one of my talks, someone will come up to me and tell me they had always wanted to write a book but didn't have the time to do so. I point out that four foolscap pages should produce about a thousand words and that everyone has time to write four pages a day. In sixty or seventy days, the book is written! That's not quite fair as editing it, planning it, typing it, can all take a great deal of time, but today with computers it really is a lot easier than in my day when for twenty-five years I banged out thousands upon thousands of words on a second-hand portable non-electric typewriter.

The other excuse would-be authors make is that they don't know what to write about. I always quote Joy, my former secretary, who said the same thing for three years and then won a prize for her novel and wrote three more. Getting a book published is, I admit, a lot more difficult these days than it was when I started. Then, if a publisher thought an author had potential, he would publish a book in the expectation that the ensuing ones would be even better! Nowadays, except in very rare cases, it is an entirely commercial decision – will the book sell well? If not, no matter its literary merit, or the fact that it could appeal to a limited market, it is unlikely to be accepted. A potential writer has to make up their mind whether their subject matter is one that interests them or a mass market! It is quite unnerving to know that the exposure in the bookshops of a newly published paperback is very limited. Miracles, however, do happen, as illustrated by the Harry Potter books.

The year of 1985, apart from the personal sadness of my mother's death, had other unhappy events such as the horrible deaths of fifty-six football fans at the Bradford ground when the stands collapsed. As many died in that dreadful event as did in the fatal airplane crash carrying the Manchester football team. Even sadder for us was the fatal heart attack Neill had only a year after my mother's death.

On a happier note I acquired another granddaughter, Jemma, Iain and Heather's second child. Their firstborn, Emily, was a delight and Mel and I loved her visits. Mel built a little wooden house with diamond paned windows for her, complete with tiny kitchen which had running water, a bookcase and a miniature ironing board. We installed the baby alarm so that she could pretend to telephone us in the house. He also made a shop with a colourful awning under which the toddlers stood to serve tiny packets of groceries and, needless to say, dolly mixtures. I think we enjoyed watching the children play as much as they enjoyed being shopkeepers. Emily is now twenty-two years old and studying economics at Leeds University!

My Spanish Civil War book, *Frost in the Sun* was published by Century in 1986. It was chosen by Leisure Circle for their Book Club edition, and a paperback edition appeared the following year. Some time later, a large-print edition was published by Thorpe and the paperback was reprinted in 2001. Like all the other historical sagas, the stories don't date as contemporary novels can do since they are fixed in time by their content. An audio version was produced a year later.

Although I was happy to see *Frost in the Sun* in print (not that I liked the covers for the hardback or the paperback versions over which I, alas, had no control) I was now totally engrossed in the preparation of a new venture – a biography. Watching a television documentary one evening, I was intrigued by the story of a woman who fostered over thirty children to whom she was their 'Mum'. Most of these children had been physically or sexually abused and it was beyond the ability of Social Services to cope with them. This woman, Jeanette Roberts, succeeded where all else had failed – and she achieved this miracle with love.

It struck me very forcibly that here was a different kind of love to the man/woman variety which was the basis of all my books. Could I, perhaps, write about this extraordinary woman who was devoting her whole life to these damaged children? I rang the TV programme producer and obtained Jeanette Roberts' telephone number. I then called her. She wasted no time telling me there was another author already engaged in writing her life story. I was disappointed – but not for long. Within a month, Jeanette rang me to say she had not liked the angle the author had adopted and would I like to go down to Essex and see her?

That phone call began a remarkable year. Every fortnight, Pennie and I would go down to Essex where Jeanette and her colleague Joyce Nash lived with all the children in a disused convent in a village outside Chelmsford. Pennie had a tape recorder and taped Jeanette's replies to my questions. Both diffident and reserved Jeanette was not the most communicative of people and it was some time before she relaxed and accepted us as friends. It was then she told me (and it was the first time she had ever spoken of it) that she had been sexually abused by her father which was why she had such an extraordinary empathy with the children. They were of all ages and abilities and without exception, were lovely kids, smiling, happy and immensely caring of each other and adoring of their foster mother and Joyce. It was one of the happiest homes I had ever been in. They all helped one another, the elder children caring for the younger and everyone assisting in the household chores. There was little or no money and they lived from day to day, supplementing their meals with charitable food that was shortly to reach its sell-by-date from Marks and Spencer.

After such a visit, Pennie would transcribe the tapes on to paper and using these for reference, I wrote the next chapter of Jeanette's remarkable life. We both became personally involved with the family and from time to time Mel, too, would come on one of our visits. The children loved him. There were few men in that establishment so the boys appreciated his interest in them. My publisher at that time, Rosie Cheetham, of Century, also became personally interested and arranged for a literary lawyer to vet my finished book, which I called *House of Tomorrow*, to ensure we were not going to be sued by any of the social workers who Jeanette so often justifiably criticised; or, indeed, by the parents who had abused their children whose stories I told. Rosie also agreed to employ Tony Mulliken to arrange a publicity tour to promote the book.

The tour turned out to be a major undertaking including as it did five or six radio or newspaper interviews a day all over the country lasting a week. Mel came with us, as by now Tony and his wife, Pam, had become personal friends and Mel and Tony's easy manner and jokes helped to put a very shy and reluctant Jeanette at ease. As a novel launch for a book, we arranged a boat trip down the Thames for all the children and I was able to persuade Jon (Pertwee) to join us which he did in his full Worzel Gummidge regalia, much to the children's delight. The reviews poured in. A popular woman's magazine published a long article about Jeanette and the book. *Everyman* television programme ran two documentaries on her and unusually allowed us to have an appeal for funds at the end.

These documentaries brought in sackfuls of letters (which Pennie and I handled for Jeanette) nearly all containing donations and or offers of help. This continued for several weeks and I was reminded of the days when sackfuls of applications for pets had arrived at Little Surries all those years ago!

Several countries in Europe bought rights and most beneficial of all to Jeanette and the children, was the formation of a Trust set up by a Christian group of London City businessmen. They were able to purchase the dilapidated convent for the family and introduce some major improvements. 'Odd Fellows' chose *House of Tomorrow* for their Social Awareness category Book Award, and the *Mail on*

Sunday's magazine featured it. With all the publicity generated, the book was enormously widely read and as a result, the subject of child sexual abuse was brought to the attention of a large number of people who had suffered similar abuse in their childhood. Letter after letter arrived stating that they had never before felt able to talk about it and how doing so now was helping them to come to terms with it. This, of course, had been Jeanette's objective when she revealed her own damaged childhood despite the fact that her revelations were proving painfully evocative.

When I had first thought of writing that book these repercussions had not crossed my mind, but I am so glad that I followed through the momentary idea to do so. Jeanette and I are still in touch and I receive regular newsletters about the children, many of whom she has adopted and who have now provided her with grandchildren.

I myself was presented with yet another granddaughter, Charlotte, this time by Graeme and Sarah. A few years later she laboriously typed her first story about a room which the sun refused to visit, using the typewriter in my study. The picture of me at work in my study was taken by the photographer of the Leisure Circle Book Club when they came to interview me.

The question I am most often asked has to be: 'Where do you get your ideas?' Not out of the ether! Usually they are sparked by some incident or happening such as the television programme about Jeanette. My next book was sparked by the hurricane in October of that following year, 1987. In Kent, we suffered a great deal of damage and personally lost a row of lovely old Bramley apple trees. However, the huge fifty foot high old walnut tree growing only a few yards from the house, did not fall on the roof as I had feared it might. It would certainly have caved in the roof as well as the south wall, and I started to imagine the after effects of such damage. This thought led to the idea for my next historical saga, *Ortolans*. Once again, I wanted to write something a little different – in this case, how an old house affected the generations of the family who lived in it, rather than the other way round. I wrote the story in three parts – the prologue set in 1588 when the house was built; part one in 1788, part two in 1888 and part three in contemporary times. In each case, the house itself played a major part in the families' lives. The book was published in 1991 and was a Book Club Associates choice for that year. Among sundry other editions, it was translated into Braille for the blind. The most recent reprint was in 2001.

By now I had acquired four more grandchildren, Graeme's two sons Thomas and Arthur and Iain's third daughter, Polly. A few years after her divorce from Arnold, Nicky had married David Goodhew, a fellow student at the Horticultural College she was attending in order to pursue her wish to become a professional gardener. Unlike our feelings for Arnold, we all took to Dave who shared Nicky's love of nature. After their marriage, they moved to Gloucester where, hardworking and industrious, Dave became manager of a nearby fruit farm. The following year they produced their first child, a little girl called Matilda, known to us all as Tilly. Three years later, their son, Max, was born. This brought the final total of my grandchildren to eight. It remains to be seen if any of them will end up with careers in writing.

My niece, Rosalind, however, by this time a lecturer in the Linguistic Department at Lancaster University, was to publish four very academic titles in the last four years of the 20th century. Her younger sister, Annabel, also published three books, one called *The Islands In Between*, on her experiences in Indonesia; and two further books during her career as a counsellor. She was further involved in the writing of two television documentaries. Their brother,

Murray, was not a writer but a seller of books and had a successful career as a salesman for Hodder & Stoughton's books to foreign countries.

The year 1988 was overshadowed for me by the death of our very much-loved Springer Spaniel Bogart (named when we had acquired him fifteen years earlier when we still had Humphrey, the Great Dane). We had all known he would not live a great deal longer but to my everlasting distress, he was killed when I, myself, ran him over. He had been underneath my car when I started it up and not knowing he was there, I moved off. It was small consolation that he died instantly but I had nightmares for a long time afterwards and my heart goes out to anyone who has the even more terrible misfortune to run over a child.

Elsewhere in the world, far more terrible things were happening – the massacre in Tiananmen Square, the Lockerbie air disaster, the deaths of over fifty young people when the river boat, *Marchioness*, sank in the Thames. Terry Waite was still a hostage in Beirut and Sadam Hussein had invaded Kuwait.

During those years in the eighties, I wrote another historical saga called *The Spinning Wheel* and had published a book of short stories called *Variations*. Quite recently, Arthur took it into his head to read several of the stories as I had told him that they were often inspired by events in his father's and my own childhood. They caused him to laugh out loud and he took the book home so he could read more of them. I am now in the process of completing a second volume.

Although I wrote every morning and most afternoons – on a word processor which all but eliminated my faithful typewriter – I always took time off when the grandchildren came to stay. Graeme had stored his hot air balloon in our garage and, now a qualified instructor, he often took us hot air ballooning which was great fun. He flew commercially as well as privately and this augmented his income which was much needed as his printing franchise was not doing at all well, which Mel had forecast from the beginning. He finally packed it up and with Sarah's patient agreement, went off to live in a caravan near Peterborough where he had a job as a flying instructor having made up his mind to become an airline pilot as soon as he had logged sufficient hours to get his licence. It took over a year but he finally achieved his ambition and got a job at Gatwick as a pilot for Cityflyers. Now, ten years later, he is a Captain flying short haul for British Airways.

During that time, Iain had been head hunted by Henderson Administration and moved his family to a beautiful house in Dulwich where the three girls went to school. It was always a great joy going to visit them as it was such a happy household. Then Heather had to have a mastectomy but the operation went well and for the four following years she was in the best of health.

I continued to write, although by 1991 I had reached the ripe old age of seventy. Not that I felt my age, although I did have to have a stent put in a blocked artery. Mel and I played golf whenever the weather was fine in England, and nearly every day when we went abroad, which we did twice a year. We always went to the same hotel knowing that apart from the perfect golf courses in the area, we could dance in the evenings in the bar where they still played our vintage dance music. I felt the time had come now for me to retire but first I wanted to write the third of a trilogy about the Rochford family. *The Chatelaine* and *The Wilderling* were my favourite books and I now settled down to write *Fool's Curtain* which was to be the last of my 'big' books. It was published in 1992 but was not after all the last one, despite my intentions.

That year I wrote *The Silver Link*. I didn't mean to but many years earlier, not long after Mel and I had moved into Chiswell Barn, during a shopping expedition, I had run into one of my new neighbours. I smiled and said 'hullo' but to my chagrin, she virtually cut me dead. I was aware that I barely knew her but it upset me that she had not even returned my greeting. I said as much to Pennie who informed me that I must have run into the identical twin sister who I'd not known existed. I thought about identical twinship on one of my walks, wondering who, if not their parents, could tell one from another. Could their husbands? Surely in the intimacies of the marital bed, a man would know if he was making love to someone not his wife?

I decided to forget about it but the possibility of a story haunted me at night-time when I wanted to go to sleep until finally, all those years later, I realised that the idea was not going to go away until I had written the story. Not, I decided, about twin girls as I didn't want to upset my neighbour! I would write about twin boys. This ended up as *The Silver Link*. I was particularly pleased with the ending which I had decided upon before I started! The book was published in 1993.

In April I had to go into St Thomas's for a second blocked heart artery. As I left the hospital and thanked my surgeon for the successful operation, he said in a cheerful voice:

'See you again soon!'

'I sincerely hope not,' I replied, whereupon he informed me that if I continued smoking (and I smoked thirty to forty cigarettes a day) I would almost certainly be back and next time I might not be so lucky as to survive. This warning coincided with the heartbreaking news that Heather not only had bone cancer, but that it was in her liver and blood, too. She had only a limited time left.

Realising that Iain's three girls would soon be motherless, I decided they must at least be able to count upon a grand-mother and I immediately stopped smoking. It wasn't easy but all our thoughts were with Iain and his family. Heather was indescribably brave, carrying on a normal life as long as she could. Once or twice I had to rush up to London to look after the children when she was having a bad day, but her two best girlfriends who lived nearby were nearly always on hand to offer support. That Easter, Iain took her and the girls on a last holiday to our hotel in Spain where, she told me, she had spent a wonderful week. I promised her I would always be there for the girls, particularly for the youngest, Polly, who was still only eight years old. Heather did not want to go into hospital or a hospice, and she died on 26th June at home.

I went up to Dulwich that morning – a beautiful sunny day, and sat in the garden with the children who were still too shocked to fully appreciate they would never see their mother again. Iain stayed rigidly in control until two days later at the funeral. It was a terrible time for him as theirs had been a wonderfully happy and successful marriage. Iain decided that despite the tragic memories the house now held, it would be best for the girls to stay in their home and at the same schools where as much as possible in their lives would remain unchanged.

For the rest of the summer, he looked after the girls and himself on his own but when he returned to work after the summer holiday, he engaged a delightful former friend of Heather's who had recently been through a divorce to look after them. Lucy moved in and for the next few years, took care of the house and Polly. Emily and Jemma were happy as boarders at Woldingham Girls School in Surrey and Polly was the most disturbed by her mother's death. Lucy was wonderfully patient and understanding. She finally left to move back to her home environment where she got married and had a baby daughter of her own.

It is difficult for me to give enough praise to my eldest son for the way in which he not only coped after Heather's death but was in every respect both father and mother to his girls. And throughout the years they were growing up, he maintained his responsible position at Hendersons and eventually was appointed to the main board of directors. Every weekend and holiday was devoted to his daughters' welfare and yet they were never spoilt. All three have done extremely well at school, and the younger two have, like Emily, gone to university. They are sweet, loving, thoughtful children, caring for one another – Emily in particular, took on a motherly, elder sister role – and are devoted to their father to whom they owe so much. I know I am not the only one whose admiration for Iain is total. If Heather were here, she would be proud of him and her girls.

The notorious death of Princess Di and her lover in Paris occurred in 1997, a mystery still unresolved; but far more meaningful for me was the death of my former secretary and great friend Joy Tait, who had played such an important role in the conception of Claire Lorrimer.

Two years later, shortly before the end of the century, my brother-in-law John, Eve's beloved husband, died. They were married during the war and in all those long years since, they had only ever spent one week apart. It was a terrible blow to my sister, although John had been ill for some time and she knew he was going to die. We were all deeply concerned about her as she seemed to bury herself in her grief and was unwilling to leave the house where she believed his spirit still hovered.

Mel rose magnificently to the occasion. We would take her to the Incosol, our wonderfully luxurious hotel in Spain, he said. Eve and John had not been well off and he would pay all the considerable expenses. If she refused to come with us, I was to say that I was so worried about leaving her, I wouldn't go if she did not come too. The ruse worked as afterwards Eve admitted she had not wanted to leave her home but did so in order that I wouldn't miss out on my holiday. When she finally reached the hotel where Mel had organised a two-room suite so she could be near us, Eve began really to enjoy the change, the sun, the wonderful food and, as she was a keen bird watcher, the wildlife. It was a holiday we repeated the following year and to which Eve could now look forward. I telephoned her at home every night just to let her know someone was interested in her day's happenings as I guessed how difficult life must be when for fifty years there was always someone nearby with whom to talk over the day.

I will always be immensely grateful to Mel for helping to make those few years of Eve's life tolerable for her as, sadly for me, she died very suddenly three years after John's death. Although she suffered from glaucoma she was never ill and would not have known of the sudden blood clot to her brain. Her eyesight had been fading rapidly and she would soon have lost her sight completely, so in many ways her death was merciful. Moreover, she never stopped wanting to join John. Anne, Eve's children and I remind ourselves of this and have agreed never to wish her back with us as she would not have wanted to come.

CHAPTER 19

'Are you going to have an 80th birthday party, Granny?' asked Emily, my eldest granddaughter.

I hadn't thought too much about it but now, seeing the expectant look on her face, I said that I was going to think of something special to celebrate this landmark in my life, something different, out of the ordinary; something the family would always remember. Emily was filled with curiosity which I could not satisfy even had I wanted to since I did not have the slightest idea what we could do.

February 1st, 2001 was only a month away. It was time I came up with a 'good idea'. Fortunately for me, that morning in the study, Pennie informed me that amongst the morning post was payment for the reissue by House of Stratus for several of my earlier titles, including *Relentless Storm* which I had written twenty-five years previously. I could not remember much about it other than that the background was of the mountains, involving an avalanche and skiers, the descriptions derived from my childhood skiing venues at school in Switzerland. I thought back to later years when I took the children skiing; when I had been with my mother to her favourite resort, Crans, where we celebrated our joint birthday; when Mel and I had been to the same place one summer to walk in the mountains. I thought, too, of the four younger grandchildren who had never yet seen the mountains let alone been skiing – and that was when I knew what I wanted to do for my 80th party – I would take the whole family to Crans for a weekend.

'That's crazy!' Mel said. 'This is February you are talking about. It will probably be snowing and no one will be able to ski.'

'It will be very expensive!' Pennie warned me when I asked her to look up possible flights from Heathrow airport or Gatwick, or from Birmingham, near Graeme's family.

'The children will be at school until four p.m. on Friday,' Graeme warned. 'We'd only have Saturday and Sunday morning to ski!'

'You'll never be able to find a chalet at the last minute,' Iain warned.

I was now determined to go; the more so when Emily said she thought the idea really cool! We would not stay in a chalet but in the five-star Golf Hotel, I decided, and Pennie duly booked the accommodation. Further enquiries showed we could all get a train from Geneva at six o'clock on Friday evening to take us to Sierre, the railway halt where a minibus from the hotel would take us up the mountain to Crans. Now it was only a matter of coordinating flights so that we were all at Geneva in time to catch the train.

'You'll never do it!' Mel warned. 'Suppose the flights are delayed. There is only a half hour after landing before the train leaves!'

'I've booked train tickets!' I told him, wondering if I was, in fact, heading for a dreadful fiasco.

I rang the sports shop in Crans and asked them to find me a ski instructor who would take the beginners. A delightful Madame Hug telephoned me to say she would be pleased to take on the children.

'I'm anxious that the boys will have learned enough by Sunday morning to go down a red run,' I told her. 'They are very athletic. Can you do it?' She would try, she promised. Charlotte had already been skiing with her school and Iain's girls had often enjoyed winter holidays skiing with their father. Nicky's younger children would go tobogganing on the nursery slopes. With everyone's agreement, albeit with Mel's misgivings, flights, train, and hotel were booked. It was Tom's thirteenth birthday within a few days of mine and I asked the hotel to be sure to organise a birthday cake.

Mel looked increasingly worried as the last of the arrangements was finalised. He tried not to show it seeing how much I, as well as the children, was looking forward to the trip. I suppose I *was* tempting Fate – there was so much which could go wrong. Apart from the weather and the possible flight delays, there were eight young children involved any one of which might develop chicken pox or measles or simply fall downstairs and twist an ankle. I determined not to think about it. Nothing ventured, nothing gained, I told myself.

On the whole, my life had been far from blameless and I had no reason to suppose that God would look down on me now! But he certainly did. Our flights to Geneva landed exactly on time. The fourteen of us raced through customs and along the corridor leading to the railway station. We boarded the train waiting by the platform with five minutes to spare. Needless to say, the Swiss train, too, was exactly on time and with its usual efficiency we reached Sierre where the hotel mini-bus awaited us. The younger children who had never seen deep snow before, peered eagerly out into the darkness as we wound our way up to Crans.

The accommodation the hotel arranged for us was faultless and when we had sorted ourselves out and unpacked, we went down to the bar where Iain had organised a champagne toast to start the festivities. The excitement mounted as by now a trifle tired, the children discussed the next day's skiing. The forecast was good, the waiter told us. It should be a fine day.

The disappointment next morning when we came down to breakfast was acute as we looked out of the windows to see a complete whiteout. It was snowing – huge white flakes falling relentlessly from an invisible sky. Not even the ski guides would be on the slopes in this weather. The waiter did his best to cheer us up. It would have stopped snowing by ten o'clock, he promised. We would have a lovely sunny day.

Madame Hug arrived and endorsed the waiter's forecast and she set off at once with the children to hire the necessary skis and boots and toboggans for Tilly and Max. Miraculously, by the time everyone was equipped, the snowing had stopped and the sun was sparkling brilliantly in a cloudless blue sky. With fresh powder snow under foot, skiing conditions could not have been better.

Mel and I met the family for lunch at the foot of one of the ski runs. Tom and Arty had made such good progress that Madame seemed confidant they would manage a red run next day. Meanwhile, Tilly and Max decided they wanted to learn to ski so Madame spent the afternoon with them whilst the boys skied with Charlotte and their mother and father. That evening, when everyone returned to the hotel, the children plunged into the indoor heated pool while the grownups sat watching them from the overlooking bar. As we went to our room to change for the birthday dinner, Mel said:

'So far so good!' He had been sleepless the night before worrying that my 80th party idea was going to be a flop. 'Now, at least there has been one perfect day,' he said.

The hotel triumphed with a magnificent meal and a wonderful birthday cake with spun sugar and enough candles for Tom if not for me! Sunday dawned as perfect a day as Saturday and, as predicted, Madame was able to take Tom and Arthur down a red run to show off their new skills to their parents. We all gathered back at the hotel to grab a quick lunch and finished packing before the bus took us down to Sierre to catch our train to Geneva.

I suppose it was a hopelessly extravagant weekend which, as a magnificent birthday present, Mel paid for. But I don't regret a single minute of it. Graeme made me a super video of the weekend from start to finish, and Iain gave me an album of pictures entitled *Mum's 80th Birthday* which is my favourite book. All the grandchildren are now, five years later, accomplished skiers and we still exchange Christmas cards with Madame Hug.

The whole family enjoyed another holiday together the following year when Iain invited us all that summer to the lovely house he'd had built in Portugal. It was on the edge of a golf course and despite our advancing years, Mel and I still enjoyed playing golf as well as swimming in Iain's pool.

Later that year, after reading an article in the newspaper about surrogacy, I decided to write one last book as the theme interested me. Was surrogacy really something new or did it go on in the past, I wondered? It did, of course, especially when an heir was desperately needed to continue the family line. So I wrote *Deception* which was published in 2003 by Severn House. They had been producing attractive library editions of a number of my past novels but this was the first new book of several more to come. Such pleasure as I might have had from its production was diminished by my very dear sister Eve's death. Not only had she been my close companion throughout our childhood, but also for the past forty years ever since Donald and I moved back to Sussex, we had grown very close and missed her deeply as did my other sister, Anne. However, Anne was consoled by her deep spiritual faith which had also helped her through Eve's funeral which, unfortunately, took place on the first anniversary of her husband, Peter's, death.

Writing had always had the power to remove me totally from real life. I lose count of time and live for a while within whatever story I am creating. I had quite seriously decided that *Deception* would be my last book but now when I was feeling saddened by the thought that I could no longer lift the telephone and speak to Eve, I decided that I needed something else to divert me. We live in a private road, a country lane which after a mile, comes to a dead end. At one end of the lane houses and cottages open directly on to the road. Further up, they have for the most part long drives up to the houses. As it is a private road, we all contribute to the upkeep and we have meetings to discuss what should or needs to be done. Because there are more or less two factions, those who want the road surface and verges improved for greater speed and those like us living close to the road who want it left in a fairly rough state, the discussions have at times become quite heated.

Walking home one evening, I remarked jokingly to Mel that if the arguments became more heated, it could come to blows – even murder! It was, of course, a joke but the idea stuck in my mind and I thought it might be quite good fun as well as an exercise for me to develop the idea and write my first Whodunit. As it was not intended for publication, I began by referring to the real residents but then Edwin Buckhalter of Severn House, who had just produced *Deception* rang me and asked what I was writing next. He said he would really like to see my Whodunit as the genre was currently popular in the States. He persuaded me to start again and use my idea for a fictional story.

It was thus that I started at the ripe old age of eighty-two to write about murder instead of love! It was great fun to do although it proved more difficult than I had imagined to keep from letting the reader know who the murderer was. The book was duly published by Severn House the following year under the title *Over My Dead Body*, and had some very pleasing reviews from America, one referring to a 'nicely done psychological suspense'; another to 'an inventive plot with plenty of reader appeal'. Despite my plan to stop writing, I now felt encouraged to write another Whodunit, this time about murder on a golf course, and this duly appeared in print with the title *Dead Centre* and was published last year.

The publication of *Dead Centre* brought the total number of books I have written in my long life to seventy-nine. Five of these were children's books, one a book of short stories, two Whodunits, fifteen historical family sagas and the remainder light romantic novels. I have not kept records of the number of short stories I contributed to magazines, nor of the number of poems I've written over the years, some serious but many rhyming accounts of the children's and grandchildren's activities. One of these about Mel's heart bypass operation was put on display by the surgeon in the hospital; another about one of Emily's sports days in a heat wave was put up in the school.

As I am now in my eighty-sixth year, I think it really is time I retired – or at least as soon as I have finished writing my autobiography. As I near the end of it, I realise how very lucky I have been throughout my life – with my family, my friends, my children and grandchildren, and all the doors that have been opened for me. So many people have contributed to my career as well as my happiness. How many writers have been blessed with two patient, hard-working, intelligent, supportive secretaries such as my late friend Joy Tait and now Pennie Scott?

I've been lucky, too, in my agents, publishers, and in particular my editor Diane Pearson who, as an author herself, was always so understanding. I am grateful, too, to the many readers who liked my stories and took the trouble to write to me – an unfailing encouragement. Of all these letters, I think I most value the ones I have received from readers who tell me my books have helped them through a difficult or tragic time in their lives. My mother used to say this, too. Certainly not least I have to say how very lucky I was to have such a loving and perceptive parent to steer me towards a literary career.

I have been fortunate, too, on a personal level – not only with my parents, my sisters, my children, my friends – but how very lucky I was that albeit by mistake, Mel chose me as his dance partner sixty-six years ago! He may not always have had faith in my good ideas but he has never failed to support them. With his sense of humour, his immense generosity, his support, care and love, he has made the last thirty years of my life so much fun, and we have grown old together. Although he has now reached the venerable age of ninety and my eighty-fifth birthday is behind me, we keep each other young even if our legs wobble as we stagger round the golf course and very occasionally round the dance floor if someone is playing one of our tunes.

I have promised him that when I have finished writing this autobiography, I will emerge from my study for good and he need no longer have to wait patiently for his supper whilst I dash off a few more words. I was about six years old when I first started telling stories to Anne, and it really is high time I retired. Tomorrow I shall start clearing my cluttered study of its mound of reference books, papers, files, book jackets, photographs. I plan to keep my typewriter, computer and photocopier for personal use.

This afternoon, the marquee is arriving for the wedding next door when Pennie's eldest daughter is to be married. It will be a gala affair and when her other daughter was married, the place was bedecked with flowers and everyone had a wonderful time. I hope for Pennie's sake that everything will go as well this year. It would be so awful if, after all the hard work, something awful happened at the last minute. Suppose she or her husband or even the bride or groom got ill? Supposing there was an accident and someone was badly hurt? Killed? Suppose it wasn't an accident and someone was murdered? Suppose . . .

No, I will absolutely NOT start plotting another book. I will not even think about the possibility that the best man could hide the body so that the celebrations . . . No! I do mean no this time. Besides, it would be totally unrealistic to stab someone with a tent peg . . . although you could possibly strangle someone with a guy rope or . . . I know I promised Mel I would not write another book. The only problem is – and it's a problem I know isn't going to go away – *Death in the Marquee* does seem quite a good idea!

I now find myself in the same position as my grandmother and my mother, neither of whom ever 'retired'. Apart from the large quantity of articles my mother wrote for over sixty years, she published over two hundred books under her own and several pseudonyms. She was never short of ideas for a new plot. I wonder now – would I have become an author if I'd had a different parent? Or have I simply been following in the family footsteps?

As I grow older, I find myself questioning more and more often whether there is a 'life hereafter'. Is my mother somewhere up there watching over my writing career with her supportive eye? Will I see them again – my parents, my sister Eve, my well-loved friends in their light and dark blue uniforms? It would be so joyful to be sure of our reunion. Sometimes when I am walking on my own through the woods, I see a shadow and just for a fleeting moment I ask myself: can that be Heinkel rushing towards me through the trees? And for that brief moment, I know that I will see them all again.

Edenbridge
May, 2006

EPILOGUE

Nine years have passed since I wrote *You Never Know* and it is now 2015. I have reached the ripe old age of ninety-four. Very sadly, Mel is no longer with me. He died on 27th January 2012, one week before my ninety-first birthday. His health had deteriorated so much he was really ready to give up the effort to keep going. To say I miss him, the best friend I ever had, is a huge understatement. However, I am luckier than a lot of other people in that I still have my writing to keep me occupied, and I have three wonderful children and eight grandchildren who all visit me and keep in regular touch on the telephone.

Not least, I have the company of my rescue greyhound Bertie – see his photograph on page 285. Apart from stealing food and occupying any vacant chair or sofa, he is literally as good as gold. I am able to take him for walks on my mobility scooter as I am fortunate enough to live on a mile long, private road with fields on either side.

Last year was a remarkably busy one. I had two books published – *Georgia* and *Trust Me,* and all eighty past publications have been re-issued as ebooks. So, too, have been the one hundred and sixty wonderful romantic novels my mother wrote as Denise Robins. This led to quite a lot of publicity – articles in magazines and daily newspapers. Even more publicity has resulted as last year was the Commemorative 75th year of the Second World War Battle of Britain, in which I participated.

You will have read earlier on page 54 that I joined the

Royal Air Force as a WAAF in 1940 and had the good fortune to be recruited to Special Duties – work so secret that it remained on the Official Secrets Act until 1976. This was long after other aspects of the Dowding System became known. I am so glad that I am a surviving veteran of the Battle of Britain from that vital year of 1940, and can speak for all those other immensely hard-working young women who so willingly gave up six years of their youth to work in the underground filter rooms. They may no longer be here but their relatives will now be able to tell their children how vitally important their work was – so vital that after the war was over, Sir Winston Churchill the then Prime Minister said:

'All the ascendancy of the Hurricanes and Spitfires would have been fruitless but for the system known as the Dowding System. But it is the pivotal role of the Filter Rooms within the system which allowed commanders at all levels to manage the battle from a common picture of the air'.

Had it not been for Lord Dowding's creation, the invasion Hitler had planned (Operation Sea Lion) would have taken place. We were unprepared. Our air force was our only real defence against the hordes of enemy planes which attacked day and night. Although we in the Filter Rooms were able with the radar system to track them, what really counted was the bravery of our young pilots who risked their lives daily, sometimes several times a day, to shoot the enemy down. Vital though our contribution was, we were never facing death as they were every time we went on duty and we honour them. Far too few survived.

Even so, as it turned out, it took six long years before the population could get rid of their gas masks, their air raid sirens, their blackout curtains; clear the bombed buildings and craters; demobilise our forces, and join in the immense struggle to get the country back on its feet.

In Chapter 6 I gave a summary of the work we did in

the Filter Rooms, but for those who might be interested, enough time has now passed for me to be more explicit about the Dowding System which came into being shortly before the outbreak of war. It was known as The Chain Link Home and we, in the Filter Rooms, were the centre link of a three-part chain.

The first part consisted of a series of overlapping RDF (Range and Direction Finding) Stations, based at intervals round the British coastline. Their radar waves extended out over the seas to Europe. When one of these beams struck an aircraft, an echo was returned to the station (radar stands for Radio Detection and Ranging). The operator read this position on a screen nothing like as sophisticated as the version now used by modern Air Traffic Control. The radar operator was able to determine the distance of the target fairly accurately but measurement of direction was much less precise. The operator now relayed the best estimate of the position of the plane by telephone to a 'Plotter' sitting at a table in the Filter Room with headphones connecting her to the station. This was the second link of the chain. On this table, known as the Filter table, (see the photograph on page 285) was a map with a grid. The Plotters each had a box of counters in the colour allotted to their positions. They placed a coloured counter on the point relayed to them. These positions were always completely accurate as far as distance from the radar station was concerned, (for example, twenty miles) but not strictly accurate for direction. The plot on the Filter table was not therefore the true position of the plane. However, the neighbouring RDF Station would also have sent out a signal. This time the plane might appear on their screen as twenty-two miles away but also inaccurate for direction. The Plotter receiving this information would put her different coloured counter where she was told.

Behind the table, not attached to a headphone, was a

commissioned officer known as a Filterer. It was their job
to place an arrow in the true position of the plane, (as in
my example: where the twenty-mile arc crossed the twenty-
two-mile arc). As the arrows continued one after the other,
the direction of the plane was quickly established. It was
designated by a small plaque 'H' (for hostile) and a number.
On the balcony above the table was a 'Teller' who was
attached by telephone to the Operations Room where there
was a similar gridded map and to whom they would relay
the arrowed position. The Ops Room, as it was known,
was the third link in the chain. The commanding officer
on the balcony overlooking the table would see from the
arrows roughly how many planes, whether friend or foe,
were approaching or leaving our shores and from which
direction. He could then alert the relevant fighter squadron
to scramble the aircraft so they had time to gain height
and be in the right position to attack the enemy planes as
they approached.

It was obvious from these operations that in all three
links, speed was absolutely essential. The Filter Room calcu-
lations were also sent to Air Sea Rescue, Barrage Balloon
and Searchlight commands and to the Observer Corps.
Planes travel fast and all three links had to be accomplished
quickly enough for enemy planes to be intercepted. This
was of truly vital importance because we were vastly
outnumbered by the Luftwaffe, as the German air force
was called. Our pilots were frequently untrained, inexperienced and very young men, who had volunteered
sometimes straight from school or university. As so many
were getting shot down, there was less and less time for
new pilots to be trained and as weeks and months went
by, some pilots had had only two weeks training and sometimes had never been up in a Spitfire or Hurricane before
going into action. Sir Winston Churchill said in one of his
memorable speeches: 'Never in the field of human conflict

was so much owed by so many to so few' and these young men thereafter came to be called 'The Few'. We now know from surviving Luftwaffe pilots that when they attacked us they were surprised to find our pilots higher up waiting for them.

Because of radar and its application of the Dowding System Hitler was unable to obtain his essential air superiority over Britain and so called off the prepared invasion – Operation Sea Lion. Instead he decided to open another front by invading Russia – Operation Barbarossa – a fatal mistake for the enemy.

The Filter Room, together with all other aspects of the Battle of Britain, has been wonderfully depicted in the museum recently opened in the former Fighter Command WW2 Headquarters, a lovely old building, Bentley Priory, in Stanmore, Middlesex. There, part of a Filter Room table has been reconstructed and bronze statues of five plotters at work are shown full size. Two of these were modelled from two of us remaining veterans as girls, myself and Eileen Younghusband, who although now ninety-four years old, still gives wonderful, colourful lectures about her activities in the war. Bentley Priory is open Mondays, Wednesdays, Fridays and Saturdays from 10a.m. to 5p.m., March–September; and 10a.m. to 4p.m. October–February as I write. On page 285 is a picture of Eileen and myself when we were asked to welcome Prince Charles and the Duchess of Cornwall in order to explain our work on the official opening day of the museum.

As one of the few surviving Filter Room WAAFs, I was much in demand last year to participate in various Fighter Command activities; for brief television interviews for the 75th anniversary service in Westminster Abbey; at Biggin Hill for the official dedication of a new coin, and for the RAF Benevolent Fund at their fund raising dinner. I also gave a speech at the unveiling of a stained glass window at the museum last summer, and was interviewed three times by national newspapers!

This all took place in August and September last year when I was supposed to be convalescing after two bouts of pneumonia. At the same time, I was finishing my new book, *Live The Dream*, for publication this year.

I called this autobiography *You Never Know* because it fits my life so well. Now, when I am nearing the end of it and I should be in my rocking chair, my life is suddenly full of these new activities. I wish Mel could be with me to share them, but you can't expect to have everything you want in life and I am immensely lucky to have so much.

Your future might be just as unexpected as mine has been. My advice if you wish to stay young is:

'Rescue a greyhound, buy a mobility scooter, don't give up but look forward to tomorrow. There might be a nice surprise awaiting you. You never know.'

Claire Lorrimer (February 2016)

Bertie

Plotters at work
on the Filter
Room Table

Me at the official
opening day at
Bentley Priory
Museum

INDEX

(Page numbers in italics indicate references to illustrations)